Jewish Power in America

Jewish Power in America

Myth and Reality

Henry L. Feingold

Transaction Publishers
New Brunswick (U.S.A.) and London (U.K.)

Library of Congress Catalog Number: 2008027792
ISBN: 978-1-4128-0835-4
Printed in the United States of America

Library of Congress Cataloging-in-Publication Data

Feingold, Henry L., 1931-
    Jewish power in America : myth and reality / Henry L. Feingold.
        p. cm.
    Includes bibliographical references and index.
    ISBN 978-1-4128-0835-4 (alk. paper)
    1. Jews--United States--Politics and government--20th century. 2. Jews-
-United States--Politics and government--21st century. 3. Jews--United
States--Attitudes toward Israel. 4. United States--Ethnic relations. I. Title.

E184.36.P64F45 2008
305.892'4073--dc22

                                                        2008027792

In memory of Herbert A. Cohen and Donald Newman
who pointed the way.

Contents

Preface

From a statement by the foreign minister of Malaysia, to a recent study of an imagined Jewish control of American foreign policy, to an ad in the nation's leading newspapers exposing a satanic plot by the "Israel lobby," the notion of a Jewish power conspiracy continues to haunt the anti-Semitic imagination.[1] The fear that Jews have a special access to power is as old as Jewish history. It was contained in the warnings given to the Egyptian pharaoh (Exodus 12). It was what Haman whispered into the ear of the Persian King Ahasuerus (Esther 8:7) in the biblical story of Purim. The late nineteenth-century fantasy that Jews control the world's money markets and the Nazi obsession with Judeobolshevism were linked to a fear of Jewish power. In the American historical context, the fear is embedded in the soft underbelly of the isolationist movement during the thirties. It was best articulated by America's favorite hero, Charles Lindbergh, who warned of it in his infamous Des Moines address in September 1941.[2]

The latest accusation that focuses on neoconservative control of the nation's Middle East policy is foreboding because the notion of a Jewish power conspiracy has found place in the mind of credentialed thinkers and policy makers. It can no longer be simply dismissed as the ravings of lunatic fringe anti-Semites. Senator Fulbright, who railed against excessive Jewish influence in the making of the nation's Middle East policy in the sixties and seventies, or former President Carter's charges that drew an analogy with the apartheid policy of South Africa are not easily dismissed as chronic haters.[3] Many reviewers of the work of Professors Mearsheimer and Walt find it primarily wanting in the quality of scholarship, rather than its anti-Semitic content. The authors tout themselves as supporters of Israel and support the right of Jews to lobby in their interest. Moreover, the focus of a special animus on Israel makes the charge of inordinate Jewish power more feasible. Unlike American Jewry, Israel, after all, has an army that has demonstrated its mettle on the field of battle. This book is not intended as a response to Mearsheimer and Walt, but when two highly accredited scholars produce a polemic dressed in scholarly academic clothing that draws upon a vintage negative image concerning Jews and power, it arouses concern.

There is Jewish power at play in the American polity that sometimes, like the American Irish in earlier decades, may seem inordinate. Yet when only seventy years have passed since two out of three European Jews were murdered in a genocidal spree, the notion of a satanic Jewish power again at work in the world needs to be treated with alarm. The charges and stereotypes attacking Zionism and Israel are strikingly familiar. We need to be clear about it; American Jewry stands accused not so much of a Rothschild-like conspiracy to control the world's money supply, but the more conceivable aspiration of projecting an inordinate influence on the nation's Middle East policy to ensure the well-being of Israel. American Jewry is, after all, well known for its deep concern for the welfare and security of Israel.

To be sure, Jewish political power exists as a separate agency in the American polity, but before we can determine whether it is inordinate, it needs to be identified and defined.[4] It is not the kind of power that is preoccupied with military armaments as associated with a sovereign state like Israel. Nor is it personal power. There are many influential Jews today who raise huge sums for office seekers, but there are none like Jacob Schiff, who, at the turn of the twentieth century, controlled the Kuhn Loeb banking interests and was totally committed to using his vast wealth to alleviate the persecution of Russian Jewry. With the exception of an abiding concern with the security of Israel, there are no overriding public policy concerns that differentiate the Jewish voter from the informed formally educated segment of the American electorate. The overwhelming Jewish support for stem-cell research, for example, is fully shared by the American voter with a similar level of education and income. Yet power there must be, not because anti-Semites have conjured it through the ages. By definition all living things have some degree of power. As a thriving community, American Jewry cannot be imagined without it. Individual empowerment and its broad distribution is, after all, a basic aspiration of the American social and political system. We are therefore compelled to begin with acknowledging the truth of the assumption that American Jews do have some political power. But what kind is it and is it inordinate compared to the power exercised by other ethnic and interest groups that thrive in the American polity? Above all, the basic charge of those who have raised the alarm about Jewish power, that it is used conspiratorially against the national interest, needs to be addressed.

This book seeks an answer to these queries, not through learned discussions about the alchemy of power, which is the province of political scientists, but by examining five recent major instances, beginning with the New Deal, when the play of Jewish power, or power exercised by Jews, was evident. This historical approach rests on the assumption that a great deal can be learned about power by observing how the American Jewish community responds to crisis or special circumstances where the use of communal power can be readily observed.

The chapters that follow are not intended as a complete study of Jewish political culture, but they contain sufficient information to illustrate the complexity of the Jewish power question. The parameters of the power problem are initially probed in the first chapter, which exposes the complexity of the problem. That is followed by five broad areas chosen because they reveal most about the play of Jewish power. The first three focus on the area of American Jewry's primary interest in foreign policy. It includes the American Jewish response to the Holocaust, which is contrasted with its response in the following chapter to the travail of Soviet Jewry. The reasons why the projection of Jewish power for the freeing of Soviet Jewry was more successful than the far more urgent case for the rescue of European Jewry during the Holocaust is probed. The third chapter in this triad concerns American Jewry's political advocacy role vis-à-vis Israel, which has triggered the current complaint about the inordinate use of Jewish political power. That discussion is followed by three chapters that deal with the manifestation of Jewish power in domestic politics. The stage for that discussion is set by an examination of the sources of Jewish political culture, with an emphasis on the historic roots of the remarkable activism of the Jewish electorate and its heightened leadership role in movements for change and reform. The remarkable engagement of American Jewry in the political process now amply documented by survey research and evidenced by the disproportionate number of Jewish officeholders on all levels of government can be traced in some measure to its relationship to the Eastern European Jewish migration and to the inherent activism of the political left.

Taken together, these three chapters present the reader with a broadly comprehensive picture of the American Jewish impingement on U.S. foreign policy. The prism is macrocosmic, which means that the selection of specific incidents is not sequential. These chapters are followed by and examination of two domestic political phenomenon, the neocons and the New Left, which I have called "Jews by accusation" because their tribal bona fides are otherwise unclear. In many cases, the conversion from Orthodox Judaism of the immigrant generation to some stripe of socialism served to conceal the process of assimilation. The neocons entered the political arena as political thinkers and conceptualizers of strategy, while the shorter-lived generational New Left entered the political arena through the developing youth culture of the sixties and seventies. It was a path into the broader world. Were they radical Jews, people whose search for roots through a Judaic conduit, or Jewish radicals, people who happened to be born to Jewish parents, but who focused their search outside the Jewish fold?

The final chapter is devoted to summarizing and further developing the observations in the foregoing chapters regarding the play of Jewish power in America. The five historical cases show that, in fact, Jewish power in America is a tenuous, fragile force that is mostly confined to the realm of ideas and values, and that the fear of its abuse is fantasy given the type of proud citizens Americans Jews have become. It is most effective in implementing its political agenda when it is in consonance with the national interest. When it is not, as in the case of advocating a more effective rescue policy during the Holocaust, even the full use of avenues of activism encouraged by the system, in which the Jewish community is well practiced, could not change the Roosevelt administration's war aims to include the rescue of European Jewry until it was too late. Allaying the fear of undue power in Jewish hands is the weakening of Jewish identity and communal affiliation. Increasingly, its agenda does not differ notably from other urbanized well educated groups. There is little specifically Jewish about it and its traditional political liberalism is becoming less outspoken.

* * *

There is some apprehension in presenting a book that can easily be mistaken for an effort to allay the concerns of those who harbor irrational fears about Jews and their power. On the face of it, such an effort is probably futile since it is, after all, an irrational fear likely to be resistant to reason or an impressive research apparatus. Footnotes are therefore confined to citations for direct quotes and statistics that would interrupt the flow of the narrative. I note, finally, that the envisaging of a demonic

Jewish power at work in the corridors of American government can appear to be rational, if one is unaware that empowerment of all groups is at the very heart of the American democratic process. We note in the following pages that Jews, like most Americans, feel themselves empowered and are conspicuously active in all phases of the American political dialogue and increasingly in the political process. Far from being involved in a conspiracy, the American Jewish citizen actually is a model of what citizenship in a democracy is all about.

Nevertheless, American Jews, especially those who witnessed the Holocaust, may become alarmed at the developing indictment, which is expected to grow shriller as the Iraq war comes to an unsatisfactory end. They remain aware of how quickly Jews were placed outside the universe of obligation during the years of the Holocaust. When a colleague learned that I was planning to write a book about Jewish power in America, he jokingly suggested that it should be a very short book. Like many who lived through World War II, he saw Jews as the victims rather than the masters of history. His fears might be allayed by reading this book, which finds that there is such a thing as Jewish power in America. It is freely exercised by each Jewish citizen and also communally. The greatest loss to the nation and to its Jewish citizens would be if, cowed by the emerging indictment and still burdened with the terrifying memory of the Holocaust, they mute their political voice to seek shelter in metaphorical hidden attics. It is in that spirit that this examination of the complexity of the Jewish power question is offered.

Henry L. Feingold
New York City
September 4, 2007

Notes

1.   Israel Lobby refers to AIPAC (American Israel Public Affairs Committee), which pressed hard for Israel's interest in opposing arms for Egypt in 1978 and the AWACS arms sales to Saudi Arabia in 1981. A fairly balanced "exposure" of AIPAC belongs to Edward Tivnan, *The Lobby: Jewish Political Power and American Foreign Policy* (New York: Simon & Schuster, 1987).

2.   Such charges predate the famous Russian forgery *The Protocols of the Elders of Zion*. During the 1970s, warnings about the inordinate Jewish influence were several times sounded by Senator Fulbright, chairman of the Foreign Relations Committee. The most recent manifestations in the academic world is an 82-page pamphlet containing 211 endnotes, "The Israel Lobby and US Foreign Policy" written by two distinguished scholars, John J. Mearsheimer (University of Chicago) and Stephen M. Walt (Harvard University). It first appeared under a similar title in

a paper delivered before the Council on American Islamic Relations (CAIR) and before that in an article in the *London Review of Books* and a working paper on the Kennedy School Website. An expanded version of the original paper was published in September 2007 by Farrar, Strauss & Giroux. The argument was expanded to include Israel's war against Hizbollah in Lebanon as part of the conspiracy. The newspaper ad posed the question "Why has the United States been willing to set aside its own security in order to advance the interest of another state?" See *New York Times,* April 16, 2006. Former President Carter's book, *Palestine: Peace Not Apartheid,* contains a harsh critique of Israel's occupation of the West Bank, but otherwise is not preoccupied with a Jewish conspiracy.

3.   Nor can General George Marshall, Roosevelt's primary military advisor and chief of staff of the U.S. Army, who led a State Department coterie of officials in adamant opposition to the proposed post-war establishment of a Jewish state.

4.   I use the term political power because the charges inherent in the Mearsheimer and Walt book, and specifically stated in coarser pieces, include complaints that the war in Iraq was begun at the behest of Jewish advisors, which goes well beyond mere political influence.

I

Seeking the Sources of Jewish Influence in America

This book seeks to determine the extent and depth of Jewish power in America where the openness of society would presumably make its play more discernible. But where to seek it? We cannot count its divisions, as Stalin would have done at Yalta. American Jewry does not possess sovereign power, as do the Jews of Israel. There are no longer wealthy Jews like Jacob Schiff prepared to use their extraordinary political leverage to realize Jewish interests.[1] With the exception of an overriding concern with the security of Israel, there are no public policy concerns that are not shared by other constituencies.

The search for the play of power in the American social order is beset with problems. We live in a society where the role of power in human affairs is concealed and at times altogether denied. Convinced of its malignant qualities the forefathers sought to separate government power and then allowed the three branches of government to check and balance each other. They also divided power between the states and the federal government. Tocqueville took note of how Americans lived with the illusion that such class distinctions as existed were not hierarchical. The doctor is "doc" the professor, "prof" and the president, "mister." The difficulty of pinning down the precise locale of power is compounded by the problem of defining what constitutes political power. Much of the play of power in American society is exercised privately and signs of its use and misuse are not readily observable. It is like a swift-flowing colorless stream of water. To be sure, there are instances of an unjust and coercive use of government powers, such as, for example, the former imposition of a system of racial segregation. But we have witnessed in our recent history how, when such public policy is no longer viable, the citizenry of a comparatively free society can be mobilized to eliminate or keep such trespasses in check.

1

The elusive search for power is made more problematic by the changing nature of power itself. Stalin did not live to see the sudden collapse of the Soviet empire in 1991, despite the fact that the Warsaw Pact fielded the largest army in Europe and the Soviet Union possessed a full arsenal of weapons of mass destruction. When at Yalta he posed the question: "How many divisions does the pope have?" the answer was none. But eventually it became clear that the pope had something that went beyond military power; something that decades later could make many of the Polish and Lithuanian divisions of the Soviet empire unreliable. In the twentieth century there is ample evidence that military power goes only so far in the conflict of nations and interests. During World War II, just before the invasion of the Soviet Union, the Axis seemed unbeatable. Then a series of strategic errors that brought the Soviet Union and the United States to the Allied side so radically changed the power calculus that at least in theory it made the Axis defeat inevitable. Similarly, after years of talk of missile gaps, the Soviet empire collapsed in spite of its military superiority and possession of nuclear weapons. Despite the formidable power of the American military, Washington did not have its way in Vietnam or Iraq. Clearly, even when the military accoutrements of power are overwhelming, so many tanks and so many guns, it does not fully encompass what power entails. There are non-military factors such as national moral, the quality of a nation's education system, the productivity of its labor force, the extensiveness of its transportation network, and above all, the quality of mind of its leaders and the spirit of its people that constitute power. There is a special ingredient that must be added to the factors that today affect the relationship of Jews to power. Conditioned by their historical vulnerability, Jews may be better mobilized than a people with a normal history in their struggle for survival.

There is Jewish power at play in the American polity that sometimes, like the American Irish in earlier decades, may seem inordinate. It is the image of disproportionate Jewish power that makes our search so intriguing. Alarums concerning the danger of power in Jewish hands and advocating its curtailment are not new in the Jewish experience. They are in conflict with the Jewish perspective that finds that there rarely is sufficient power that could be mobilized to protect a threatened Jewish community abroad. Such communities seem to exist in almost every period of Jewish history. American Jewry, which began to assume a leadership role in the interwar period, is continually overextended in relation to the power available to it. It may be that Jews simply feel a greater need to generate power or more likely, appeal to governments that possess it to act for them.[2] For most of their history in the Diaspora, Jews were bereft of the normal accoutrements of power in a world that was, at best, indifferent to their fate and, at worst, murderously hostile. One could logically reason that the Jewish people would not have survived for millennia in a hostile world without some kind of power at play. For devout Jews, their millennial survival was taken as a sign of divine intervention for "His" people. The Holocaust undermined that comfortable belief. By the end of World War II, American Jewry had bitter evidence of what the absence of sovereign power could mean for individual and communal survival. Had there been a Jewish state, or had American Jewry been able to convince the Roosevelt administration to include the rescue of European Jewry in its war aims, it would have been possible to rescue many more of their kin. It was that awareness that lay behind the mobilization of as yet a non-Zionist American Jewry for the establishment of a Jewish state. Before the Biltmore convention of May 1942, the idea of a Jewish state was by no means an agreed upon goal of the world Zionist movement.

There is an additional ingredient that must be added to the factors that today affect the relationship of Jews to power. The will of a people to survive and go forward after radical losses may not register on the instruments that calculate power, but it is nonetheless real. It is that will to survive as a people that fuel the initiative they take in their own defense. It acts like a silent witness to the historic factors we probe and wonder about in the pages that follow.

*   *   *

But for the moment we are primarily interested in the American Jewish political voice. From where does it emanate, and does it have a special message? A good place to begin is with the American political process, which sorts out the relationship of the various interests that compose the polity. It is well known that those who understand and use the political process, which includes such things as maximizing voter turnout, fundraising and effective public relations can amplify their political clout beyond their numbers. It is also no secret that beyond their high voting rate and the location of Jewish voting blocs in pivotal states, Jews are among the most engaged political constituencies in the nation. Surveys indicate that the Jewish voter is better informed about the issues, especially in foreign affairs. They are more likely to write to their congressmen and to the editors of the local newspaper. They are also disproportionately involved in the emerging profession of politics as pundits, speechwriters, poll takers, fundraisers, strategists and, campaign lead men. In recent years they have emerged from these behind-the-scenes activities to run for office, mostly in districts and states where Jews are a small minority. Of the four religious denominations whose congressional representation has risen between 1964 and 2006, Catholics, Mormons, Baptists, and Jews, the Jewish increase from 17 to 43 has been steepest. In contrast, mainline Protestant denominations, like Presbyterians and Episcopalians, have shown the sharpest decline. (See Figure 1.) Their presence in the judiciary and upper echelons of the federal civil service has become conspicuous. In a word, Jews use the political process well and as a result have maximized their political influence.[3]

The role of campaign contributions given by Jews deserves special mention. Over 60 percent of the campaign funds collected by the Democratic party and a respectable percentage of Republican campaign funds stem from Jewish sources.[4] But precisely what that means in terms of enhancing influence is difficult to determine. One wants to believe that major policy decisions are not for sale and, even if influence can be bought, there are competing moneyed interests and no assurance that "big-givers," Jewish and otherwise, have a common agenda. Yet money is a crucial ingredient of campaign politics and Jews are a voting bloc that has a time-honored tradition of giving as well as having more to give. The penchant for political fundraising is associated with the Jewish tradition of political engagement and activism, as well as the habit of giving, which stems from the religious culture of Judaism. Money cannot, by itself, determine the outcome of an election or change a heartfelt support of public policy like Social Security. If the American people concluded that their staunch support of Israel no longer serves the national interest, no amount of Jewish money funneled into the coffers of either party could long forestall that consensus being translated into policy. Engagement and money and activism and the myriad of other factors in the political arsenal can bring an interest group's influence to its full permissible level where it contends with other interests. Projecting influence on the policy making process is still a far cry from controlling it.

We will note in the following chapter that even the fortunate location of communal leaders near the seat of power cannot assure government action. A disproportionate share of Roosevelt's inner circle of advisors were Jewish, yet when diplomatic intercession and intervention were

Figure 1
Here are the religious affiliations of the 535 members of Congress elected in 1964
and 2006, as self-reported. Ranked by 2006 affiliations.

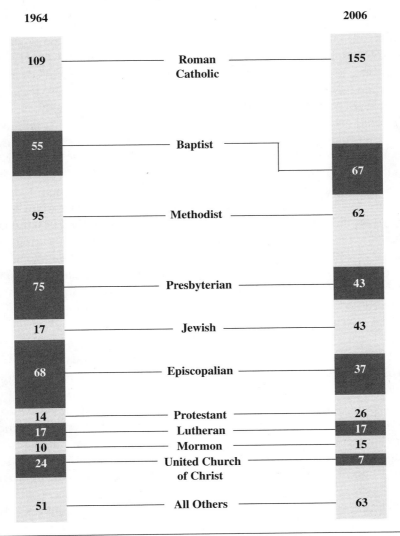

1964		2006
109	Roman Catholic	155
55	Baptist	67
95	Methodist	62
75	Presbyterian	43
17	Jewish	43
68	Episcopalian	37
14	Protestant	26
17	Lutheran	17
10	Mormon	15
24	United Church of Christ	7
51	All Others	63

Source: Michael Luo, "God '08: Whose and How Much Will Voters Accept?" New York
Times, News of the Week in Review, July 22, 2007.

desperately needed, in the immediate years before and during World War II, for the protection and rescue of European Jewry, they were not forthcoming. Most Jews close to Roosevelt did not feel that their position could be used to further a Jewish interest, even when its humanitarian purpose was shared and ultimately became part of the war aims of the nation. Clearly, a notable presence in the decision-making strata does not yield sufficient influence to pull public policy out of what is perceived to be the national self-interest. In those rare cases where a communal consensus is attainable, a group that represents less than 2.2 percent of the electorate and is overshadowed by much larger black and Hispanic voting blocks, must conceive of its implementing its political goals through coalitions with like-minded partners. It begins with the assumption that it does not possess sufficient power to impose its will on the making of policy.

Still, effective use of the democratic political process cannot alone explain Jewish influence in American politics. It seems that when Jewish goals and interests are conceived as serving the American national interest, when there is consonance between the ethnic and the national aspiration, then the Jewish influence can easily be mistaken for being supreme. It enables Judeophobes to argue that the national interest has been co-opted by a Jewish group interest as it concerns U.S. policy in the Middle East.

*   *   *

We come next to examining the source of Jewish political power. We have noted that there are few clues in American Jewish political circumstances that suggest a special source of power or influence, except for the fact that Jews usually use the American democratic political system effectively. In the past that may partly account for government support for purely communal interests, such as the Holocaust memorial museum on the capital mall or the pursuit and prosecution of war criminals who have found haven in the United States. But despite an increasing frequency of Jewish officeholders elected in areas where few Jewish voters cast their ballots, Jewish representation in Congress would actually decline in the decades ahead if it remained dependent on Jewish voters alone. Much depends on how well the Jewish interest meshes with the national. In the case of ending the war in Iraq, there is such a common interest that should ultimately be translated into public policy. The case of the Jewish interest in the security of Israel is easily misconstrued, since the strong government support given to Israel is not given at the behest of an imagined Jewish interest alone. Does Israel get diplomatic and military support because of the influence of a Jewish lobby, or are Jewish lobbyists welcome on Capitol Hill because Israel is a crucial link in upholding American strategic interests in the Middle East? Can both be happening simultaneously? The issue is far from clear.

Moreover, as a growing number of American Jews eschew communal and congregational affiliation and identify themselves as "just Jewish," the problem of determining who speaks for American Jewry has grown more complex. Historically, the picture of Jewish communal governance and advocacy was dominated by high-powered wealthy individual Jews like Jacob Schiff, Louis Marshall, Cyrus Adler, and later by men like Rabbi Stephen Wise, Nahum Goldmann, Edgar Bronfman, and others who acted as the communal leadership by agreement or preemption. They were able to do so by dint of great wealth, which they placed at the service of the community. Sometimes, as in the case of Rabbis Stephen Wise and Abba Hillel Silver, it was based partly on oratorical ability when it still counted or, as in the case of Rabbi Wise, a penchant for creating new organizations. The common denominator was money, either from one's own estate or access to those who possessed it. Such self-appointed leaders could be assets to the community, but at the same time created confusion about where actual communal authority was located. It was hard to determine for whom people like Nahum Goldmann or Stephen Wise spoke.[5] At the turn of the twentieth century, Jacob Schiff's efforts to use his position as head of Kuhn Loeb investment house to wring better treatment for Russian Jewry was a truly amazing example of the use of direct economic pressure on Moscow. On an individual basis, Schiff undertook alone what became a communal effort in the seventies and eighties to gain the release of Soviet Jewry. His personal private efforts did not noticeably improve the Jewish condition, but any fair estimate would have to conclude that Schiff's predemocratic effort was in some respects more effective than the later communal effort led by the Soviet Jewry movement. For our purposes here, the episodes are interesting because they illustrate the actual exercise of Jewish power directly, rather than through the agency of government. Finally, even in the unlikely instance when a precise Jewish interest is determinable, there is little that compels a legislator who happens to be Jewish to expend political capital on it, especially when the number of Jewish voters in his district is negligible.

Since the turn of the twentieth century, the Jewish agenda has grown
more complex and larger than when Jacob Schiff and Louis Marshall
spoke for the community. In those years, Jews pushed for liberal immigration laws, expressions of diplomatic concern for their brethren in
Eastern Europe, and strict interpretation of the wall separating church
and state. With their special connections to the American ruling elite, the
shtadlanim, could make Jewish communal needs known to the administration.[6] Today Jewish leaders are unable to present the Jewish agenda in
such precise terms. The American Jewish political persona has grown less
distinct, making the determination of a communal consensus problematic.
In the natural course of things, they have become more American and
less interested and committed to purely ethnic communal interests. We
shall note later that most American Jews probably do not see eye to eye
with the neoconservatives (neocons) whose origins were in some measure
rooted in the malaise of the Jewish left and who had some influence in
the Reagan and Bush, Sr. administrations. There has also been a change
in communal governance as the newly arrived eastern Jews rallied under
the banner of communal democracy to speak for themselves. It did so in
the case of winning the Wilson administration's support for the Balfour
Declaration in 1917. The nascent American Zionist movement, which
claimed to represent the idea of Jewish peoplehood in its most pristine
form, trotted out Louis Brandeis, the newly appointed Supreme Court
justice, to make their case. The Congress movement came into existence
over the question of representing the Jewish interest at the Versailles
negotiations. But rather than going out of business as the negotiations
concluded, Rabbi Stephen Wise the founder of the movement, made it
a permanent feature of American Jewish political scene. The resultant
democratization, combined with the political turmoil on the Jewish left,
made for greater political diversity, including such heartfelt issues as
the security of Israel.

Jewish communal governance is extraordinarily complex. Embodied
in agencies like the Joint Distribution Committee and the American
Jewish Committee, the dominance of the descendants of the nineteenth-
century German Jewish immigration, sometimes referred to as "uptown,"
persisted for many years. But on the operational level German Jewish
communal leadership came to an end with the death of Louis Marshall in
1929. The final cause of its decline was democracy itself. The "uptown"
leadership could no longer command adherence from the separate constituencies and the new generational cohorts that composed the organized

community. It had to rely on the less certain rewards of persuasion. The American Jewry that was governed by "Marshall law" had a clearer line of internal authority.[7] The moneyed piper played the tune.

Its decline left a leadership vacuum that became apparent with the rise of the Nazi threat in the thirties. The new "downtown" leadership coming out of the fractious politics of the immigrant generation could not speak to power with one voice, as had its predecessors. The resultant incoherence was one of the reasons for American Jewish ineffectiveness during the years of the Holocaust. Communal inchoateness was still present when an imagined analogous "rescue" case for Soviet Jewry came to the fore. By the 1970s, the transition from representation of the Jewish interest by well connected "court Jews" to a popular leadership supported by a professionals cadre of communal workers had been completed and the results were more satisfactory.

Yet, even during the governance of the *shtadlanim* at the turn of the twentieth century, control was far from complete. The Jewish governing threshold varies from generation to generation and it may be that the seriousness with which ideology was taken by the immigrant generation made communal governance difficult under any circumstances. So raucous was the continuous protests from the congested ghettoes where the immigrants settled that the German Jewish stewards sometimes referred to it as the "noisy quarter." Political leaders realized that dealing with Jews was not like dealing with Catholics immigrants where the church itself could give communal interest some shape. There was a cacophony of sound emanating from different quarters divided religiously, politically, by economic class, and even by the distinctive regional cultures from which they stemmed. The political culture of American Jewry became so variegated that it takes an act of fantasy to imagine that it could serve as the basis for a conspiracy to seize and exercise power. There was no paucity of aspiring leaders among Jews, but followers were in short supply. During the thirties, the raucousness of Jewish communal life, especially over the issue of fundraising made it difficult for political leaders to determine who spoke for Jews and what the message was.

Had those who fear that Jews were wielding too much power fathomed how dependent Jewish communal leadership was on the recognition of the administration in power their apprehensions might have been allayed. The presidents, governors, and mayors reserved for themselves the right to choose the communal leaders with whom government business could be transacted, or even whether they would talk to the leadership of the ethnic group at all. Teddy Roosevelt had his Oscar Strauss, but Wilson had few Jews in his administration. Governor Alfred E. Smith of New York had a bevy of Jewish advisors that included Henry and Belle Moscowitz, Robert Moses, and Samuel Rosenman. By the election of 1928, Jewish voters abandoned their allegiance to the Republican party. Herbert Hoover, who won the election with little support of Jewish voters, had few Jews in his administration. Franklin Roosevelt's "little New Deal" in New York State first won the hearts of Jewish voters when he expanded Smith's "Jew Deal." Richard Nixon made a special effort to attract Jewish voters, but the strategic positioning of Henry Kissinger, Max Fisher, and Leonard Garment did little to allay fears regarding his character and his anti-Semitism. In the post-war era, the administrations in Washington addressed the community through their own Jews, who were often hardly known to community leaders. Ford, Carter, Reagan, and Bush all tapped into the Jewish talent pool for appointments. But generally Jews, like other ethnics, were more accepted in the inner circle of the Democratic party than that of the Republicans.

The ability of American Jews to win a place in the power structure came at a price. Once part of the inner circle of key decision makers in the administration, their ability to wield power to realize communal needs was severely limited. The members of Roosevelt's "Jew Deal" would not openly advocate a more active government rescue role for the threatened Jews of Europe without calling into question their own bona fides as enablers of the American national interest. When Henry Morgenthau, Jr., Roosevelt's loyal secretary of the treasury, submitted his plan for the harsh treatment of post-war Germany in 1944, the cries that he was motivated by ethnic rather than the national interest were not long in coming. Being near the seat of power did not translate directly into Jewish power. Such persons had usually already negotiated the path to acceptance by placing their Jewish identities on a low-flame backburner. They had become government officials who happened to be Jews, sometimes unhappily so.[8] Morgenthau was the exception that proved the rule.

For the aspiring candidate at the precinct level, it was the Jewish vote that counted. Unlike other ethnic voting blocs, Jews also experimented with organizing their own political party to intrude directly into the political process. The most noteworthy example is the organization of the American Labor Party (1935) in New York State and its successor, the Liberal Party (1944). The ALP did not label itself as a Jewish party, but its financing by the Jewish labor movement gave the impression that it was. While the ALP's sponsorship and leadership were Jewish, it viewed itself as an American political party and addressed welfare state and labor issues, rather than specific Jewish ones, such as the refugee crisis. They were political parties organized by Jews, rather than Jewish political parties. With the exception of votes garnered for Herbert Lehman in the gubernatorial election of 1936, the ALP had little impact on national politics.[9] During the fifties, the Liberal Party could sometimes hold out the promise of marginal votes to make a difference in the politics of New York State. In its time, the ALP played an important communal role by offering a political instrument that allowed the socialist-oriented Jewish voters to cast their ballots for a high-born Episcopalian without compromising their principles. It served as a bridge drawing the Jewish voter into the American political process. That there existed sufficient communal skills and resources to organize a statewide party indicated an operational level well above that of other ethnic voting blocs, a lesson not soon forgotten by political leaders.

* * *

The story of Jewish political power would be incomplete if it failed to touch on the enhancement of Jewish political influence attributable to the disproportionate Jewish presence in the nation's professional and cultural elites, such as law, the sciences, the professoriate, medicine, theater, and the visual arts. The notable Jewish presence in these elites does not affect political power directly, yet it clearly enhances a Jewish political presence, particularly in the modern Western democracies. In the Weimar Republic, it became a lodestar for anti-Semitism and the charge that Jews were corrupting German culture. In America, where the cultural elites, especially the stars of Hollywood, are well integrated, it is difficult to imagine a *Judenrein* (Jew-Free) American popular or high culture purged of Jews, as was the case in the Reich. The scientists, artists, and other sundry culture carriers of Jewish origin tend to be only nominally Jewish and communally unaffiliated. Albert Einstein is prototypical. He was celebrated among Jews as an ideal Jew and drew greater crowds during his visit to New York City than the traditional revered rabbis. But while the great scientist lent his name to the endorsement of various Zionist causes, he was careful to keep his distance from playing a communal role. An offer to become the president of the newly organized Hebrew University in Jerusalem was rejected, as was a later offer to become the president of the newly established Jewish state of Israel.[10]

Such Jews seemed most comfortable in the unpreemted space found on the margins of both cultures. They were not fully accepted in the elevated circles of the host society, while at the same time they were no longer fully comfortable in the Jewish world. It is perhaps their "outsidedness" that allowed them to become especially receptive to certain universalistic "civilizing" ideas concerning human fraternity and the need to limit the play of naked power in human affairs. Such Jews became prominent in the founding of peace movements, and today worry about global warming and vanishing species, and all problems of survival that confront mankind. They are citizen of the world as well as a specific nation in it. It became the image of the Jew as liberal and global-minded that became a mainstay of the anti-Semitic imagination at the turn of the twentieth century. Fear of Jewish prominence in the film industry, for example, was based not on its impact on the profit margin, but its potential impact in shaping national values. Jewish representation in basic industries such as mining, the automobile industry, petrochemicals, or pharmaceuticals remained minimal. It was their prominence in the universities, the publishing industry, and especially the communications industry that proved worrisome. That was where Jewish talent and entrepreneurship seemed to be concentrated. The anti-Semite imagined that a Freud or an Einstein or a Walter Lippmann transmitted a specifically Jewish message that could in some mysterious way mislead the nation.

The actual exercise of political power by Jews is best observed within their communal organizations, like their labor or their Zionist movement. Historically, the most intense power struggles were played out within the Jewish ethnic economy and were frequently solved within the community. When Jewish unions went on strike against Jewish "bosses" in the twenties, such strikes were often accompanied by physical conflict for control and had an ideological dimension. The rivalry between Jewish communists and social democrats for control of the garment unions culminated in the catastrophic strike of 1926, which almost destroyed the Jewish labor movement. Strangely, the existence of such bitter intracommunal strife did little to challenge the notion of an organized Jewish power conspiracy. Few ethnic communities have been so plagued by perennial divisive political strife. It is only in recent years that Jews have finally succeeded in cooling the ideological "hot" posture that plagued the immigrant generation.

Jewish intracommunal politics also remains fierce today because there are spoils to win in the form of millions of dollars of philanthropic funds. Few ethnic groups in America can boast of possessing an informal internal taxing system like the United Jewish Communities (UJC), formerly the United Jewish Appeal (UJA). The UJC, the major communal fundraising agency, alone reaches into all Jewish communities. Millions are raised each year to finance the communal needs, which range from care of the aged to education, from resettlement aid for Israel to retraining of Soviet emigrants. Jewish communal politics is budget politics, who gets what. There is even something resembling communal governance in the annual General Assembly meeting of the CJF (Council of Jewish Federations) and its fundraising arm, the United Jewish Communities (UJC), where many of the conflicts between competing communal interests are settled internally and an agenda of priorities is established.

We will note later that it is difficult to classify the occasional foray of ostensibly Jewish interest groups, like the neoconservatives or groups associated with the New Left, into the national political arena. As in the case of the American Labor Party, aside from the prominence of Jews in their formation and membership, determining the Jewish identity of such groups is problematic. That does not prevent classifying such groups as Jewish by people who for whatever reason need to establish such a link. In the case of the neoconservatives the problem is compounded because they do not represent a Jewish communal consensus, and the causes they advocate are not realizable through the use of normal political instruments. The American Israel Public Affairs Committee (AIPAC) lobbies for what it believes will help Israel, but one cannot imagine lobbying for neoconservative causes such as democratic nation-building or the war in Iraq. The confusion is abetted when some agencies associated with the extreme Jewish left or right, like Jewish members of the Communist party or the Jewish Defense League cover themselves with a Jewish communal mantle and claim to be the voice of the Jewish community. In the absence of a formal mechanism whereby an ethnic constituency makes its will known, the possibility for a well organized interest group to preempt the community voice is a distinct possibility. In the case of the Iraq war, however, there was no concerted effort to speak for American Jewry nor could there be.

The New Left of the sixties and seventies, whose core organizations, Students for a Democratic Society and the Berkeley Free Speech Movement were initially overwhelmingly Jewish, had a considerable impact on the peace and civil rights movement.[11] Yet stopping the war in Vietnam and extending civil rights were not exclusively Jewish aspirations. We note later that neither the neocons nor the New Left can rightfully claim support in the Jewish community. Most Jews were appalled when the SDS allied itself with the Black Panthers, and today one hears few Jewish voices supporting the war in Iraq. Yet since the problem of who speaks for the Jewish community or any American ethnic group has never been formally resolved the preemption of the Jewish communal voice by small group intent on doing so seems unavoidable.

*   *   *

The Jewish political voice is especially audible when all the elements that compose the American Jewish power nexus are supported by a strong communal consensus. One such moment occurred when enormous communal pressure was projected on the Truman administration to extend diplomatic recognition to Israel in May 1948. It also is likely to occur when the Jewish communal and national interest correspond to a popular national cause such as Roosevelt's declaration of war after the bombing of Pearl Harbor. But usually such instances are associated with "liberal" policy measures in the domestic sphere, such as proposed legislation for support of stem cell research or raising the minimum hourly wage. Its preferences here correspond roughly to what the educated urbanized elements of the general population support. When these optimum conditions for confluence exist, then the Jewish influence appears much greater than it is to Judeophobes who overestimate Jewish power and underestimate the power of the majority. Far from being a Jewish conspiracy, the reality is that a coalition of forces, usually liberal, has come together to amplify support for a specific policy. That is the real story behind the rising pressure for a national medical insurance plan. It is far from a Jewish conspiracy. Remaining unanswered for the moment is why Jews are so active in the leadership and rank and file of these coalitions.

When Jewish advocacy does focus on a "tribal" goal there still is no assurance that there will be total agreement on all aspects of a given policy. Jews overwhelmingly support the security and well-being of Israel, but that does not necessarily extend to support of the wall or settlements on the West Bank. On key issues, Jewish communal support remains divided so that no clear mandate to communal leaders can be given. The "Jewish lobby," headed in this case by AIPAC, often comes down at a considerable distance from where the Jewish political center of gravity may actually be.[12] We will note later that there have been several instances when it also did not represent the policy of the government of Israel. There is consensus on the desirability of peace, but little agreement on how best to achieve it. Unburdened by the actual responsibility for security held exclusively by the government of Israel, American Jewish public opinion tends to be more flexible on the requisites for a permanent peace. At the same time there are voices within the community that are more strident and less prone to compromise than even the most security-minded Israeli. American Jewry is a variegated tribe. With all, the interest in Israel, strengthened by kinship, religion, and history, is sustained and deep, so that any demand for compromise that is seen as threatening the security of the Jewish state can overnight radically alter the American Jewish political profile. When Mearsheimer and Walt complain, as did Senator Fulbright before them, that Jews control the dialogue that sets Middle East policy so that opposition voices cannot be heard, they seem unaware that the Jewish state founded in 1948 has not yet experienced a single year in which its survival did not go unchallenged. A bloody suicide bombing in an Israeli city or a heightened security threat can alter the Jewish political profile overnight.

* * *

For reasons that go beyond the urgency of their communal interest, American Jewry has been fairly successful in its transaction with its government. One scholar observes that "the movement of Jews into the American political elite marks a radical social transformation in Jewish history, for that matter in history in general."[13] But that movement has in it a paradoxical element. The potential of Jews or any other interest group to project influence is associated with its ability to fit into the society, to be part of the commonweal rather than a "foreign" group. The Jewish political voice is heard best precisely at the juncture when American Jewish group identity is in the process of being transformed so that it is more American in its focus and interests. Though still effective, the number of Jewish activists that were mobilized by the Soviet Jewry movement was comparatively small for a community of 5.2 million.[14] That transformation from hyphenate to full-time status as Americans also accounts partly for the reluctance for the Jews of Roosevelt's "Jew Deal" to press him on the rescue issue. Jews close to the seat of power, like Felix Frankfurter, Sam Rosenman, Ben Cohen, and Isador Lubin, would not advocate a specific Jewish cause that could be perceived as favoring an ethnic rather than a national interest. At the time there existed a gulf between the two interests. Up to the bombing of Pearl Harbor, and for a considerable period thereafter, Roosevelt and his advisors felt that the primary goal of foreign policy was to get a reluctant nation into the war. The American people could not have been mobilized for war if it was projected as one to save the Jews. Not until the light of victory could be seen at the end of the tunnel did Roosevelt relent and order the establishment of the War Refugee Board in January 1944, which brought him closer to the Jewish interest of rescue of their European brethren.

We shall note in the following chapter, in the most urgent case for the exercise of its political influence during the years of the Holocaust, American Jewry could not convince the Roosevelt administration to act until it was too late. It was ineffective despite the fact that conditions to influence policy were seemingly optimal. When it was most needed, no special power such as then fantasized by Roosevelt haters, could be brought into play. In reality, those who see extraordinary Jewish power are dealing with a complex tapestry in which Jews acting in confluence with others seem to exercise such power. Their efficient communal organization may sometimes allow a more effective organization of public pressure, but it is a freedom to organize available to all ethnic subcultures in a democratic society.

* * *

It is possible that the imagining of a satanic Jewish power persists through the ages because the image has been around for so long that it has taken on a life of its own. Jews are disproportionately prominent in American politics, which may go beyond the fact that they use the political process effectively. There may be factors outside the normal configuration of power that go beyond organization and activism that strengthen the Jewish political presence. For some, like the British historian Arnold Toynbee, the very defiance of the normal lifecycle of civilizations, makes it suspect. For others it may be fueled by their conspicuous presence in the world of science and communications.

The persistence of the fantasy that imagines a historically vulnerable people as all-powerful would be less puzzling if "soft" power were considered part of the picture. That is a term used here to refer to "civilizing" ideas based on shared values about how a worthy life is best lived, which today is universally embedded in divergent societies. In Western civilization these ideas based on the Judeo-Christian tradition they are stated in much abbreviated form in the Decalogue. Jews have played a primary but not exclusive role in advocating such civilizing ideas in the public square.[15] They include everything from the panoply of values propounded by major religions to the idea of justice, freeness, and the rights of the individual found in Western democracies. Today, some version of these life-affirming values are inherent, often in subterranean form, in all societies, where together they compose what might be called a universal moral grammar. In a word, there exists, openly in some parts of the world, and in subterranean form in others, a shared set of values and rules, a moral grammar, concerning how life should be lived and the preferable direction of public policy. In a suppressive society, like the former Soviet Union, it may simply be a unarticulated sensibility that says, "Gulag, 'No,'; Freedom of movement, 'Yes.'" In American political culture, one can locate them in the ideas associated with the liberal persuasion whose list of what needs liberation is continually expanded.[16] Since Jews, for historic and security reasons, have an interest that the host societies where they live adhere to the highest moral level of behavior, that hidden grammar forms an indirect buttress of Jewish influence. In the end, the rescue of Jews from the death camps, the struggle to win the right of emigration for Soviet Jewry, or today, the campaign to stop the genocide in Darfur, in which Jews are deeply involved, are issues that gain an extra measure of influence because of their connection to the wellsprings of human rights that have become part of the assumptions by which we live. Jewish liberalism would hardly be a flicker on the monitor of human events if it were not amplified by this subterranean stream.

Years of suppression by authoritarian regimes does not seem able to suppress this concealed code. Preceding the bloody suppression of the protest in Tiananmen Square, the students carried a papier mâché representation of the Statue of Liberty, the most familiar icon associated with free societies.[17] The release of Soviet Jews by a reluctant Kremlin had a great deal to do with upholding the freedom of movement idea reiterated in the Helsinki accords. It occurred after Communist parties in France, Italy, the United States, and other countries apprised their comrades in Moscow that it was virtually impossible to argue against the idea that emigration is a natural right. Governing systems and degrees of freedom and control vary enormously from society to society, but there seems to exist an almost intuitive understanding even in the most suppressive social orders of where the path of progress should lead. Yet soft power finds little sanction in law. There are no military units to support its mandate. Its impact is long-range and rooted in a universal human preference that freedom is better than slavery.

Though Jewish voters customarily support every foreign policy initiative that contains such a moral dimension, from Wilson's Fourteen Points
to Roosevelt's Atlantic Charter, with the exception of the two Jewish
lawyers who pushed through the Briand-Kellogg Pact in 1928 outlawing
aggressive war, there is little direct evidence that Jews alone have advocated the moralization of public policy. The democratic socialism of the
Western world has inherent in it a moral imperative that grows out of the
underlying moral grammar in its assumption that the world must be made
better, kinder, and more humane. Jewish voters are far from being alone
in their quest for a world of peace and a concern for a moral dimension in
our foreign relations. The listing of other constituencies including Quakers, liberal Protestant churches, and ordinary public interest advocates
dominate the newspaper ads advocating such positions.

That is what is so strange about the view that the invasion of Iraq is
part of a Jewish grand strategy to bring democracy to the Middle East.
We shall note in chapter VI that the invasion is attributed to the plotting
of the neoconservatives, ostensibly a Jewish group, imbued with a vision of a muscular, confidant, crusading democracy ready to abandon
the reactive foreign policy to which democracies are heir in favor of
democratic nation-building. The notion that the invasion of Iraq to be
followed by its democratization becomes part of a Jewish plot to end
the Middle East conflict and finally bring security to Israel. That theory
has now collapsed under its own weight. A full accounting of motivations for the invasion of Iraq will become known only years from now
when the archives are opened, but it is already clear that Israel was far
more concerned with the threat from Iran and its quest for the bomb.
Rather than unidentified Jewish interests pushing for the invasion, the
reverse seems to have been the case. American policymakers sought the
support of Israel for the planned invasion, which was reluctantly given.
The Iraq war that has heightened the notion of a demonic Jewish power
acting behind the scenes conceals the fact that the strategy of bringing
democracy to the Middle East by force of arms if necessary conceals a
mix of motivations familiar to students of Theodore Roosevelt's "Big
Stick" policy. Upset about the failure of the Santo Domingo (now the
Dominican Republic) to pay its debt to Germany in 1904, Roosevelt is
purported to have acclaimed that he would teach the Dominicans democracy, even if he had to break every bone in their bodies. That penchant
for imposing democracy by force is not so distant from events in recent
American diplomatic history, and has consistently failed to win support

among American Jews. There are some who point out that the invasion of Iraq is atypical from many vantages, especially in its preference for hard rather than soft power. America's premier place in the world was achieved in an unprecedented non-coercive way. The historian Charles Maier coins the term "empire of consumption" to indicate America's non-coercive consensual ascendancy.[18] If it is true that the democratic American society serves as a kind of natural home of the moral idea we have classified as "soft" power, and that American behavior in the international arena, while far from perfect, has generally achieved a higher moral level, then there is no need to find a Jewish conspiracy to impose it on the nation. The quest for the moral high ground and the accompanying play of soft power is something that Americans, Jews, and men of goodwill everywhere, share.

Lest the reader detects an ethnic hubris, let it be clear that Jewish prominence in advocating "soft" power may go beyond moral standards embedded in its religio-culture or a special saintliness. It stems from the long-range effects of powerlessness, the inability of exilic Jewry to protect itself from physical assault. It is, after all, in the interest of a group that has historically had little assurance of communal security to ask the world to be better than it is or perhaps wants to be. One finds little evidence of such moralistic tendency where Jews possess sovereign power, as in Israel. Members of Israel's peace movements and of her Kibbutzim, where such soft ideas germinate, are overwhelmingly the children of European Ashkenazi Jews. What puzzles many is that despite clear evidence that those with murderous intent are deaf to a moral outcry, the enthusiasm of Jews who submit such civilizing ideas to an unhearing world does not diminish. It is possible that rather than the classical scheming demonic image drawn, the Jewish political persona is characterized by an innocence born of not possessing sovereign power and its corruptions during its long exile.

* * *

American Jewish influence in world affairs, especially in the Middle East, seems formidable because it is projected within a democratically conceived American foreign policy. The increase in American Jewish leverage in politics generally, and in Middle East policy particularly during the Cold War years, occurred simultaneously with the growth of the United States as a world power. But it accounts in some small measure for the protective American diplomatic and military mantle that shields Israel in the dangerous neighborhood it lives. The need to maximize that support has shaped much of American Jewry's post-war political culture, but there was little evidence of American concern until the administration of John F. Kennedy who promised military protection, but rejected Ben-Gurion's proposal for a formal alliance. The Truman and Eisenhower administrations were more concerned with keeping the balance of forces in the Middle East. The closeness between the United States and Israel, which became manifest before the administration of George W. Bush, is more apparent today because the threat has become more manifest. But it has not been forced to go to an extreme, such as counseling a preemptive war against an oil-rich Arab nation. That grand design, which was ostensibly conceived by neoconservative counselors, found little support among Israel's strategic thinkers who viewed Iran as the greater threat. Moreover, Israel prides itself in never having had to request direct American military intervention. To some extent she has become self-sufficient in the production of the high-tech weapons that have become part of modern warfare. During the war in Lebanon in 2006, much of the Israeli ordnance, including cluster bombs and drones, was manufactured in Israel. In the end, major weapons systems, such as fighter aircraft and anti-missile defenses, remain beyond Israel's financial capacity. During the ' 73 war, the question of resupply became crucial and highlighted Israel's need to become completely self-sufficient in security matters.[19] That was the original strategic thinking behind the development of its atomic bomb. For the time being, Israel is the only state of its size permitted to maintain its own atomic arsenal. Israel's possession of the bomb has become a major talking point in the troubled American relations with Iran. Its regional monopoly on the ultimate weapon to assure its security is now on the verge of being broken. What will happen then haunts Israel's strategic thinkers. Given the depth of hostility and the intractability of the half-century-old conflict, one can doubt that the traditional Jewish reliance on the moral idea, on soft power, will avail. There are signs at the United Nations and other forums of the international community, like the European Union that, with the exception of the United States and Germany, the Jewish presence remains outside the universe of obligation, as it was during the World War II. That is the stark reality embedded in the collective Jewish memory. From an internal Jewish communal perspective, the belief that somehow the security of Israel is a reality, because American Jewry has a lock on American foreign policy, may be a consummation devoutly to be wished, but too incredible a fantasy to be credible.

The chapters that follow tell us that even in the instances when Jews were seemingly successful in enlisting the support of the American government, the Jewish impact on policy was minimal. The outsized role played by American Jewry in opening the gates for the emigration of Soviet Jewry was not based on its political power. The Soviet Jewry movement did not possess the leverage to alter the immigration regulations of a superpower. But it was able to call upon the influence of the United States to act as a kind of proxy in a peripheral area of the foreign affairs arena. It is an example of the resonance that the idea of free emigration possesses in its own right. In the context of the Cold War, the human rights trespass represented by the Kremlin's reluctance to "let my people go" was a cudgel in the hands of the government in the propaganda war.

In general, however, American support for Israel in the protracted negotiations with the Palestinians has become so apparent that it has to some degree compromised its status as "honest broker." It is that special relationship which accounts partly for the complaint that Jews have special access to American power. Rarely considered, by those who complain that Jews control American policy in the Middle East, are the ties of mutual interest reinforced by shared principles that make that friendship possible. There is also a question of how dependable power wielded on her behalf based solely on Washington's goodwill could be. Nations, we are informed, do not have permanent friends, only permanent interests. American support has been withdrawn by a sudden change of circumstance and long-range interest. There are examples of several communities, including the South Vietnamese regime in 1975 and the Kurds of northern Iraq, as well as the Shiites of the south, who suffered grievously as a result of such abandonment. American aid to its clients is not extended exclusively out of largess. Relations with other nations are by their very nature transactional. Something is required in return in turn for aid or diplomatic recognition or a lucrative trade agreement. It is sometimes exacted in the form of reciprocation as in Nixon's request that Israel position its armed forces to stop Syrian tanks from rolling into Jordan in 1970, or merely diplomatic support for fragile states as during the Cold War.

The reader will note that the ability to influence policy in marginal cases such as the release of Soviet Jewry rests on persuading American decision makers that it is in the national interest to do so. Jewish NGOs, like the National Conference on Soviet Jewry, are not by themselves able to convince oppressive governments to change their ways. Their case must be made for them by the American government, which must be persuaded to act. How persuasive Jewish leaders can be depends only partly on their political leverage and the use they are able to make of the democratic political process. Much depends on the proximity of the Jewish interest to the ability of Jewish leaders to persuade decision makers of that mutuality.

We deal with an ominously familiar image with which Jewish communities through the ages have had to contend. An American ethnic constituency, increasingly challenged to sustain itself as a community, stands accused of a Machiavellian scheme to control American foreign policy in the Middle East and by extension elsewhere. The image is seductively simple. Jews are imagined to possess inordinate political power and the satanic will to use it against the national interest.

* * *

These chapters are not intended as a counterpolemic, but rather to illustrate the many facets of the power question. We begin with a historic episode that in American Jewish history probably represents the greatest need ever experienced by Jewish leadership to influence foreign policy. In that era too, nurtured by some not fully understood need to believe the demonic, the caricature image of Jewish power surfaced undeterred by persistent rumors, eventually confirmed, that European Jewry was being subjected to an industrial murder process. The reader will learn that the accusations that are surfacing today are not innocently submitted. The myth of Jewish power and evil intent is deeply embedded and enormously dangerous.

Notes

1. George Soros who recently entered the Jewish arena to counteract the "baneful" effects of the "Israel Lobby" possesses wealth on the scale of Jacob Schiff, but heretofore has shown little interest in Jewish philanthropy.
2. The following are only a sample of American Jewish requests for diplomatic intercession: the Damascus blood libel case in 1840, the Mortara kidnapping (1858), and the passport question for Jews of Russia (1890-1914). See Cyrus Adler and Aaron Margalith, *With Firmness in the Right: American Diplomatic Action Affecting Jews, 1840-1945* (New York: Arno Press, 1977 reprint edition). More recently, requests for intercession included the threatened Jewish communities in Europe during the Holocaust and intercession for Soviet Jewry (1964-1989), and since 1948, the overriding need of Israel whose legitimacy and existence is perpetually challenged by its neighbors.
3. See Tom W. Smith, *Jewish Distinctiveness in America: A Statistical Portrait* (New York: American Jewish Committee, 2005), 15-18. Jews were particularly success-

ful in the election of 2006 in which two Jewish Democrats, Sen. Chuck Schumer (NY) and Rahm Emanuel (IL) chaired the Democratic campaign committees that reclaimed control of Congress. In the House, Jews will chair key committees, Bob Filner (CA), Veterans Affairs Committee; Barney Frank (MA), Financial Services Committee; Henry Waxman (CA), Government Reform Committee; and Howard Berman (CA), Standards and Official Conduct (Ethics) Committee. In the Senate, the list of Jews in leadership positions is equally imposing: Carl Levin (MI), chair, Armed Services Committee; Barbara Boxer (CA), Environment and Public Works; Joe Lieberman (CT), Homeland Security and Governmental Affairs Committee; Herb Kohl (WI), Special Committee on Aging; Arlen Specter (R-WI), senior Republican on Judiciary Committee. There will be at least two Jewish governors, Ed Rendell (D-PA) and Lind Lingle (R-HI). Jews elected to local governments and courts is equally disproportionate.

4.   Max Fisher was merely one of several Jewish money raisers for the Republican Party. See Peter Golden, *Quiet Diplomat*, New York: Herzl Press, 1992

5.   Goldmann became head of the World Jewish Congress and a member of the Jewish Agency, but did not have a popular constituency in the community. Wise founded and became head of the American Jewish Congress and occupied most leadership posts in the American Zionist movement, and also developed a "jolly pulpit" in his own "Free Synagogue" and the Jewish Institute of Religion (JIR), which he founded.

6.   Hebrew for the "court Jews" with special influence with the king. Today, the term refers to Jewish leaders, who by dint of class and wealth and personal power, have access to power holders.

7.   "Marshall Law" was an appellative that exaggerated the authority commanded by Louis Marshall as head of the American Jewish Committee. It pertained more to an imperious attitude than to the command of actual power.

8.   See Henry L. Feingold, "'Courage First and Intelligence Second': The American Jewish Secular Elite, Roosevelt and the Failure to Rescue," *American Jewish History*, 424-458. The classic example of that transaction entered into by Jews in the inner circles of power is that of Walter Rathenau, who, at the pinnacle of his career following his appointment as German foreign minister in May 1922, continued to believe in the divinity of Christ, but thought it would be considered opportunistic to convert.

9.   Roosevelt won the election of 1936 with the largest majority in American history and did not need the extra votes from formerly socialist voters to carry New York State. Lehman had won a special place in Jewish labor's heart because of his great financial aid to the movement after the debacle of the strike of 1926 and the subsequent struggle with communist infiltration.

10.   The pattern of disaffiliation among scientists was not uncommon. Only 17 percent of the refugee scientists in the Manhattan project who could be classified as Jewish under the Nuremberg Laws considered themselves Jewishly affiliated.

11.   The problematic connection between the Jews and the New Left is developed in chapter VII.

12.   For example, during the Ehud Barak Labor party administration, AIPAC lobbied against funneling financial aid to the Palestinian Authority so that it might be strengthened against the Hamas onslaught. Its position was more closely aligned with Likud than the Israel government.

13.   David Biali, *Power and Powerlessness in Jewish History*, (New York: Schocken Books, 1986), 181.

14.   No count was ever taken. The highest number gathered in one place occurred during the great rally at the Capitol in December 1987 and was less than 220,000, among whom there may have been 8,000 to 10,000 activists, only a handful of whom were fulltime. See Henry L. Feingold, *Silent No More: Saving the Jews of Russia, The American Jewish Effort, 1967-1989* (Syracuse, NY: Syracuse University Press, 2007). The author concludes that the American branch of the Soviet Jewry movement was a distinct minority. Most American Jews remained unaware of a Jewish problem in the Soviet Union.

15.   What seems today to be eternal and universal may not always have been so according to Lynn Hunt. She views human rights as having gained currency during the enlightenment and not fully embedded until the compilation of the Universal Declaration of Human Rights in 1948. The earliest version of that "moral grammar" lacked universality. English common law had no sense of the inherent equality of man first put forward by Thomas Jefferson and the French Declaration of Rights (1789). See Lynn Hunt, *Inventing Human Rights: A History* (New York: W. W. Norton, 2007).

16.   For example, the strictures against murder of innocents are to some extent present in all cultures and societies, even those that practice human sacrifice or genocide. The idea of a preexisting "moral grammar" for which all civilizations are wired is similar in some respects to Noam Chomsky's theory for the inherency of the rules of language, except that one cannot conceive that societies are "wired."

17.   That such could be the case in a nation with a comparatively weak democratic tradition and much suppression, especially during the years of the Cultural Revolution, attests to the strength of this underground stream. The case of Czechoslovakia, which after a brutal wartime occupation followed three years later by a Soviet model socialist state, snapped back with a Prague Spring in 1978 and aspired to "Socialism with a human face," reflects its persistence.

18.   Charles S. Maier, *Among Empires: American Ascendancy and Its Predecessors* (Cambridge, MA: Harvard University Press, 2005).

19.   There is still a lingering suspicion among Israeli strategists that the lateness of the resupply was part of a conscious strategy by opponents in the State and Defense departments to allow Israel to "twist in the wind," so that she might realize the limits of her influence on U.S. Middle East policy.

II

Saving the Jews of Europe:
The Failure of the "Jew Deal"

American Jewry's ineffectiveness in rescuing its European brethren was not for lack of concern, but lack of sufficient political power. That insufficiency is difficult to recognize because the conspicuous Jewish presence in the Roosevelt administration made the opportunity for rescue seem propitious. In the earliest phase of the crisis, when a more generous policy of admission of refugees was urgently needed, opening the gates wider for the Jewish refugees was politically virtually impossible. During the Depression, the nation's restrictive immigration policy gained new popular support to supplement the original nativist national origins formula on which the quota system of the Reed Johnson immigration law (1924) was based. How could refugees be admitted when "one third of the nation [was] ill-housed, ill-fed and ill-clothed?" argued restrictionists, using the president's own ringing phrases.[1]

The closing of the doors to virtually all refugees, which began during Hoover's administration by a strict interpretation of the "likely to become public charge" (LPC) provision of the immigration law, was continued by Roosevelt. The administration of the immigration law went beyond what the law required so that only in 1939 were the relevant quotas filled. Despite the fact that Jewish leaders seemed in a good position to at least gain a more generous administration of the existing law, State Department directives ordered an ever stricter policy for the issuance of visas. The Jewish electorate was Roosevelt's most loyal ethnic constituency and remained so after the election of 1936 when the ardor of other ethnic voters waned. Leading Jews maintained an especially close relationship with Roosevelt who, like Al Smith, his predecessor as governor of New York, sought talent wherever it could be found. Though Roosevelt equalized access to the federal civil service for all ethnics, and may actually have been more prone to appoint Italian Americans to the judiciary, the predominance of Jews in the Roosevelt administration became fodder for the anti-Semitic propaganda mill.[2] But the three congressional committees that could play a role in rescuing the hapless Jewish refugees were chaired by Jews, the House Judiciary Committee (Rep. Emanuel Celler), the House Foreign Affairs Committee (Rep. Sol. Bloom), and the House Committee on Immigration and Naturalization (Rep. Samuel Dickstein). Moreover, from an ideological perspective, the shaping ideas behind the welfare state, such as public housing, social security, and medical care were first incubated in the Jewish labor movement and among Jewish social workers. American Jewry had an almost proprietary interest in the New Deal. Yet, aside from allowing the extension of visitor's visas, Roosevelt would allow no exception to the restrictive provisions of the immigration law, even for Jewish children stranded in France.

Viewed from a distance, the rescue of German-speaking Jews from central Europe, the first victims of Berlin's excesses, seemed within reach of American Jewish power. The Nazi threat was, after all, perceived from the outset as threatening all Western civilization, including the United States. American Jewry was well known for its philanthropic network, so that at least some portion of the cost outside of the family support required by law could be absorbed by Jewish philanthropic agencies like HIAS (Hebrew Immigrant Aid Society) and the JDC (American Jewish Joint Distribution Society). In the end, it was the inability of American Jewish leaders to convince the Roosevelt administration that the rescue of Europe's Jews warranted a place on the list of war aims, indeed that at Auschwitz it was also their world that was burning, that produced a listless rescue effort until 1944. When leaders like Rabbi Stephen Wise dared to make a special plea for help in Congress or the Oval Office, they keenly felt the impropriety of pleading for the Jewish interest when the entire Western world was threatened.[3] They witnessed first hand the futility of trying to change policy solely on the basis of moral principle.

After the attack on Pearl Harbor and Germany's declaration of war, there was a glimmer of hope that Roosevelt might recognize the confluence of interest between American war aims with the need to do what still might be done for European Jewry. Jews were, after all, early to perceive the mortal danger of a rampant Nazi Germany to the security of the nation. Roosevelt assumed the political risk in related areas like the Destroyer–Bases deal with Britain (September 1940), enacted by executive order, and the Lend Lease Act (February 1941). He decided together with Churchill at their meeting in Argentia, Newfoundland in August 1941 that the war was about defending democracy and the Atlantic powers. The nation became a virtual silent partner in the war against Germany. Yet the overarching moral crusading character of the impending struggle, which was stated even before America entered the war in the four freedoms of the Atlantic Charter, did not recognize the deportations and the developing death camps. There was little recognition that if Nazi race theory prevailed, the formula of pluralism that delicately bound America together would be undermined. A more generous refugee policy, and later a policy of direct intervention to stop or at least minimize the slaughter as an integral part of that moral crusade, were not considered. The information strategy of the war meant the avoidance of talk of the "Final Solution," lest the war become a war to save the Jews. No ringing statement regarding the genocidal character of the Final Solution was ever issued from the Oval Office. The fate of the Jews was not mentioned in any of the wartime conferences at Teheran, Cairo, Casablanca, or Yalta, which determined war aims and strategy. Allied propaganda rarely spoke of Berlin's penchant for genocide. Somehow the datum that most clearly demonstrated the difference between the two sides was allowed to slip out of the public dialogue. One wonders if it could ever have been otherwise. European Jewry was never included in the "universe of obligation," which in Western civilization ostensibly bound all of Europe's people together in a web of protection and concern. Strangely, six decades later the myth of a formidable Jewish power at work in the world persists and shows signs of becoming stronger.

* * *

In order to determine the play of Jewish power, we need to know what was possible and what would have been sufficient. To this day, no agreement has been reached on whether such steps as the bombing of Auschwitz and the rail lines leading to it might have saved lives. Similarly, only today's moralists set unrealizable standards on what needed to be done to earn the moral high ground. Most researchers have come to realize that given Berlin's genocidal passion, there were limits to what might have been done. In a catastrophe of such scale, it may well be that enough could never have been done to satisfy the moral athlete. The flood of anti-alien legislative proposals in Congress in 1938 was, in fact, an example of the cherished democratic process producing an unacceptable response. So adamant was the opposition to the admission of refugees in the electorate that it became one of the redlines Roosevelt would not cross. He read the political reality accurately and any influence possessed by American Jewry would have made little difference. It reveals a basic truth about special interest power such as Jews are purported to possess. The practical estimate of the effectiveness of such power is related to the feasibility of implementing the goals proposed. In the case of the refugee crises, no such relationship could be established. On a practical level, some mutually agreed upon standard concerning rescue possibilities must first be in place. That may involve not only determining the possibility of negotiating with Berlin concerning Jews, but also some determination of the leverage available to the United States. Until 1944, when there were the first intimations of Berlin's willingness to bargain seriously about what they called the "Jewish question," the possibilities to pressure for action from the Roosevelt administration on the refugee crises, and later externally, to elicit a response from Berlin regarding the halting of the industrial murder process, were minimal. While rescue was at most a footnote to wartime strategy for Roosevelt, the Final Solution was a priority goal for Berlin, which became an even higher priority after it became clear that the war was lost. Before the war began in September 1939, and almost two years thereafter when America was neutral, the Roosevelt administration did take advantage of the possibility of transacting business with Berlin concerning the refugee crisis its policy had generated. Roosevelt's old Groton crony, George Rublee, actually negotiated a "Statement of Agreement" containing the terms for mitigating the crisis. But the agreement could not be implemented because the amount of capital required to "ransom" and resettle German Jewry was not available to Jewish leaders, nor were there havens where German Jews might be resettled. A policy to change the immigration laws to allow Jews to enter, and after the U.S. entry into war, to make the halting of the slaughter a major Allied war aim became possible only in 1944, when it was clear that Germany faced utter defeat and various proposals for ransoming the Jews resurfaced.[4]

The Evian Conference and the Rublee-Schacht negotiations that followed can serve as the earliest evidence that, contrary to the anti-Semitic rhetoric that spoke of inordinate Jewish power, America Jewry was in fact almost powerless to fulfill the responsibility kinship had assigned to it. In the years between the advent of Hitler to power in January 1933 and 1940, it would have taken the expenditure of a considerable amount of the administration's political capital to convince the American people that the Nazi threat would have to be confronted, and even more to convince them to allow European Jewry to find haven among them. Beyond the strength of the isolationist block, it took time for Americans that felt they had been duped into entering World War I by gruel propaganda and Allied duplicity to change. Protected by the moat of the Atlantic Ocean, Americans were not inclined to recognize much less counter the threat emanating from Berlin. German Americans were the nation's largest hyphenate group and there had been signs that the influence of National Socialism had made some inroads among them.[5] Roosevelt's primary task was to convince the reluctant Depression-ridden American people to prepare for war. By the time of the London "blitz," much of the isolationist strength in Congress had been eroded, but the final step of actually going to war remained elusive. Berlin spoke endlessly of the "Jewish question" and its propaganda converted Roosevelt to the Jewish faith. But in order to keep the Jewish question on a low level back-burner the State Department preferred the euphemism "political refugee." The term Jew never appeared in the title of the several agencies involved in the listless rescue effort such as the War Refugee Board. As late as 1940 the American people remained reluctant to become involved in the war for any reason, much less to rescue European Jewry.   To this day, it remains difficult to envisage the U.S. entrance into the war without the Japanese attack on Pearl Harbor and Berlin's surprising declaration of war that followed.

The cry heard in the immediate pre-war years that the Jews were pushing the nation into war was much louder than the similar cry today regarding the role of Jewish neoconservatives in getting the United States into the war in Iraq. It was audible enough to influence Roosevelt, who had a sensitive ear for what would roil racial and ethnic tensions and redound badly for his administration. That may have been behind his rejection of the Wagner-Rogers Bill (1940), which would have admitted 10,000 Jewish refugee children outside the quota system. Eleanor Roosevelt, the president's hyperactive wife, tried vainly to get his support for the measure. But her efforts were futile. Jewish leaders watched in dismay as Roosevelt shelved the Wagner-Rogers Bill they advocated, only to witness a congressional craze a year later to grant haven outside the law to Christian British children, victims of the "Blitz." In the 1930s anti-Semitism was a given part of the nation's political climate. The president's ability to use the power of his office rested ultimately on the support of public opinion, which in fact opposed admission of Jews under any circumstances. Roosevelt, to whom Jewish leaders looked for succor, possessed neither the power nor the inclination to respond to their urgent request. Unlike the later case for admitting Soviet Jewish refugees during the seventies and eighties, during the World War II period the political environment worked against rescue. During the Cold War the reverse was the case.

Aside from public opinion, the actual power arrangements in the international arena also militated against a more active rescue policy. American military power was so degraded during the twenties and thirties that there were serious doubts whether the nation could defend itself, much less take on added responsibility towards the growing number of victims of Nazism. The president understood that the war would eventually come to American shores and that the nation was woefully unprepared. The inauguration of the nation's first peacetime draft in September 1940 was a sign that the lesson was being absorbed. The national budget now paid some heed to building up defense industries. But the realization that U.S. entry into the war was inevitable came too late to strengthen Roosevelt's hand on the question of refugees, which remained on the margins of the administration's concern. In that sense, the invitation of thirty-two receiving nations to convene in Evian, sent by the State Department in June of 1938, to find a solution to the refugee crisis, was little more than a political gesture. The invitation clearly stated that the United States itself would not change its immigration laws and was not requesting other receiving nations to do so. If one adds to this the privatizing effects of the Depression, which in 1938 showed signs of reverting to the unemployment rate of the early thirties, the prospects for mitigating the refugee crises looked bleak as the war approached. The failure of the countercyclical strategy on which the New Deal was based, and Roosevelt's seeming loss of his political touch after the failure of the court packing scheme, generated a loss of confidence in the administration. By the early months of 1939, the prospects were remote for winning the administration's help for a foreign minority whose kin were not winning popularity contests at home. The Roosevelt that ran for a third term in 1940 was not the Roosevelt of the "hundred days." The political price tag for a more active rescue policy was higher than his administration was willing to pay.

The president Jewish leaders had to address regarding the rescue of their European brethren was preoccupied with the unfolding events in Europe. Given limited options about the disposition of a foreign minority, Roosevelt treaded carefully. He chose first to face the Nazi threat, but his reading of American public opinion made him wary, lest his entrance into the war be imaged as a war to save the Jews. The Jewish leaders who were called upon to make the case for a more active rescue policy were aware of that the case for intervention had to be made first on the basis that the Reich posed a threat to the national interest, rather than to rescue European Jewry. In effect, public opinion severely limited not only the projection of Jewish power, but also the possibility of Roosevelt acting unilaterally on behalf of Jews.

Jews had voted the Republican ticket as late as 1920. It was the party of Lincoln and Theodore Roosevelt's name was on their citizenship papers. But once they switched their allegiance to the Democratic party, they became the most loyal of the ethnics that supported the New Deal. They did not change their allegiance after the election of 1936 as did other ethnics whose ardor declined.[6] For various reasons the Jewish love affair with FDR was more ardent than the support of other ethnic blocks. But in a strange way, the attachment of the Jewish voter to the New Deal militated against the political leverage of its leaders. Roosevelt was aware that Jewish leaders could not threaten him with the loss of the increasingly important Jewish vote which, in any case, had no place else to go. They soon became dependent on the less certain rewards for political loyalty. So loyal was the Jewish electorate to Roosevelt that the creation of the American Labor Party by Jewish labor unions in 1935 allowed the socialist-inclined Jewish workers of New York state to vote for a highborn Episcopalian without betraying their socialist principles.

The Jewish love affair with the New Deal, and Roosevelt particularly, continued throughout the war years. The case for rescue was not boldly pressed until 1944, when Henry Morgenthau, Jr., his Jewish secretary of the treasury, submitted evidence of the State Department's efforts to block even those rescue efforts that might have been undertaken. Those Jewish advisors, whom anti-administration forces had taken to calling the "Jew Deal," were careful not to undermine their positions by seeming to advocate a Jewish need at the expense of the national interest. They were men of high station whose transaction with the majority culture required a playing down of their Jewish origins in favor of patriotism. That was certainly the case in the career of Henry Kissinger. Nor was it peculiar to the American polity. Walther Rathenau, who was the highest-ranking Jew in Germany during World War I, was above all a patriotic Prussian. "Rathenau has not overcome Judaism as a religion," observed the Jewish theologian Franz Rosenzweig, "he just thinks that he has."[7]

Like Rathenau, Felix Frankfurter, Isador Lubin, Ben Cohen, did not deny their Jewishness, but considered it merely an accident of birth. Jews who reached the highest rank in Western parliamentary democracies, like Rathenau and Disraeli, were inevitably only marginally Jewish and disinclined to use their influence to support a Jewish need. Yet there was a slight departure in the American model. Morgenthau, Roosevelt's secretary of the treasury and the Jew closest to Roosevelt, involved himself deeply in the rescue effort during the Holocaust. He exposed Breckinridge Long, the assistant secretary of state who spearheaded the Department's blocking efforts and was instrumental in bringing the War Refugee Board into being. His fate was not as drastic as that of Rathenau, who was assassinated. After Morgenthau submitted a "hard" plan for the post-war treatment of Germany, he lost favor in the Truman administration. Those policymakers who already sensed that the threat to the American national interest would now emanate from Moscow pointed out that the secretary was motivated more by an ethnic than a national interest. Morgenthau was not reappointed when Harry Truman became president in February 1945.

Being close to power did not mean that when high-placed Jews spoke at all they would necessarily speak with one voice. By the 1930s, the effect of developing in a free society had encouraged variegation and loss of content in group identity. American Jewry entered the crisis as a divided community. It lacked cohesiveness and coherence and could no longer speak to power holders with one voice. The issues that divided Jews concerned everything from communal governance, to the interpretation of the tenets of Judaism, to the question of Zionism. Every nuance of ideology had its own organizational expression and the fragmentation was compounded by the triangulation of the religious community. During the New Deal period, the only thing that Jews could really agree upon was the support of Roosevelt and the need to defeat Nazi Germany. Everything else was in flux. The four attempts to overcome these deep divisions were failures. As late as 1943, the newly organized American Jewish Conference failed to hammer out a unifying platform that could be transmitted to power holders. Not only was there no Jewish organized conspiracy as imagined by some, there was really no organized American Jewry. Instead there were hundreds of organizations, each representing a different interest, each with a different program of what might be done. American democracy released new energy and talent in American Jewry, but it also fragmented its coherence as a people. Power moved from the community leaders to individual members of the community.

Had all the problems of projecting Jewish power been magically resolved, had the American people been convinced that the need to rescue Jews served the national interest, had the Jewish communal voice retained its coherence and transmitted that need to rescue to power holders, had Roosevelt understood that the Final Solution also posed a dire threat to Western civilization, there still can be little assurance that the Holocaust could have been prevented. Beyond the inability of American Jewish leaders to persuade Roosevelt to act for much of the war, the kind of power the Roosevelt administration required to stay the hands of the Nazi executioner was not available to it. Berlin gave a far higher priority to liquidating the Jews than could be mustered by the Allies for rescue, even under the most favorable circumstances. The decision to liquidate Hungarian Jewry in 1944, the last surviving Jewish community in Europe, when it was clear that the war was lost gives us some indication of the high priority the Final Solution had in Berlin. The Allies had finally exerted some effort to rescue Hungarian Jewry through the War Refugee Board, yet within full view of the world over half of Hungary's almost one million Jews went up in smoke.[8] Berlin was deaf to moral suasion and sufficient physical force on the ground to convince the leadership in Berlin to abandon the Final Solution did not begin to develop until after D-day in June 1944.[9] In the case of the rescue of Soviet Jewry, the reverse was the case. After the suppression of the revolt in Hungary (1956), which followed the uprising in Berlin (1953), and especially after the invasion of Czechoslovakia in 1968, the knowledge that an unwelcome communist regime was being imposed from without in Eastern Europe was inescapable. After the crushing of the Prague Spring, loss of confidence in Moscow's leadership grew even among the faithful. It was the almost universal sense that the path of progress pointed in the direction of the principles of human rights stated in the Helsinki Accords that ultimately freed the Jews of the Soviet Union. In wartime Berlin, such moral pressure would have been of little avail. Even after it became clear that the war was lost, the National Socialists remained in total control of Germany until the bitter end.

One might have imagined that once it was certain that Germany was defeated and the moral power the Jews could bring to bear was fully in consonance with the nation's war aims there would be a more active rescue policy. But impending victory had little effect in changing public policy, which remained largely indifferent to the rescue of European Jewry. The decimation of Hungarian Jewry and the death marches claimed additional hundreds of thousands of lives within full view of an alerted world.

The conclusion that moral or ideational power, the kind Jews could bring to bear, was wholly inadequate to prevent a crisis wrought by the decision to make genocide part of the public policy of the state is unavoidable. European Jewry was never incorporated into the universe of obligation that serves as a benchmark of civilized life. It is in the indifferent response of the witnessing nations and agencies to genocide that the conviction held by so many that civilizing ideas and moral suasion count for little in the real world are based. It would have been better had the Jews had some of the divisions Stalin queried about at Yalta or failing that, persuaded Allied strategists and decision makers that it was in their national interest to stop the death camp mills from grinding.

If there were such a thing as usable Jewish power, surely the Holocaust would have been the moment to use it. But that did not happen. Until the final months of the war, the kind and amount of power available to American Jews was inadequate to save their European brethren. It is that reality that makes the conjuring of a Jewish power nexus particularly problematic. In what might have been the litmus test of the existence of such power, the destruction of European Jewry, there is little evidence of its play.

* * *

But in 1944, when the war was turning in favor of the Allies, and some of the major physical impediments to the rescue effort were gradually removed, the sense that something might be done to impede the slaughter was in the wind. In January 1944 the Roosevelt administration created the War Refugee Board, and initiated a policy of more direct intervention in the rescue effort. A few months later, the seemingly immutable American immigration law was circumvented by executive order and temporary havens were established in Oswego and several other countries to allow those in the refugee stream to find haven. But rescue did not follow immediately. Berlin's passion for genocide remained intact, as did control of the killing grounds which enabled it to do so. A specific focus on saving of lives remained absent from the military campaign and Allied war aims. The family of Anne Frank and many others were deported on September 3, 1944 just three months after D-Day in June 1944. The WRB and the temporary havens policy came too late to save the millions. The rescue of European Jewry never became part of the

Allied war aims, which continued to be based on the idea that nothing must be undertaken that would interfere with the speedy achievement of victory. Most steps proposed by rescue advocates, from bombing Auschwitz to sending food packages to the camps, fell into that category. The change of the military situation on the ground did not notably soften the hearts of decision makers. Even the announcement that the savaging of German cities from the air was in retribution for what Berlin was doing in the east was rejected on the grounds that such an announcement was prohibited by the Geneva Convention. Had it been possible to mobilize Allied military power after D-Day, perhaps as many as a million lives might have been saved. But such power is precisely the kind that a stateless people does not possess.

It was the imminence of physical defeat, especially as the Red Army approached from the East, not moral suasion, that changed or softened German policy. That led to the "Blood for Trucks" ransom offer carried by Joel Brandt, and the dismantling of the Auschwitz gas chambers in November 1944. The signs that the logjam was breaking in Washington were also perceptible. Particularly noteworthy was the aforementioned case of Henry Morgenthau, Jr., who proposed a "hard" plan for the postwar treatment of Germany. His activism leads one to wonder what might have happened had the Jews close to Roosevelt shown more courage in advocating the rescue of European Jewry.

Clearly, whether it was members of the so called "Jew Deal" during the New Deal era, or neoconservatives during the Republican administrations of Reagan and the Bushes, the fact that Jews hold high positions near the seat of power does not assure that they recognize a so-called Jewish interest or that government will do their bidding. The successful projection of power has a great deal to do with the political context within which such a projection is made. The domestic political environment that militated against the admission of Jewish refugees in the thirties had also changed by 1944. Roosevelt had decided to run for a fourth term and Jewish support would be called upon. Paradoxically, in 1944, the year when the expenditure of resources to defeat the Nazi Reich, which had made anti-Semitism the mainstay of its national ethos, had reached astronomical proportions, organized American anti-Semitism also reached its zenith. But strangely thereafter it rapidly declined until it virtually disappeared from the graphs. It proved to be difficult to maintain an anti-Semitic passion when the nation's sons were fighting and dying on the field of battle against a foe that made such a hatred the center of its belief system. The war itself acted to mute overt domestic anti-Semitism, which reverted to a latent form. In this case, a change in government policy preceded ideological change, not the reverse as one might have expected. When the first photos of the camps began to appear in the press, the price of such unbridled hatred became clear to many. General Eisenhower ordered that as many as possible should be exposed to the camps. There are thousands of personal testimonies by American soldiers who first understood what they were fighting for when they saw the death camps. Even then the credibility problem that haunted rescue advocates, the unwillingness to believe that a "civilized" government could make genocide part of its public policy and had used modern industrial processes to produce death as on a production line, was never fully dissipated. Public opinion surveys conducted in April 1945 show that most Americans did not conceive of an industrialized killing process that took millions of lives. It beggared the imagination.

But as the war drew to a close the confluence of interest between America and its Jews had begun to take shape. Jewish organization like the American Jewish Committee had discovered that tolerance could be marketed just as ethnic and racial hatred were. In 1944 an American troopship, the *SS Dorchester*, was sunk in the North Atlantic. Out of that incident came a poster, followed by a postage stamp, showing four chaplains including a rabbi who, after having given their life jackets to the men who had none, arm in arm went down with the ship. Like the Atlantic Charter, the four chaplains poster expressed the unity of the nation in the face of the Nazi threat. In 1940, the Detroit race riots showed that the mobilization for war barely concealed the deep class and racial rifts that divided the nation. By 1944, racial and religious tolerance were everywhere propagated as desirable national goals. But it would not be until years later that the civil rights movement brought the ideal closer to reality. The stage for the struggle for civil rights, which would occupy center stage in the sixties, was set during these later war years. It was disproportionately fueled by Jewish activists. For Jews an important sign that acceptance had been achieved came when the Carter administration agreed to extend financial support for the building of the Holocaust museum on the Washington Mall. The permanent exhibit of the museum does not hesitate to expose American government indifference to the possibility of rescue during the war.

*   *   *

A situation *en extremis,* like the Holocaust, that urgently calls for the use of all available American Jewish power can tell us a great deal about the extent and nature of that power. It reveals a situation full of paradox. On the one hand the anti-Semite continues to imagine that the Jews have too much power while, on the other, the American Jewish witness observes that the requisite power to do all that needed to be done was not available to Jews. In both the refugee and rescue phase, the actual play of Jewish power is difficult to detect.

That all ethnic groups use the power available to them to further communal interests is a given. After World War II Polish-Americans complained bitterly about "the crime of Crimea." Greek Americans pressed for the restoration of Greek rule in Cyprus. Cuban Americans continue to press for the continuation of the economic embargo of the island. The role each group is permitted to play in the making of policy is limited not only by its own political leverage, but also by structural factors inherent in the foreign policy making process which is made by the president with the "advice and consent" of the Senate. Since treaties have the power of law, a two-thirds vote is required for their passage. Special interest pleading is customarily confined to subsidiary details that are settled early in the process. In the case of the Holocaust and World War II, for example, Roosevelt determined early that the nation would ultimately be compelled to enter the war. It took several years to convince an isolationist Congress to follow his lead. Rescuing European Jewry, which was of primary interest to Jews, was a subsidiary aspect of that interventionist policy. It could be accommodated only to the extent that it was in consonance with the major policy of winning the war. During the rescue phase (1941-1945) Jewish advocates were repeatedly told that the best way to save the Jews was to win the war quickly. The American Jewish advocacy for the admission of refugees concerned immigration policy, which was solidly in the hands of restrictionists. When military assets had to be expended, as in the case of bombing Auschwitz, or when major strategy was concerned, as in the case of planning the invasion of Europe, it had to be integrated with the end goal of winning the war as quickly as possible with a minimum loss of life.[10] That made the prospects of success remote from the outset. We have noted that a more active rescue policy became manifest in 1944, when Allied leaders could be fairly certain of victory and such steps as warning the Szalazi regime in Hungary not to deport the Jews did not interfere with the major goal of winning the war. The prospects of rescuing Hungarian Jewry in

1944 were far better than rescuing Polish Jewry in 1942 and 1943. But even here the "Blood for Trucks" proposal, which held out a remote prospect of saving thousands of lives, could not be accepted since one of its purposes was clearly to hasten the break up of the "strange Alliance" between the Allies and the Soviet Union. During a war for survival, even after victory is within reach, the needs of the military operation override other elements that are part of the power calculus. The kind of moral power Jews brought into the arena during World War II played a minor role at best.

Similar priorities obtain in domestic policy. We have noted that American public opinion did not support a change in the immigration laws and refugee policy that would have permitted more Jews to enter. The Freeports policy, which finally brought over nine hundred mostly Jewish refugees to a War Relocation Authority facility near Oswego in July 1944, still had to be implemented by executive order. Even at that late date it is doubtful that, had the administration requested consent from Congress, it would have been granted. Much depended on public opinion, so the ability to educate Americans to develop a more humane response on the admission of refugees should be considered an important part of Jewish power. We shall note later that the skillful use of public relations went far to assure the success of the effort to win the release of Soviet Jews. Of all the elements of Jewish influence in America, the power of communications and public relations is perhaps the most developed, but breaking through the curtain of silence that surrounded the operation of the Final Solution in the hope of changing the mindset of the American public during wartime proved to be beyond its power. The anti-refugee policy remained in place until 1944 and physical intervention to halt the slaughter was never considered. Yet the news of depredations did leak out and received coverage in the back pages of newspapers. There were hundreds of protest rallies and marches on Washington and theater pageants, like "We Shall Never Die", which featured Edward G. Robinson and Paul Muni. But muted by the story of the war itself and unable to differentiate what was happening to European Jewry from other victims of the Nazi occupation, the story of a government-sponsored genocide using the industrial process was not heard. Even after photos of the camps strewn with emaciated bodies appeared in *Life* magazine, the American public did not fathom the depth of the catastrophe. The Bergson group's most successful efforts, page-long ads, sometimes composed in the dramatic prose of Ben Hecht and illustrated with the breathtaking art work of Arthur Szyk, did more to disturb anti-rescue officers, like Breckinridge Long in the State Department, than reshaping general opinion.

By 1944 the Oval Office had become somewhat more accessible, but that did not mean that the crises could compel Jewish leaders to set aside their differences and speak to the president with one voice. After seeing several Jewish delegations each separately pleading for its own rescue clients, Roosevelt is purported to have murmured that he wished the Jews would have a pope like normal religions. In fact, he once spoke of Rabbi Stephen Wise as the "pope of the Jews."[11]

The long-standing issues that divided American Jewry seem particularly irrelevant today in light of the Holocaust. During the refugee crises, Jewish organizations could not agree on what should be done on issues like mass resettlement. When the Bergson group suggested that the rescue and homeland goal should be separated to enhance the possibility of rescue there was adamant opposition from mainline Zionists. The Zionist movement, which had organized the most successful resettlement experience in the twentieth century, could not support the State Department-sponsored resettlement scheme in Sosua in the Dominican Republic. For Zionists, Palestine was the only suitable haven that actually welcomed the Jews of Europe. Nothing should be allowed to interfere with resettlement in their ancient homeland. But Roosevelt would not challenge the British White Paper that limited the prospect of such resettlement. Not until the Biltmore Conference of May 1942, when Ben-Gurion pushed for a commonwealth resolution, did the American Zionist movement reach a tenuous agreement to press for a Jewish state rather than merely a cultural center.

We have noted that the Jewish voice that spoke to power lacked coherence and the community it spoke for had lost some cohesiveness in the free atmosphere of America. The conspiracy envisaged by those who see a Jewish will to control and dominate requires at the least some modicum of unity that did not exist during the years of the Holocaust and does not exist today. There occasionally appear men, like Secretary of the Treasury Henry Morgenthau, who break all the rules to speak out. Morgenthau was probably more responsible for the creation of the War Refugee Board, the high point of government rescue effort, than any other American Jew. But such voices were rarely heard in the Oval Office. His activism presents a disturbing vision of what might have been achieved, had it proved possible to mobilize the Jews close to the administration in the rescue cause. Such highly placed people can act as a bridge to power holders and facilitate and accelerate the slow moving democratic process. Yet having Jews in high places does not necessarily translate into direct power over basic policy. Morgenthau was an exception created by the horrendousness of the Holocaust and the imminence of victory. Moreover, in a situation like the Holocaust, or the rescue of Soviet Jewry, or the need for diplomatic and military support of Israel, American Jewry has no independent means of projecting power. It is compelled to rely on the sovereign power of the American government which acts as its proxy, but only when it is in its national interest to do so.

In a democracy, an aroused public opinion is the essential beginning of the policy and law making process. In the case of the Holocaust, it was essential that American public opinion be converted to the cause of refugee admittance and to rescue where possible. But for various reasons, American public opinion remained largely indifferent to the fate of European Jewry. The problem for American Jewish leaders then became how to generate such influence outside the normal political process. The principle weakness of the American Jewish effort in the thirties was its inability to convince public opinion that something needed to be done. Polls taken as late as 1940 placed American Jewry as either the first or second least popular group in the country, and also showed solid opposition to the admission of more refugees. Had there been such a public outcry as developed later for British children, Roosevelt's rejection of the Wagner-Rogers Bill to admit largely Jewish children stranded in France might not have happened.

The problem was that the kind of ideals and aspirations Jews brought into the political arena might have clarified why America fought, but had only a long range or impact, when what was needed were the divisions that Stalin sought at Yalta to gain physical control of the killing grounds. It takes generations to reshape the public mind. Sometimes a cataclysmic defeat can accelerate the process. The German people offered little resistance to Nazi tyranny, even when they became aware that the war was lost. It was only the complete military defeat that finally broke the Nazi spell.

Finally we face the gloomiest truth of all. In this case there was no substitute for the possession of physical military power. Had American Jewry been unified in the face of the crises and spoke to power with one voice, had the American people mustered their customary generosity and humanity, had the Roosevelt administration recognized the need to prevent the genocide of the Jews as a major war aim, if all these things had magically fallen into place, there is still no guarantee that the mass murder of European Jewry would have been prevented, though many more might have been saved. Unlike the Soviet regime, which ultimately was persuaded to listen to its normally sycophantic Communist parties in France, Italy, and the United States that continuously cautioned the Kremlin that it was losing the moral high ground, the Nazi regime remained immune to moral suasion. There was no power in the Jewish or Allied arsenal that could have convinced Hitler not to kill the Jews. Some power beyond civilizing ideas proffered by Jews is required to stay the hands of the Hitlers, Pol Pots and Bin Ladins who dwell among us.

For those who rely on American Jewish power for security, as well as those who use it as grist for the anti-Semitic mill, this episode reveals its limitation. Historically, no American ethnic group ever felt a greater urgency to mobilize itself and put into play all its power or influence. But almost no signs of the use of such power appear on the historical monitor. We have probed some reasons for the lack of effect—the Depression, the war itself, the disunity and lack of Jewish communal coherence, anti-Semitism, the fanatic will of the Nazi regime to liquidate the Jews. By the time some of these roadblocks were removed in late 1944 it was too late, most of Europe's Jews were already in ashes. If Jewish power existed at all there is little evidence of its play during World War II. But that startling fact has not put a crimp in the imagination of those who need to believe that there is among Jews a demonic power to somehow damage the nation that has an unprecedented record for allowing Jews the full expression of their talent and energy.

Despite considerable influence in the Roosevelt administration, Jewish leaders had little success in moving the Roosevelt administration to a more active rescue policy until 1944, when it became possible to conceive of an Allied victory. Its inclusion here is also an illustration of the futility of "soft" power, the power of moral suasion, in the face of a maniacal will for genocide. Armed only with such power, European Jewry was utterly vulnerable to the misuse of state power. The Holocaust, which posed the most urgent need for the mobilization of Jewish power in recent historic memory, yielded no evidence of the existence of such a secret power. The victory of the Allies came too late for European Jewry. That dilemma that encompasses all the uncertainties of the Jewish power question has become one of the most hotly debated issues in American Jewish history. Can responsibility be assigned to Jewish leadership or, for that matter, to the Roosevelt administration if we have no agreed upon gauge to tell us how much power and what kind they actually possessed? In the debate concerning the role of Jewish leadership during the Holocaust, the power and weapons to stop the slaughter physically were never in the Jewish arsenal. Their failure consisted rather in their inability to persuade Allied leadership, and beyond them world public opinion, that Jews should be considered part of the universe of obligation that defines mankind.

* * *

Yet while civilizing ideas and moral suasion proved futile for the rescue of European Jewry, they have a remarkable staying power. The Atlantic Charter of August 1941 proved to be a formidable instrument in focusing the war aims of the Allies. It told the man in the street that he was fighting a just war. There is some evidence that lack of largess during the Roosevelt administration as it concerned refugees in dire need of havens was not permanent. During the Carter administration, 800,000 Indo-Chinese refugees were admitted, and Clinton later gave temporary shelter to 10,000 Bosnian Moslems in Fort Dix, New Jersey. That a change in the nation's mentality had taken place came when the American government was called upon to help extricate Soviet Jewry from another pending human catastrophe. That is the subject of the following chapter.

Notes

1. This paraphrases Roosevelt's well-known phrase delivered in his second inaugural address in January 1937.
2. The impression that Roosevelt appointed a disproportionate number of Jews to federal positions in the civil service and the judiciary was created by the fact that Jews were appointed to agencies dealing directly with the public and therefore were more visible. In reality Jewish appointments to the judiciary were slightly below those granted to Italian Americans but, to the dismay of Irish Americans, Jews did gain more positions in the state and municipal civil service as the merit system was implemented.
3. Wise and Rosenman in particular mention such feelings. But Henry Morgenthau, Jr., the secretary of the treasury who was closer to Roosevelt and secure in the relationship, finally did make the breakthrough in 1943. See Henry L. Feingold, "'Courage First and Intelligence Second,' The American Jewish Secular Elite, Roosevelt and the Failure to Rescue." *American Jewish History*, 72 (June 1983): 424-460.
4. In fact the crises began with an offer to "ransom" the Jews of Germany, which grew out of the Rublee/Schacht/Wohlthat negotiations in 1939. It was called a ransom proposal by the columnist Dorothy Parker and was far beyond the Jewish organizational world to redeem. (See Henry Feingold, *Politics of Rescue, The Roosevelt Administration and the Holocaust, 1938-1945*, New Brunswick, NJ: Rutgers University Press, 1970.) The Yishuv also maintained a transfer agreement,

which permitted wealthy Jews to bring out some of their capital in the form of capital goods, which would then be redeemed in pounds sterling.

5.   The arrival of new German immigrants who had experienced the collapse of the Reich in the twenties and were more likely to accept the "stab in the back" legend tipped the balance in the German American community. It dominated the liberal German '48ers represented by Carl Schurz and went on to produce the virulent anti-Semitic and pro-Nazi German American Bund. As a result of the efforts of a Jewish congressman, Samuel Dickstein, the leader of the Bund, Fritz Kuhn, was imprisoned in 1940.

6.   The allegiance of Italian Americans was particularly affected after Italy's invasion of France in April 1940 triggered Roosevelt's famous "the hand that held the dagger...." speech.

7.   Peter Lowenberg, "Walther Rathenau and Henry Kissinger: The Jew as a Modern Statesman in Two Political Cultures," The Leo Baeck Memorial Lecture, Nr. 24, (1980), 3.

8.   The establishment of the War Refugee Board (WRB) and the passage of the Freeport temporary shelters in the early months of 1944 mark the high point of the administration's rescue effort. It took four years to reverse the inclination to do little. That attitude would not change until the Allied victory was assured.

9.   The question of whether bombing Auschwitz and the rail lines leading to it was the key to rescue is handled in my article "Bombing Auschwitz and the Politics of the Jewish Question during World War II" in Michael J. Neufeld and Michael Berenbaum, eds., *The Bombing of Auschwitz: Should the Allies Have Attempted It?* (New York: St. Martins Press, 2000), 193-203.

10.   A hypothetical example of such a change in strategy might have been to open the second front in June of 1943, as the Soviets requested, rather than a year later. If successful, the loss of life might have been considerably reduced.

11.   In fact, by 1943 Wise's leadership was challenged by Rabbi Silver, and he was only a shadow of the stentorian voice that once spoke for American Jewry.

III

Jewish Power and the Freeing
of Soviet Jewry

Despite the many well-placed Jews in high places, the effort to enlist the Roosevelt administration in the rescue of European Jewry was not successful. In contrast, there were fewer influential Jews in the Nixon, Ford, and Reagan administrations, yet the campaign to "free" Soviet Jewry was effective. The projection of American Jewish power acting together with Israel seemingly compelled the reluctant Soviet government to release its Jews.[1] For the untrained eye, the confrontation with a regnant totalitarian power may seem analogous, but historical context make comparisons misleading.

Nazi Germany's program to push its Jewish citizens out of Germany was implemented with such determination that it threatened the dislocation of the German economy, especially in the critical area of foreign trade.[2] It aspired to nothing less than to make the Reich *judenrein* (cleansed of Jews). But after its invasion of Poland in September 1939, Berlin found itself with 3.1 million additional Jews, making the fulfillment of that goal more remote. Berlin then turned seriously to consider genocide as a "final solution." In contrast, consumed more by class than race, for the Soviet regime, Jews were considered one of many suppressed ethnic and religious groups within its empire whose ultimate position in the governing arrangement was yet to be determined. Stalin had earmarked the nationality question for himself and considered Jews not to be a nationality. In the years between 1967 and 1990, almost as if they loved them, the men in the Kremlin did everything to retain their Jews. Over the long term, the number of deaths in its Gulag matched that of the German death camps, but a systemic murder process, featuring such things as the salvaging of hair and gold fillings, did not develop. The Soviet campaign against its Jews had different roots and produced less lethal results. We shall note later that the difference between Nazi and

45

Soviet depredations was often lost on activists who viewed the travail of Soviet Jewry through the prism of the Holocaust.

* * *

The effort to extricate Soviet Jewry saw the deployment of all the components of American Jewish power. These included the skilled use of public relations and associated communications skills, a high level of voter engagement, and a talent for fundraising and, (as noted in chapter I), political lobbying and a good knowledge of the workings of the American political system. When times called for an extreme effort, as in the case of diplomatic recognition of the Jewish state in the early months of 1948, the communal effort to influence political decisions could be formidable, but such mobilization of resources was confined to extreme circumstances. It was the use of these instruments that brought the Soviet Jewish story to world attention. It was not an easy task. The challenge for the public relations effort was not only to get its special message to the public, but also to differentiate the plight of Soviet Jewry from that of other captive people. Only after the special case of Soviet Jewry was established could the emigration question be elevated to a higher place on the Cold War agenda. The popular slogan of the movement, "let my people go," became for organizational insiders, "let my people know." Yet a public relations campaign, which is often at the core of what passes for Jewish political power, brings certain drawbacks with it. It requires high visibility, which acts like a Post Office "wanted" poster on the anti-Semitic imagination, which sees Jewish influence everywhere.

The idea that Soviet Jewry, like its European counterpart during the Holocaust, had to be rescued helped mobilize communal energy. Yet the analogy also posed problems, since the notion that Soviet Jewry faced a threat of physical destruction similar to the Jews of Europe was a dubious one. The Nazi intention for Jews was far more murderous and, whereas it was nigh impossible to find a haven for the Jews of Europe in the 1930s, during the eighties American Jewry and Israel vied to have them.[3] The threat to Soviet Jewry was considered primarily as one of communal and cultural obliteration rather than a threat to life.[4] If one did not openly challenge the regime's efforts to reconstruct Judaism to fit into the socialist mold Soviet Jews could "pass" into the majority culture. It was more a question of the survival of Judaism, the religion and culture, then the physical rescue of threatened Jewish communities. The majority of Soviet Jews did not choose to emigrate until after 1989 when Gorbachev's liberalization loosened the regime's control mechanism and social and economic chaos became imminent.

Than why did the two such different events become so linked in the Jewish imagination? Post-Holocaust American Jewish political culture, the historical habits and preferences a group carries into the political arena, cannot be fathomed without awareness of the impact of the Holocaust on the American Jewish psyche. That mentality is a key part of our story. If the American man on the street thought of the Holocaust at all, it was as part of the atrocities associated with World War II that, for many, were best forgotten. But for Jews who were deeply traumatized by their radical losses such a cleansing of memory was not available. They considered the Soviet threat to their brethren as not only real but imminent. When rumors of the deportation and perhaps liquidation of Soviet Jewry surfaced in 1953, the year of the Doctor's Plot, Jews recalled the earlier failure of witnessing nations and international agencies, like the International Red Cross and the Vatican, to intervene. The perception that what was happening to Jews in the Soviet Union was analogous to what had happened to German Jewry haunted the activists of the movement, so it took little to convince them that they were saving Soviet Jewry the way their parents had failed to save the Jews of Europe.

* * *

From the outset there existed a dual focus in the organized worldwide movement, the desire to rescue the threatened Soviet Jewry and the need to reinforce the security of Israel by increasing its Jewish population. That duality made the projection of Jewish power problematic, since most secularized American Jews were concerned that there be no repeat of the Holocaust and less with using Jewish influence to allay Israel's demographic deficit. The mixing of the strategic Cold War goal concerned with reinforcing democracy in the Middle East by strengthening Israel with an ethnic goal of saving Soviet Jews *qua* Jews raised doubts regarding the integrity of the movement. It was the first mentioned objective rather than the second that first attracted the support of certain legislators around Senator Henry Jackson. Predictably, the two goals sometimes became hopelessly entangled. The division acted to cloud the focus of the American movement, especially when the question of resettlement came to the fore and it became evident that many Soviet emigrants were not fleeing the Soviet Union for particularly Jewish reasons.

Historically, the desire for Jews to leave Russia was of long standing, as was the American Jewish desire to support them. The archives are full of letters and petition of American Jewish communities requesting legal redress and intercession from the American government after the Tsarist government required special standards for Jews who returned to Russia for visits or business. The turn-of-the century notes to the Kremlin penned by Alvin Adee, the State Department's master of penmanship and noble sentiments, are worth reading today for their eloquent statement of humanitarian principles. Looking forward from 1900, a researcher might have been more likely to predict greater involvement with the fate of Russian and east European Jewry, which seemed always threatened, than the Jews of Western and Central Europe. It was, in fact, the children and grandchildren of the turn-of-the-century immigration from Eastern Europe who were now called upon to help these potentially new Jewish immigrants from Russia.[5] Like most Diaspora Jews, American Jewish leaders viewed German Jewry as a model of successful emancipation and the accompanying benefits of modernity. Though there were many portents of the failure of emancipation in Germany, history had disarmed American Jewish leaders, who were unprepared to accept the sudden turn of fortune that plunged the splendid German Jewish community to its doom. In contrast, after the Bolshevik Revolution and the "Iron Curtain" cut off Soviet Jews from world Jewry, they were viewed as a "lost" Jewry which, in the prevailing Zionist thought, would one day be found and ingathered in the Jewish homeland. The existence of Israel changed the complexion of the perennial phenomena of Jewish refugee-ism and of the way Jewish power was projected in its behalf. Israel could not acknowledge that there could be a refugee problem once the Jewish state, anxious to welcome all Jews, was in existence.

In this discussion, we are primarily interested in discovering how such an unlikely bending of Soviet emigration policy in the direction of Jewish interest came to pass. Were the Kremlin and the American government acting on behalf of Soviet Jewry responding to Jewish power? Clearly a communal movement of NGOs, like the National Conference for Soviet Jewry (NCSJ) and the Union of Councils for Soviet Jewry (UCSJ) and the dozens of affiliated groups, could not alone have compelled a change of emigration policy of a superpower. Without the intercession of the American government, the efforts of the American Soviet Jewry movement and its allies would have remained a "cry in the wilderness." That enlistment of American government help was made possible by a confluence of interests between the objectives of the Soviet Jewry movement and the Cold War goals of American foreign policy. It was the Jackson-Vanik amendment and later the Stevenson amendment that catapulted the Soviet Jewish emigration issue onto the Cold War stage.[6] That allowed a relatively minor trespass committed by the Soviet control system to gain the attention of the American government. The confluence of the government and Jewish interest was inherent in the situation. The Soviet resistance to emigration became a natural part of the indictment of Soviet suppression of human rights, like the freedom of movement. Senator Henry "Scoop" Jackson may have had his own political interest in pushing the amendment forward, but he couched the struggle in terms of the denial of human rights. Emigration, a right recognized by the Universal Declaration of Human Rights, a version of which the Soviets had finally signed in 1972, became a Cold War cudgel to bludgeon the Soviet system by calling attention to its rejection of universally accepted standards of national behavior. That denial of a universally recognized right gave the struggle for emigration its focus, but Henry Kissinger, Nixon's national security advisor, was wont to point out that the United States too would not countenance outside pressure seeking to determine its immigration policy.

On the face of it, the Jackson-Vanik amendment seems like clear evidence of Jewish control of American foreign policy, but the microhistory presents evidence of a complex story that shows an uncertain Jewry allowing itself to be used for Cold War purposes.[7] Far from being a Jewish cabal holding American foreign policy hostage to compel the Soviet government to grant emigration visas to Soviet Jews, the leadership of the Soviet Jewry movement was hesitant to enter into such a transaction. Some thought that Kissinger's back channel agreement to allow 40,000 to 60,000 to emigrate annually would satisfy all who wanted to leave, while not unduly straining the capacity to resettle them. By 1979 there was pressure within the community to abandon support of the amendment. The group of Jewish congressional assistants led by Richard Perle who conceived of the amendment was motivated primarily by the sense that it offered a strategy to subvert Kissinger's policy of détente. It used the pressure to free Soviet Jewry to toll a Cold War victory. The release of Soviet Jewry would be an additional dividend. As it was, the rescue of Soviet Jewry never became a primary goal of American foreign policy.

But the price of the amendment entailed the abandonment of the moral high ground since it was, in fact, a thinly disguised ransom offer that proposed to exchange credit and access to the America market for the release of Jews held captive.[8] The human rights position was that freedom of movement was a natural right belonging to each citizen and it was therefore immoral to enter into such transactions with a tyrannical power. More telling was the reason given by Andre Sakharov, the highly regarded leader of the Soviet dissidents, who spoke of the impropriety of letting some gain their freedom at the expense of others who would continue to rot in the Gulag. But the strongest opposition to the Jackson-Vanik idea of exchanging trade privileges associated with the Most Favored Nation status for Jewish emigrants came from commercial interests, and from within the foreign policy establishment. Henry Kissinger, who was confident that in the rivalry between the socialist and capitalist system the latter would prevail, considered Jackson's pressing of his amendment as an attempt to derail the key plank of his policy of détente. It was a matter of policy priorities. For Kissinger and his policy strategists, it was more important to arrange mutual disarmament agreements than to gain the release of a handful of Jews. Immigration policy, he maintained, had always been an internal affair. The United States, for example, would not countenance Mexico having a hand in determining American immigration policy, but Jackson would not be moved. Ultimately, Kissinger proposed an elaborate face-saving device in which the Kremlin would agree to let a certain quota emigrate annually, in exchange for MFN treatment and access to credit that went with it.[9] It was all done informally by letters. The Soviets never spoke to negotiators in Jackson's office and Jewish leaders spoke only to Kissinger. Conflict over interpretation of the non-existent formal terms was not long in coming. How many would be allowed to emigrate, 60,000 yearly or was it only 40,000. Jackson insisted on a precise figure. Finally, when news of an agreement was made public, Andre Gromyko, the Soviet foreign minister, denied that he had ever agreed to such an outlandish pact. The Jackson-Vanik amendment remained on the books until 2002.

To this day there is disagreement about whether the amendment, which marks a high point in the projection of by the U.S. government on behalf of Jews, actually pressured the Kremlin to release its Jews. By 1979, some Jewish leaders concluded that the amendment hindered, rather than aided, the flow of emigrants and favored its modification or complete abandonment. But others argued that it was necessary to maintain a drumbeat of pressure on the Kremlin. There was a tendency for supporters of the amendment to overestimate its impact on trade. Compared to the restraints on Soviet American trade generated by security factors, the Jackson Amendment did little to interfere with the flow of goods. The real contribution of the amendment was to cast media attention on the Soviet Jewry emigration issue. It became a problem to be solved, one of several on the Cold War agenda.

*   *   *

From the perspective of Jewish power, the amendment is instructive because it revealed a new source of political influence stemming from congressional assistants to Jewish senators Jacob Javits and Abraham Ribicoff and others, like Henry Jackson and Charles Vanik, who were friendly to Jewish interests. It was these assistants, led by Richard Perle, working out of Jackson's office who conceived of the strategy of using economic pressure to wring better treatment for Soviet Jewry, first to protect their rights in place and, failing that, through a liberalization of Soviet emigration policy for those Jews who wanted out. The strategy was a virtual repeat of the one that guided Jacob Schiff at the turn of the century, except now it would become a matter of government policy, rather than a private affair of a Jewish banking house. The informal group met periodically and had a changing membership.[10] There was no official Jewish caucus in Congress, but unlike the Jews near Roosevelt who carefully down played their ethnicity, there was a mutual recognition among Jews in Congress and the upper echelons of the federal civil service, of a special Jewish need. Listen to Morris Amitay, an Israeli-born former student of Kissinger at Harvard, who became a congressional assistant to Senator Ribicoff and played a key role in bringing the Soviet Jewry issue to the attention of Congress: "There are now a lot of guys at the working level up here who happen to be Jewish," he observed, "who are willing to make a little bit of extra effort and to look at certain issues in terms of their Jewishness, and that is what has made this thing go very effectively in the last couple of years."[11]

Interesting too was that the relationship was not confined to getting government to help Soviet Jewry. The Jackson-Vanik amendment served a dual purpose. It was not only Jewish power wielders calling upon the use of American power for a Jewish purpose, but also American power holders using a Jewish need for what they believed was the national interest. Richard Perle and other neoconservatives were as much interested in subverting the détente policy as they were in bringing Soviet Jews out. Few members of the Bunker group were involved in Jewish organizational life, but they were committed Jews who believed that there was a confluence between the Jewish and the national interest.

Even in the development of the Jackson-Vanik amendment it is difficult to find a direct exercise of Jewish power. It seemed more like power projected by strategically positioned officials who, in some cases, happened to be Jewish, but focused largely on national issues. Most legislators who became involved were not Jewish, but had been made aware that the emigration question was becoming an important issue for the Jewish electorate.[12] The dozens of legislators who became involved in the Soviet Jewry issue had first to be made aware that there was an issue. The Jackson-Vanik amendment would not have happened if lawmakers had not first become aware of the significance of the emigration problem in Jewish and Cold War affairs. That awareness can be partly attributed to Jewish activism, which began a decade before the amendment came to the floor of the Senate in 1974. Developing such awareness fell to the handful of activists who assumed the leadership of the Soviet Jewry movement, and behind them was the favorable response of the American people. "Ultimately, the real underpinning of the lobby's success," observed Morris Amitay, who was the prototypical Jewish lobbyist, "is the fact that most Americans consider a secure Israel to be in the best interests of the United States."[13] That was true of Jewish activism for the release of Soviet Jewry as well.

* * *

That task Jewish activists set for themselves was not an easy one to realize. The political reality faced by the Soviet Jewry movement was that for much of its existence, the White House was occupied by Republican administrations that Jews supported neither with their votes nor their money.[14] Nixon's "hit list" contained a disproportionate number of Jewish names and many wondered how Henry Kissinger, his principal foreign affairs advisor, as well as chair of the National Security Agency, could continue to serve under an outspokenly anti-Semitic president. During the Nixon administration, bringing the Soviet emigration issue to the highest echelons of government decision making faced formidable obstacles. The Nixon administration aspired to leave its mark in history by ending the Cold War on terms favorable to the United States. But armed with its own weapons of mass destruction and intercontinental delivery systems, the Soviet Union, in effect, had achieved military parity with the United States and had no incentive to make concessions to

Washington without getting something in return. That meant not only trade and credit concessions, but also some easing of the troublesome noise emanating from the Jewish public relations campaign.

During the years of the Johnson administration, alarm about continued Soviet expansionism in the Horn of Africa and the oil-rich Middle East increased. The fragility of the existing peace arrangements came to the fore in 1962 when the two superpowers came perilously close to a nuclear exchange during the Cuban Missile Crisis. The Nixon administration's response was its policy of mutual de-escalation and peaceful competition in non-strategic areas. But after the crisis in Cuba and aggressive Soviet moves in the Middle East, opposition to any concessions to Moscow hardened. Leading the Senate in advocating a firmer policy opposing détente was Senator Jackson, the Democratic senator from Washington. His amendment projected the emigration issue into the middle of the Cold War dialogue by positioning it firmly in the anti-détente camp. When Kissinger, in an effort to thwart Jackson's hard-line position, fashioned a back channel informal agreement for yearly emigration quotas with Moscow, Jackson insisted that emigration was a human right that the Kremlin should acknowledge at the outset. The scheme was hastily abandoned by Moscow.

Whatever the human rights motivation, on the national political level the amendment was more about Cold War positioning than it was about extricating Soviet Jewry. Paradoxically, as the nation's least enthusiastic Cold War supporters, most Jewish voters in 1962, when the two superpowers came perilously close to a nuclear exchange, would probably have agreed with the reasoning behind détente. But Moscow's military support to Syria and Egypt, especially the suspicion that it had planned and sponsored the Yom Kippur war in 1973, placed many a growing number of Jewish voters on the anti-détente side. Moving towards the political center, American Jewry's former attraction to democratic socialism and, in some cases, to the Soviet "experiment" itself had faded back into history.

An interesting story in its own right, the mobilization of congressional support for the amendment, did not give the anti-détente forces a stranglehold on Soviet-American relations, but it went far to strengthen the Soviet Jewry movement as a formidable pressure group. The task was now to convince American public opinion of the justice of the Jewish emigration cause. The implementation of that essentially public relations objective marks the Soviet Jewry movement's finest hour. Aware that the headlines over the trial of the Leningrad hijackers and the Soviet effort to impose an education head tax on the emigrants and now the Jackson amendment had prepared the groundwork for creating a favorable public opinion, the Soviet Jewry movement used the free media attuned to activism to develop a supportive public opinion with a strong emphasis on human rights. The primary challenge became how to differentiate the persecution of Jews from that of the dozens of other subject people of the Soviet empire who had been deprived of human rights.

The campaign for doing so rested on a communal tradition of political activism which, when combined with a special talent for public relations, gave the Jewish message unusual resonance. In Jewish immigrant political culture, becoming informed of an injustice was considered merely a first step for achieving justice. Although a secular mentality was making inroads into the traditional culture, the idea that Judaism was a religion of deeds had not fully disappeared. It served as motivation for young modern Orthodox activists, usually members of the Student Struggle for Soviet Jewry (SSSJ), who served as the movement's most militant group. Secular Jews mustered an unusual optimism about the possibility of changing the political system through the democratic process, using the existing levers for change. In a word, the need to act, to do something, was ingrained in Jewish religious culture and strongly reinforced by the ethnic liberal secular culture. We have noted previously noted that their confidence in, and knowledge of, the political process allowed them to use it effectively. Jewish NGOs missed few occasions for social justice and reform causes. There always seemed to be some Jewish community somewhere in need of succor, nor was their activism confined to Jewish causes. Jewish communal mobilization to prevent the execution of Sacco and Vanzetti was a portent of the development of what someone called "a community of whistle blowers." When the need to come to the aid of their brethren in Russia developed, the experience in getting the government to intercede was already part of their political experience. American Jewry was well prepared by its historical experience to take up the cudgels for Soviet Jewry. Diplomatic correspondence and letters of concern regarding the treatment of Jews were a well established part of America's diplomatic practice since the Mortara kidnapping case in 1858.[15]

The major portion of these notes concerned the victimization of Jewish communities abroad. That led naturally to reminding government officials that inherent in the American ethos derived from its shared

Judeo-Christian roots was concern for the downtrodden. The appeals sought to exploit the inherent moral content in American foreign policy. The appeal for Soviet Jewry fit snugly into a preexisting pattern. It also reinforced the impression that Jews inevitably called on the nation to live up to its principles, and perhaps to be better than it could or wanted to be. Whether they spoke of, the genocide of the Armenians or famine in Eastern Europe after World War I, American Jewry, together with such groups as the Quakers, earned a reputation of being morally involved minorities, which gave its public relations a recognizable liberal coloration.

By the 1970s, Jewish concern about the fate of their brethren was also better understood by the general public, which had been made aware of the Holocaust. Awareness was reinforced by communal activism, which is also rooted in the socialist tradition that drew many Jews by its insistence on *praxis,* the conviction that theory must be followed by action, lest the movement cease to make actual history and revert merely to moralizing. Some members of the Soviet Jewry movement had witnessed and sometimes participated in physical confrontation with police and other civil authorities during the civil rights struggle and then in the anti-war movement. The tactics of going limp, of getting arrested and dragged by the police while photographers were taking pictures, a ritual taught in training sessions, was also a source of prestige and group status for the participants.

* * *

The organizational expression of the movement, which came fully into being in the early seventies, was based partly on the far-flung Jewish organizational infrastructure, which was the envy of other ethnic groups. Hundreds of chapters, permanent and transitory, sprung up wherever there were aggregations of Jews. Some were attached to chapters of national organizations already existing or the local religious congregation. Others developed completely independently. Eventually, two umbrella organizations developed to undertake the challenging work of bringing the case for Soviet Jewry to Jewish and national attention. One was the National Conference for Soviet Jewry (NCSJ), which encompassed most of American Jewry's major defense and fraternal organizations, whose delegates sat on its executive board and determined its budget and policy. The NCSJ's programs and strategy reflected American Jewry's close link to Israel and the world Zionist movement. That may be the reason why a competing umbrella group called the Union of Councils for Soviet

Jewry, based on voluntary grassroots activism, soon labeled the NCSJ the "establishment." Both organizations advocated the need to protect Soviet Jews in place and to gain for them the right to emigrate if they so desired, but the UCSJ, with weaker ties to the world Zionist movement and Israel, showed less concern about specific location for their resettlement in Israel. They often took their signals directly from the tightly knit *refuseniks* group in Moscow. Predictably, the two agencies competed for funds and headlines. In addition, there were numerous ad hoc groups and specific interest groups, like those affiliated with the Student Struggle for Soviet Jewry (SSSJ), that made up the movement.

Though it came to be called a movement, it was from the outset fragmented with only a limited sense of the goals they held in common. That lack of cohesion seemed to work at the grassroots level, where enthusiasm counted for more than focus. Organizational disunity was, in fact, the signature of Jewish organizational life, and had a negative impact on the earlier rescue effort for European Jewry. That internal communal division suggests that the vision of a Jewish conspiracy controlling American foreign policy is far removed from reality, since the American Jewish organizational world does not possess the coherence to mount such a conspiracy. The disputatiousness of Jewish communal life is legendary, and is illustrated in Jewish folk humor by the maxim, "two Jews, three opinions." During the Soviet Jewry episode, the addition of a sovereign Jewish state to the mix considerably strengthened the movement, while at the same time compounding its disunity.

Unity was not essential for the public relations aspect of the campaign—protest rallies, posters, stories of heroism and suffering that were widely syndicated in the English-language Jewish and American media, and the dozens of techniques and slogans to create public awareness of the emigration issue. The more attention called to the plight of Soviet Jewry, the better. The brilliance and energy of its public relations was the movement's finest hour. Some tactics, like the wearing of bracelets with the names of imprisoned *refuseniks*, were borrowed from the civil rights and anti-war movements in which Jewish youth were disproportionately active. Slogans with a familiar biblical ring, like "Let My People Go," well known to all familiar with the Negro spiritual, gained national popularity. But "Never Again," the most effective slogan of the movement which was ultimately adopted by others, came from the Jewish Defense League that had been marginalized because of its illegal means of gaining media attention and its penchant for violence. Unlike the failing efforts to get the Holocaust story known, rarely a day passed without a story concerning some Soviet depredation committed against *refuseniks* carried in the media. In effect, the "iron curtain" on information within the Soviet empire had been penetrated. The public relations campaign was so coordinated that if a Jewish foot was cruelly stepped on in Moscow on Monday one could expect an immediate reaction to it in New York on Tuesday.

In contrast, during the years of the Holocaust there was an eerie silence as the cattle cars rolled to the death camps with their hapless human freight. The depredations committed against those Soviet Jews who opted to emigrate became well known and eventually posed serious problems for Soviet authorities. Compared to Soviet suppression in Czechoslovakia in 1968, or its treatment of the Crimean Tartars, the depredations aimed at Jews were on a minor scale, an internal story. The public relations campaign succeeded in raising the level of attention. In the setting of the Cold War, Soviet Jewry became a problem that required remediation.

* * *

Nevertheless, it is difficult to determine to what extent the public relations campaign breeched the wall of public indifference regarding the emigration issue. What was being done to Jews in the Soviet Union had to compete with a series of stories, like the war in Vietnam, the civil rights struggle, Watergate, and especially the Yom Kippur war, that monopolized media attention. The impact of the Soviet Jewry story was predictably greater within the Jewish community, but even here communal mobilization was far from total. The "saga" of Jewish victimization may also have reached a saturation point beyond which yet another story about persecution of Jews, imposed on the hundreds of Holocaust stories that were surfacing in the personal memoirs of survivors and in TV docudramas like Gerald Green's "Holocaust," would have little impact. Some could no longer muster enthusiasm for yet another humanitarian crusade. By the mid-seventies, early contact with Soviet emigrants, who were sometimes found not to share the standard liberal Jewish mindset as well as being ungrateful and insufficiently Jewish, caused some disaffection. "They lie, they cheat, anything to get what they want," observed a rabbi in Queens, "[many] lack the basic concepts of humanity let alone Judaism."[16]

In the half decade following the failure to modify the Jackson amendment in 1979, little movement on the emigration issue could be observed.

The issue seemed dead in the water. Given the resistance of the Kremlin, the assumption that Jewish organizations abroad, in conjunction with the American government, changed Soviet emigration policy is a dubious one. How Soviet compliance with the right of emigration was finally achieved goes beyond American Jewish advocacy to the growing role the human rights question played in the Cold War. The release of Soviet Jewry after 1985 occurred simultaneously with the liberation of other groups. For the full answer to that liberalization process, we need to know more about the reasons for the collapse of the Soviet Union and what role the failure of its control system, particularly regarding the right to emigrate question, played in it. Comparatively few Sovietologists predicted that human rights could become a crucial issue for the men in the Kremlin.[17]

By the election of Ronald Reagan in 1980, a considerable momentum had been built up to gain the release of those who wanted to leave. Clearly, without the Cold War conflict, which amplified the Jewish grievance, the Soviet Jewry movement, which was one of several organized efforts challenging Soviet authority, would not have come to world attention. It moved a relatively minor issue to stage center in the Cold War dialogue and gave Washington a chip in the diplomatic game that heretofore had been part of the Kremlin's arsenal. The possession of over three million Jews within its borders in theory gave Moscow the ability to totally alter the Middle East problem. The emigration of almost one million Russian Jews to Israel could help relieve its demographic deficit, and thereby change the power calculus in that strategic oil-rich region. That much was understood from the very outset of the movement in the mid-sixties. When the election of Reagan intensified the tensions between the contending superpowers, Moscow responded by cracking down on its Jews and virtually halting the flow emigrants. In a sense, the Soviet Jewish issue became a harbinger of the crises within the Soviet Union. Some maintain that it also acted as an intensifier.

Calculating the precise role of Jewish power in gaining the release of Soviet Jewry when a multiplicity of factors was involved is problematic. The world might never have learned that such a problem existed, were it not for the movement outside Soviet borders. But public awareness does not automatically result in remediation. After five years we are no closer to easing the well known genocide in Darfur. In the case of freeing Soviet Jewry, not even the enlistment of the sympathy and cooperation of the American government and the action of Congress could pry open the closed doors of a totalitarian power that considered the desire to emigrate a rejection of its sense of self. It requires much more than power projected by American Jewry through the American government to achieve such a change.

A broader range of historic factors needs to be considered in the final accounting regarding the emigration of Soviet Jewry. It took more than three decades of effort to bring it to fruition and then it came incrementally. American Jewry did not do it alone. The actual finding of the "lost" Jews of Russia and the establishing of an internal network and contact with the outside world was first achieved by Israel, through a special office located in its foreign ministry, but directly responsible to its head of state. Not only was Israel first on the scene, but the existence of a sovereign state that could make the case for Soviet Jewry in the international forums was important, despite the fact that for much of the post '67 period, the Soviet Union did not maintain diplomatic ties with Israel. Israel's ideological and biological drive proved far stronger than that of American Jewry, whose interest and passion for "rescue" had first to be rekindled by Israel. Together they composed a formidable but contentious partnership for pressuring the Kremlin.

The real makers of history were the activists within the Soviet Union whose cries for relief challenged the system. The outside activists in America, Israel, and other countries were merely enablers. If the story of Soviet Jewry's exodus has any real heroes, it is these "refuseniks," people who dared to apply for a visa and were refused. An interesting division of labor developed. Israel found the "lost" Jews and created an apparatus that allowed them to communicate with each other and with the movement abroad; the activists within the Soviet Union kept us aware of their desire to emigrate and their willingness to risk imprisonment to make their case known. It was American Jewry that possessed the resources, the political linkage, and skills to enlist the help of the Congress and high officials in the executive branch to push the emigration movement forward. Without the ability of American Jewry to convince the American government to play the role of "rescuer," a role that it rejected during the Holocaust, the free emigration of Soviet Jewry would not have happened. It was the first example in post-World War II Jewish history where three separate Jewish communities in the United States, Israel, and the Soviet Union, armed with different kinds of power, made their presence felt on the world stage. As it turned out the sum made each of its parts seem stronger.

* * *

Our interest is to discover the nature of Jewish power and its play in the public policy arena. There are several ways in which the play of power can be noted. It can be observed in the ability to take a comparatively minor case of a Soviet trespass against Jews, differentiate it from other persecuted groups, and elevate it as a problem deserving the special attention of the concerned world. To do that, an awareness of the emigration problem had first to be established in the minds of American Jewry and the American people.[18] That was achieved by a brilliant public relations campaign, which culminated in the largest popular demonstration in American Jewish history convened on the Mall in Washington, DC in December 1987. The second factor relates to the confluence of interests that developed between the American government and its Jewish citizens concerning strategies and goals during the Cold War period, which extended from protecting democracies where they existed to safeguarding human rights. We have noted that it has been confluence of interests, rather than the pushing of an agenda of one upon the other, that has shaped the relationship between the two. The best example of that is the financial and military support given to Israel during the Nixon years, which was based not so much on a special concern for Jews, as little love was lost between American Jewry and the Nixon administration, but on the belief that America's national interest was best served by a strong democracy in the Middle East. The influence of that confluence varies with time and place. The Roosevelt administration could not be convinced that a more active effort to rescue the Jews of Europe, or even to acknowledge the primacy of the Jewish question in the war, would serve the war effort. But during the Cold War the reverse was the case. The persecution of Soviet Jewry was coupled with the ability of Jews to get word of these depredations to the outside world, where they served as additional evidence that the Soviet regime lacked a "human face." We witnessed a mutuality of interests, rather than a conspiracy to tear policy out of its national self-interest grooves. The rules governing the play of power do not permit an ethnic community armed with a measure of power, even when it is disproportionate, to dictate policy to a powerful host nation. It is this confluence of interests, rather than the imposition of Jewish power, that we see at work in the Soviet Jewry case.

But even after the movement had gained the attention of the administration and all the agents that could be brought to bear in support of the Jewish interest, which included a favorable Cold War context, it still required something more to convince Moscow to release its Jews.

Countervailing interests in the grain trade and other business forces that sought improvement of relations with Moscow often prevailed. Moscow remained adamant on the emigration question until 1987 when the process of liberalizing, or better said, Westernizing, its immigration law was finally put in place.

That extra something that brought Gorbachev to power is rooted in an internal dynamic that has little to do with Jewish power. It acts cumulatively so that its effects are felt only in the long run, and yet seems to be present even in the most closed and suppressive of societies. The long-range influence of the human rights movement that came to fruition in the eighties to weaken the Soviet control system acted as a major activator of that latent moral consciousness. American Jews viewed the emigration issue as quintessentially one of human rights. There is a paradox here because one of the earliest positions taken by the organized Jewish activists in the Soviet Union was to insist that theirs was an emigration not a human rights movement. They separated themselves from other Soviet dissidents on the human rights issue, perhaps because they had become convinced that Soviet anti-Semitism was so deeply rooted that the only answer was to emigrate. Nevertheless, there was much crossing over between the "refuseniks" and dissidents, and also within the general Soviet intelligentsia.[19] Many Jews were involved in the Helsinki watch groups and some non-Jews became part of the *refusenik* community. The human rights current affected the movement despite its policy of separation.

The values embodied in the human rights movement, which we have identified as the visible part an underlying moral grammar that exists in all societies, were shared by some portion of the opinion-making elite in virtually every country. It took different forms and had different emphasis as if it was inherent in the wiring of a given society. Somehow, as if by some social instinct, the direction of progress was known. One of these principles, that people should have the right to move, taken for granted in the West, was shared by many ordinary Soviet citizens. It seemed a humane and proper course. When the right of emigration was included in the Helsinki accords promoted and signed by Moscow the circle was complete. The Helsinki watch groups, which monitored Soviet compliance with the rights listed in Basket III of the accords, bore the brunt of the KGB crackdown. But the sense that human rights, despite the unevenness of the struggle, should be the direction of societal development was present in all the closed societies of the communist world, including

China. Assuming that in the end it would be the sovereign government that would determine who should exercise these irrepressible rights and to what extent, Moscow supported the third basket of the Helsinki accords that monitored them. It too wanted to bask in the warm glow of public approval generated by the human rights issue. Even tyrannical regimes have somehow to garner the goodwill of their subjects. Men like Gorbachev and Shevardnadze were aware that it would take more than *agitprop* to engineer popular support that had been diminishing since Khrushchev's confessional speech before the 20th Party Congress. In July 1988, Shevardnadze spoke before officials of his Foreign Ministry to complain of the heritage of low popular esteem he had inherited from his predecessors: "We cannot exhibit indifference to what others are saying and thinking about us for our self-respect, our well being, our position in the world hinges largely on the attitude of others towards us...."[20]

In the end, it was not the power of American Jewry, or divisions and missiles of the United States that brought about the release of Soviet Jewry, but the power of an idea concerning the direction of human progress. The reality of Jewish victimization would not by itself have altered the mindset of Soviet authorities. The Soviet Union was, after all, full of victims. Yet by 1985, its ruling elites, unlike those of Nazi Germany, were no longer immune from the effects of moral suasion. The Helsinki accord placed the Jewish emigration issue in a worldwide context of human rights. For the first time in modern Jewish history, a sovereign Jewish state, whose role in shaping American Jewish political culture is the subject of the next chapter, could plead the cause of the emigrants. As the Soviet authorities weakened the control mechanism that held their citizens in check, the freedom of movement became the norm as it was in the West. The rest is history.

Notes

1.   I say seemingly because there is some question whether the change in emigration policy was a response to outside pressure, sometimes called the barometer theory, or whether Soviet changes in emigration policy rested purely on internal factors. In the immediate five years before the collapse of the Soviet system in 1989, when the Soviet economic and political situation was dire, Soviet resistance to Jewish emigration became more determined. Clearly, when matters of prestige or ideology were concerned the barometer thesis was inoperative.

2.   Unlike the Soviet Union, there was no regard for a "brain drain" in Berlin. Scientific teams that had taken years to assemble were dissolved and often the released Jewish physicists were forced to find new positions. There is some doubt that the Manhattan Project, which developed the atomic bomb, could have done so with such speed without these refugee scientists.

3. The German Jewish immigrants of the thirties shared with the Soviet Jews a reluctance to settle in Israel (then Palestine). Had they had a choice, only 10 percent of German Jews would have settled in the Yishuv, about the same rate as the Soviet Jews after 1980.

4. The Jews that chose this alternative was probably numerically larger before 1989 than those who chose to emigrate.

5. The legal basis for allowing some Jews to leave was the Soviet recognition of that kinship. It was based on "family reunification," for which documentary evidence, a *vyzov*, was required.

6. The Jackson-Vanik amendment offered Moscow Most Favored Nation (MFN) status and access to the credit that accompanied it in exchange for releasing those Soviet Jews who desired to emigrate. It also assured those who chose to remain protection of their human rights. The Stevenson amendment later raised the credit limitation.

7. The earliest version of the amendment proposed a forgiveness of the wartime Lend-Lease debt in exchange for the right of Jews to emigrate.

8. Interestingly, the release of German and Austrian Jewry negotiated in 1939 was also based on a ransom offer and so labeled by Dorothy Parker. The sequestered property and wealth of German Jewry would be used as collateral for special bonds issued to resettle Jews elsewhere. Few such havens could be found. In the German case it emanated from the kidnappers.

9. Again, there is an uncanny resemblance with the German treatment of its captive Jews. It signed a "statement of agreement" with an NGO that would have permitted the staggered immigration of German and Austrian Jewry. The Rublee, Schacht, Wohlthat agreement came to little since the international money market could not accept bonds backed by stolen Jewish property and Jews had insufficient capital to pay the ransom required. Moreover there was no place to settle the Jews once released.

10. Sometimes called the "Bunker" group, at its heart were Jackson's assistant, Richard Perle, and Morris Amitay, who played a similar role in Sen. Ribicoff's office, and Mark Talisman, Sen. Vanik's assistant. Included also were Kenneth Gunther and Roy Millenson, who worked for Sen. Javits, Jayson Berman, Sen. Bayh's administrative assistant, and Richard Gilmore and Judith Davison, Sen. Humphrey and Mondale's foreign policy advisors respectively. Their informants from the Jewish organizations varied greatly in membership and interest. Included were L.I. Kennen and Morris J. Amitay of AIPAC, Jerry Goodman of NCSJ and occasionally Yehuda Hellman of the Presidents Conference. Some are convinced that the beginnings of neoconservatism on the congressional level were incubated in Jackson's senatorial staff. For Perle's background and his relationship to Jackson and also to Albert Wohlstetter, the leading theoretician on nuclear war, see Jay Winik, *On the Brink: The Dramatic Behind-the-Scenes Saga of the Reagan Era and the Men and Women Who Won the Cold War* (New York: 1966), 35-50.

11. Quoted in Stephen D. Isaacs, *Jews in American Politics*, (New York: 1974), 174.

12. Two of the most prominent legislators were Reps. Millicent Fenwick and Dante Fascell. Both were tireless in their efforts to help the "refuseniks."

13. Google: Soviet Jewry, "Correspondence Re: The Israel Lobby." (Originally appeared in the *Middle East Quarterly*.)

14. That was in contrast to the case of the admission of German Jewish refugees where the Jewish electorate had an ongoing love affair with the Roosevelt administration. Of the five administrations in power during the 1970s and 1980s—Nixon,

1969-1974; Ford, 1974-1977; Carter 1977-1981; Reagan, 1981-1989; Bush, 1989-1993—only Carter was a Democrat. The Republican Party was not totally bereft of Jewish support. It could receive anywhere from 25 percent to 35 percent of the Jewish vote. Nixon never stopped trying to win Jewish support and granted special access to the Oval Office to Max Fisher and other moneyed, influential Jewish Republicans. But Fisher was less comfortable in the Reagan White House. See Peter Golden, *Quiet Diplomat: A Biography of Max M. Fisher* (New York: Herzl Press, 1992).

15.   For a description of this intercession, see Cyrus Adler and Aaron Margalith, *With Firmness in the Right: American Diplomatic Action Affecting Jews, 1840-1945* (New York: Arno Press, 1977). American Jewry wrung a note of concern from the Buchanan administration regarding the refusal of the Vatican to return a kidnapped Jewish child after a secret baptism by his nurse.

16.   Quoted in Howard Sachar, *History of the Jews* (New York: Random House, 2002), 927.

17.   In 1989, the year of the collapse of the Berlin Wall and the subsequent unraveling of the Soviet empire, there was no loss of the Soviet ability to defend itself and use weapons of mass destruction. In some areas of military strength, Moscow actually outpaced the West and the Warsaw Pact could muster greater number of ground forces. While there were control problems in the satellites, there was little penchant for physical resistance within the Soviet Union itself.

18.   See especially Albert D. Chernin, "Making Soviet Jews an Issue: A History," in Murray Friedman and Albert B. Chernin, eds., *A Second Exodus: The American Movement to Free Soviet Jews* (Hanover, NH: University Press of New England, 1999), 15-69.

19.   In the twenties and thirties the Soviet intelligentsia included a substantial number of ethnic Jews and comparatively few detractors. In addition, the security agencies, such as NKVD, had a disproportionate number of Jews in leadership positions, while the Soviet Foreign Service was considered a Jewish specialty.

20.   Quoted in Don Oberdorfer, *The Turn: From the Cold War to the New Era: The United States and the Soviet Union, 1983-1990* (New York: Poseidon Press, 1991), 372.

IV

The United States and Israel:
Jewish Power or National Interest?

The protective embrace that characterizes the American Jewish relationship with Israel serves as the necessary background to understand the charge that the "Israel Lobby" has gained control of American Middle East policy.[1] Rooted as it is in the low-level war waged against Israel by its Moslem neighbors, the American Jewish interest in the security and welfare of Israel is sustained and intense. Its concern also lies behind American Jewry's efforts to project its political influence on policy making as one of the most active ethnic constituencies in the American political arena. The accusers, who in recent years have grown in number and gained academic legitimacy, view the projection of Jewish influence as controlling policy, which militates against the interest of the nation. The accusation that they now exercise too much power does not sit well, especially among survivors who hold an important position in the American Jewish polity. We have already noted that it was precisely the failure of the Allies to include European Jewry within the "universe of obligation" that generated the circumstances leading to the birth of Israel. At the historic moment when the help of the Roosevelt administration and other witnessing agencies was desperately needed, Jewish leaders found themselves with insufficient power to convince them to at least make an effort to rescue their European brethren. Our task here is to unravel the seamless strands that bind the American Jewish and the national interest regarding American policy in the Middle East, so that some sense can be made of it.

* * *

That disentangling is not a simple matter. Israel is an anomaly in the Jewish power category. In contrast to Jewish communities in the Diaspora, it actually possesses sovereign power, which enables it to act

65

through its own agency and not through others. To do so, it has an army, courts, and a legislative body, which makes laws defining the social and economic society within which its citizens live. That is the meaning of the frequently heard claim that, with the establishment of the state in 1948, Jews reentered history.[2]

That notion of Jewish reentry into history by an unprecedented return to its historic land after a protracted absence complicates our power problem. Not all accept the legitimacy or possibility of such a return. The Arab/Islamic world views the Jewish returnees as an outside non-Islamic people settling on their land. Many ultra-religious Jews deny the quasi-religious rationale on which that return is based, and the Zionist founding fathers originally spoke only of a Jewish cultural center. The Holocaust convinced many that the only answer for survival is to establish a state of their own. American Zionists who faced adamant opposition on the statehood question were convinced to agree to it at the Biltmore Conference in May 1942. The new state would face many challenges including the prospect of invasion by its Arab neighbors, but few foresaw that the bona fides of American Jewish communal rule might be undermined by the existence of a sovereign Jewish state. It required an agreement with Judge Joseph Proskauer, leader of the American Jewish Committee, to resolve Ben-Gurion's claim that Israel inherited a natural right to speak for all Jews.[3] Though Jewish nationalism was baked in the same nineteenth-century liberal oven as other nationalisms, it would be compelled to draw its population stock from the Jewish Diaspora. Once the state was established, a vision of primacy over the Jewish communities in the Diaspora anchored in its founding Zionist ideology took hold. The highest priority was given to the "ingathering" of settlers, not far behind was the new state's strategic and economic needs.

The intensity of American Jewish feeling regarding Israel lies behind the accusation that its influence dominates American foreign policy in the Middle East. During the early testing years of the state, American Jewry did not have to be convinced to support Israel. After the Holocaust, the meeting of Israel's needs was more urgent for American Jewry than comparative demands faced by Irish or Polish Americans. Financial aid, often given at the expense of its own needs, was freely extended. When a move occurred later to direct more of the UJA dollar to domestic needs, supporters of Israel argued that American Jewry intended that Israel's needs should be met first and that general giving would decline, should the distribution formula be changed. When it became clear that Israel would not easily be accepted by its neighbors, the need to support Israel financially and diplomatically remained intense.[4] For some American Jews, Israel's beleagueredness marks a continuation of, rather than a break with, Jewish history. It serves as a sign that the Jews of Israel share the insecurity of the Jewish condition. Rather than becoming the solution to perennial anti-Semitism as was intended by its founding fathers, Israel has become a lodestone attracting it. That paradox too binds American Jewry and Israel in a special relationship.

Here our task is not to probe the problems faced by the Jewish state in using its power to secure itself against hostile neighbors, but rather to examine how a sovereign Jewish community interacts with a Jewry which owes its first allegiance to America. What impact has Israel's state power had on the political culture of American Jewry? How does the play of American Jewry's "soft power" on the American scene interact with Israel? Behind these questions is the troublesome charge posed by opponents that American Middle East policy has become Israel's proxy.

*   *   *

We should note at the outset that there are some who question whether Israel's possession of sovereign power translates to full autonomy. There are degrees of sovereignty, they argue, and Israel possesses the very lowest. They view Israel as simply a client state that earns a modicum of security through its friendship with the United States, which covers it with a protective mantle. The accusation of Jewish dominance is, in fact, based on the opposite supposition, that America is a client state of Israel. There are many instances one could cite that demonstrate that Israel is as much bound by it self-interest as any sovereign state. It is not a failed state, as are so many founded in the post-World War II years, but it faces a continuous challenge to its very existence. After sixty years it remains unacceptable in the region, and has been compelled to defend its existence more than any other nation-state. Despite triumphs on the field of battle sufficient to establish its bona fides as a viable state, Israel seems no more secure than the pre-World War II Jewish communities of the Diaspora. The obligations its citizens are forced to assume are abnormally high. That is something that a relatively high standard of living cannot mitigate. As long as the Arab world remains unwilling to come to terms with the existence of Israel, there will be uncertainty regarding its future. The American Jewish community's role vis-à-vis Israel is shaped by that uncertainty. There is an imperative need to do everything in its power to keep Washington's bond with Israel strong not only for the sake of kinship, American Jewry could not endure the loss of yet another center of Jewish culture.

Israel's political dialogue with America and its Jewry is therefore not an ordinary one. It occurs against a backdrop of the Holocaust, during which one-third of the Jewish people were slaughtered. Every thinking Jew has at one time or another conceived that Israel may at some time in the future again be compelled to turn to the witnessing world for protection and experience again the indifference which suggested that Jews were not considered to be part of the universe of mutual obligation. It was to guard against such a contingency that Israel was the first of the small nations to develop an atomic bomb. That makes the Iranian threat, which funds low-level war on her borders and threatens mass destruction, ominous. When all else is peeled away, the existential question that Israel has faced since its birth can no longer be limited to its own survival. Israel is armed with weapons of mass destruction, which she will use if pushed to the wall. That gives the question of Jewish power a special salience beyond the confines of American politics. If for some reason America is no longer willing to maintain its protective mantle in place, the resultant danger would be worldwide. In a word, American Jewry's advocacy role, which its critics have conflated into the "Israel lobby," has implications far beyond American politics. It is at the very heart of the question of the survival of civilization as we know it. The Middle East is on the way to becoming the most likely region for a thermonuclear exchange.

*   *   *

We turn next to the complex relationship between American Jewry and Israel, without which the charge against the "Israel lobby" cannot be understood. It is something of a paradox that the American Jewish identity, which Zionists predicted was destined to fade together with that of other Diaspora communities, was actually strengthened by the establishment of the Jewish state. It generated a sense of group pride, buttressed by Israel's victories against its Arab neighbors. Unlike the supposed passivity of Diaspora Jewry, American Jewry shared with Israel a desire to be part of a winning team. That pride in Israel's feat of arms reached a peak during the '67 war. Israelis living here were wont to observe that American Jews were more patriotic and less critical of Israel than its own citizens. The sense of attachment went beyond pride and faith. The Irish reminisced lovingly about "the old sod" and the Germans talked endlessly about the "fatherland." Both sang the old songs of home. But while many European Jewish immigrants fondly remembered their youth and mimicked the cuisine of their hosts in Kosher style, few felt precisely at home in these countries. American Jewry had always missed something that other hyphenates possessed, a mother country they could call their own. They were more likely to recall hostility and rejection. That was especially true of Holocaust survivors who had become a highly committed and active element within the community. The "old country" was no "mother country" for them, just as it had not been for the immigrants from Eastern Europe who arrived in great numbers after 1880.

For these reasons, the place of Israel in the American Jewish psyche went beyond love to a kind of religious adoration that was different from the relationship of other hyphenates to their former homeland. So popular did Israel become in the American Jewish mind that some were concerned that "Israelism" would become a new form of idolatry. It went beyond the gallantry of Israel in battle, or pride in the modernity of Tel Aviv, or the sense of kinship derived from stemming from the same population stock. It was also the fulfillment of an age-old longing that was mentioned in Jewish prayers. The fact that Israel's right to exist was challenged awakened powerful emotions behind which lay American Jewry's sense of ineffectiveness during the Holocaust. Given its outward tilt to help the Jews of Eastern Europe, and its dependency on the Jews of Russia and Poland for cultural and biological supplementation, the characterization of American Jewry as indifferent to the fate of their brethren was highly unlikely. American Jewry is, after all, an eastern Jewry by derivation and its political and religious culture can be traced back to those communities. The realization that its power was insufficient to change national priorities during the Holocaust had a traumatic effect on its sense of self. In a word, American Jewry has good reasons to be fully aware of the limits on the exercise of ethnic power in America. It had born witness to its own failure during the Holocaust. The Jewish Defense League had coined the slogan "Never Again" and while the JDL never gained acceptability, the influence of its slogan was pervasive.

In the early years of the Jewish state, American Jewry's passionate commitment can be seen as a compensation for that failure. It would do for Israel what could not be done to save the Jews of Europe. As noted in the case of the rescue of Soviet Jewry, that sense of guilt and loss is at the center of its political culture. Little can be understood about its political behavior generally, and its activism particularly, without an awareness of it. The Jewish state became a substitute for the destroyed Jewish cultural center in Europe from which it derived much of its cultural and political style. Its formidable fundraising apparatus was focused on assuring Israel that she would never be in need if American Jewry could help it. The money was raised within the community, but much Jewish political influence was also devoted to assuring that the American government would see its own reasons to fill the financial gap.[5]

We have already taken note of the impact the very existence of the Jewish state has on the American Jewish psyche. Israel gives American Jewry focus and a much needed sense of unity, at least on the question of Israel's security. For a community that in the free atmosphere of America tended to ever greater diversity, such cohesiveness was crucial. The slogan later popularized by the UJA, "We Are One," may have been more a wish than a reality, but there was one matter that almost all American Jews agreed about: Israel was the centerpiece for the hope of their survival as a people in the post-Holocaust world. Candidates for office learned that to forget Jerusalem may not have led to their right hand loosing its cunning, but it could mean loosing a close race for office. That too was classified under Jewish political power, but the truth is that a change in policy could rarely be achieved by the threat of loosing the Jewish vote alone. Yet the fact that Israel was perceived to be continually threatened by its neighbors added certain intensity to the Jewish voice in the American politics. That intensity and persistence, coupled with a developed sense of public relations, assured that that voice was heard above the din of other ethnic voices.

Ironically, if American Jewry "adored" Israel, there existed ideological reasons why that love was not always reciprocated. It is probably a psychological truism that the most difficult love to bear is the one owed to those on whom we are dependent. For Israel, the relationship to its affluent brethren in America, based as it was on economic aid and political support, was less heartfelt. The ideological conflict felt with a competitive Diaspora community could not be eliminated at one stroke. But while Zionist leaders, like Ben-Gurion, learned to still the tendency to "negate the Diaspora," Jewish life in the Diaspora never earned a high place in the prevailing Zionist mentality, which insisted that professing Zionists belonged in Israel, which represented the cutting edge of Jewish life. There had always existed a demographic competition between the two communities, which surfaced again during the DP crises after the war, and again with the Soviet emigration "drop out" problem explored in the final sections of this chapter. But Israel's economy in the early years was not developed enough to absorb the waves of immigrants from the Mahgreb which, in the absence of settlers from Europe, would become a crucial element in the population stock of the new land. Israel needed all the help it could get from American Jewry, which extended it with an open heart. But Israel's early dependency barely concealed its Israelocentrism, which was requisite for keeping the new society going. Its elevated sense of self did not always sit well with American Jewish leaders. The model is startlingly different today where a developed self-sustaining Israel rarely needs to call on the support of American Jewry to negotiate the terms of its relationship with the United States. While the political presence of American Jewry is always there, in most cases, such as the details of weapons delivery or the focus on Iran's Atomic weapons program, Israel's needs are negotiated directly with Washington. The conspiratorial image of Israel controlling a powerful lobby that cleverly manipulates an innocent State Department to do Israel's bidding with the help of American Jewish political power and which agrees with everything Israel does, is far removed from reality. American Jewish influence in the corridors of American power helps, but Israel relates to Washington as an independent state. It cannot take for granted that American Jewry will automatically follow its lead.

The historic tie between the two communities is forged by a mutual dependence in a world, which viewed through Jewish eyes, is often hostile, sometimes murderously so. That historical experience cannot be easily forgotten. Incorporated into the Jewish worldview, it may seem paranoid, yet it is not far removed from reality. Jews, after all, lived in a world that wanted to murder them and gave them no quarter—a classic paranoid nightmare. It may be that Jews proposed "civilizing ideas" because it is in their interest to live in a more civilized world. After the Holocaust, American Jewry needed the emotional prop represented by a young fighting nation to generate the cultural energy that formerly emanated from European Jewry. In turn, Israel needed the political and economic support that American Jewry could provide. American Jewry would have to hone its political power to better play its advocacy role before the America seat of power. For American Jewish leadership, it was not a situation without precedent, but Israel's needs acted like adrenalin. American Jewish leaders had called on the American government for diplomatic intercession on behalf of Jewish communities abroad since

before the turn of the twentieth century.[6] Over the years, a ritual of diplomatic gestures had developed whereby the State Department's diplomatic
dispatches echoed the humanitarian sentiments dear to American Jewry.
It was a response designed primarily to retain Jewish political support by
demonstrating concern for the welfare of their brethren abroad. At one
point after such a dispatch had been sent to the Kremlin, Secretary of
State John Hay was convinced that "the Hebrews ... poor dears" would
show their appreciation in the voting booths during the forthcoming
election.[7] Still in place in the thirties, the ritual of Jewish request and
administration gestures of concern proved disastrous, since it obfuscated
the fact that there was little intention of interceding on behalf of Jews
during the refugee crisis of the thirties. It was one of several reasons for
the insufficiency of the American Jewish response during the Holocaust
and the DP crises which followed.

That inadequate Allied response to the industrialized killing process
strengthened the urge to establish a Jewish state. The communal campaign to gain recognition for the new state marked a high point in the
projection of Jewish influence on foreign policy. The Zionist movement
led the extraordinary mobilization of American communal resources to
help bring the state into being. At one point, Rabbi Abba Hillel Silver,
in a boastful mood regarding his leadership of the American Zionist
Emergency Committee (AZEC), claimed that he could flood Washington
with the cables of 10,000 irate citizens within an hour's notice. With the
exception of the Council for American Judaism and some ultra-Orthodox
groups, all formerly anti- or non-Zionist movements and agencies, from
the American Jewish Committee to the Reform Movement, had fallen
into line. American Jewry had never witnessed anything like it before,
an almost total unanimity on a major objective. The unlikely success in
convincing Truman to recognize the State of Israel, against the advice
of George Marshall and other close advisors, served as a later model of
what could be achieved by the timely deployment of communal power.
Even the hint that America's and Israel's interests were not necessarily
identical, the rationale used to win such support, brings a passionate
denial in the English-language Jewish press that points out endlessly that
Israel is, after all, the only democracy in the Middle East.

The development of the community's political instruments, especially
the skillful use of public relations, was undertaken to buttress Israel's first
line of defense, its bonds and alliance with Washington. Israel's security
during the years of the Cold War rested in some measure on the fact that

it could count on the backing of American power. Before 9/11 and the war in Iraq ushered in an enthusiasm for nation-building, America's aim in the Cold War period was to keep the region stable and outside the Soviet sphere. Washington's Middle East policy reached beyond Israel's security needs to assuring its energy requirements and playing the role of honest broker for hoped for negotiations to settle the Israel-Palestine conflict. Lobbies, like AIPAC, and defense agencies, like the American Jewish Committee or the National Conference on Soviet Jewry, did not in themselves have sufficient power to pull public policy in their direction if they worked against these broader interests. Those that accuse AIPAC of doing precisely that fail to understand that the goals of American foreign policy in the region and those of Israel are confluent and that there have been some notable failures. It could not prevent the arming of Jordan with Hawk missiles in 1970 or the arming of Saudi Arabia with F-15 jets in 1978 and AWACS radar planes in 1981. On the emotional issue of recognizing Jerusalem as the capital of the Jewish state, AIPAC has been a total failure. That is balanced by its success in other areas. "To my mind," notes the former head of AIPAC, Morris Amitay, "the truth about the influence of "the lobby" lies somewhere between being an all-powerful force and being largely irrelevant."[8] Such differences as exist are largely confined to matters of timing, intensity of effort and tactics. AIPAC's influence has been vastly exaggerated. AIPAC extends financial support to candidates who have a record of supporting Israel. It withholds support from candidates who don't. But compared to other lobbies, its spending is small. In 2004 pro-Israel political action committees (PACS) contributed six million dollars to federal candidates. It ranked thirty-ninth out of eighty in size and expenditures.[9] Under normal circumstances, AIPAC contributes about ten percent of the campaign costs of a selected group of candidates. That figure may rise as Arab-American money continues to find its way into the political arena.

The realization of American Jewry's policy goals concerning Israel depended on its ability to convince the American public and the administration that there is a confluence of interests between the two states that called for America to maintain a protective mantle over Israel. It is based on common strategic goals, as well as democratic values. Its workings can also be seen in the case of the emigration of Soviet Jewry, Jewish advocacy was successful when, in the context of the Cold War, the existence of a strategic confluence was undeniable. American support strengthened Israel, which had become its most reliable ally in the region, while earning political dividends at home.

For our inquiry, the exercise of American Jewish power in relation to Israel creates as many problems as it solves. As within the Israeli electorate, there is little agreement among American Jewish voters on what precisely improves Israel's security, which now contains forebodings of a nuclear holocaust. At the same time, unburdened by the responsibilities of power, American Jews may be more willing to make concessions in order to win the much-sought peace in the region. Moreover, the confluence of interests between Israel and the United States leaves in its wake a chicken-or-the-egg problem. In calculating Jewish power, which comes first, the American Jewish leadership convincing Congress and the Oval Office that American interests are best served by extending diplomatic and military support to Israel, or a realization by American strategists that the small democracy in the Middle East shares American values and is a dependable ally in a hostile Islamic world? But Israel and American Jewry must also consider that despite their long endurance, the strong ties to Washington are transitory. Nations, we are told, do not have permanent friends, only permanent interests. There are some signs that in the post-Iraq war period America's conception of its regional interests may change. A lost war in Iraq could foreshadow a loss of confluence. Israel may be asked to make certain concessions, like the return of the Golan Heights to Syria or the resettling of Palestinian refugees, which the Israeli voter views as running against their national interest.

* * *

It was then the urgency of Israel's needs that compelled American Jewry to project its influence in Washington. In the early decades of the state, ties with American Jewry went beyond its philanthropic dollars. Political activism on behalf of Israel became the hallmark of its political persona, and was one of the components candidates for office considered in their campaign strategy. Israel's growing military power became one of the sources for Washington's growing influence in the region and partly accounts for the decline of Moscow's influence. The American-Israel link became a major datum in international relations. At the same time, it also became a target for anti-Semitic propaganda during the recent wars in Iraq and Lebanon.[10] The close relationship becomes the centerpiece for imagining a conspiracy to control American Middle East policy. Such imaginings are not dissuaded despite the fact that the very contrast in the weight and kind of the power involved makes the image of the United States as a pawn in Israel's hands appear surreal. Israel is a diminutive power compared to the United States and its very existence is at stake in the outcome of the perennial Middle East conflict. Israel is something more than merely an American pawn in a Middle East chess game. Its relationship to Washington has developed into a kind of partnership comparable to Britain's wartime relationship with Washington. It seems highly unlikely that such a relationship could be manipulated into existence by an all-powerful American Jewry and its "Israeli lobby." A more likely model is that the preexisting strong mutual interests allows American Jewry broad range of options and an important voice, one of several, in determining strategy in the region.

Though we cannot conceive of it at present, there may come a time when the national interests of the two nations are no longer confluent and each feels compelled to go its own way. Some already imagine that the imminence of Iran's development of an atomic bomb that threatens Israel directly could set the stage for such a parting of the ways. Similarly, it can no longer be assumed that American Jewry will automatically follow Israel's lead. While basically still strong, in recent years the American Jewish consensus on Israel varied considerably from its Likud variant. American Jewry has been consistently more flexible on issues like the efficacy of the "land for peace" formula and the disposition of the West Bank settlements. The Zionist consensus in American Jewry never included its extreme left wing, which, while much diminished, still opposes the existence of the Jewish state.[11] In an op-ed piece in the *Washington Post*, Richard Cohen, a well known journalist, ended his article by noting that "the greatest mistake Israel could make … is to forget that Israel itself is a mistake."[12]

* * *

The future of the American Jewish-Israel relationship is of great concern in Jerusalem. Israel today is able to sustain itself economically and politically, so the need to call on American Jewry is less urgent. But in its sixth decade of existence, the filial ties and the occasional need for political support remain. That is not unusual. There is a long history of former "mother countries" making such use of their hyphenates in America. The Irish endlessly "twisted the lion's tail" at the turn of the century and Germany tried to make use of its ethnics during both world wars. Still, American Jewry is not an ordinary hyphenate group, much as Israel is not an ordinary nation-state. The community was in existence three centuries before the state was founded, so the assumption that it was a parent or at least a midwife to the newborn state was not a fantasy. A parent-child relationship, in which Israel took its behavioral cues from American Jewry, was not conceivable for ideological and political reasons, but the reverse, in which the newborn state dominated the parent, was almost inevitable. The problem of meshing two different kinds of power, the ideational, moral, non-corporeal power of American Jewry, whose weight in the international arena is felt through the American government, with the state power of Israel, which, theoretically at least, needs to consult no one before it acts, seems insurmountable. Israel's power seemed more real and robust, so it consistently outclassed American Jewry in the international arena, where American Jewish agencies, like the Joint Distribution Committee or the American Jewish Committee, have no independent standing. On the ascendancy and less dependent on economic aid, Israel might realistically aspire to normality were it not for the seemingly irresolvable problem of living in a hostile Islamic neighborhood convulsed by religious and nationalist passions at whose center is the Arab-Israeli conflict.

The tensions between American Jewry and Israel emerge clearly in the confrontation with the omnipresent specter of anti-Semitism. The *raison d'être* of Zionist ideology was the quest for relief from anti-Semitism, which was persistent in every period of their exilic history. It was reasoned that once Jews returned to their homeland, and were able to abandon their visitor "middle man" status, the anti-Semite would be deprived of a target for his animus. But as an irrational passion anti-Semitism did not follow Zionist logic. Instead, Israel itself became the lodestone for anti-Semitism, especially in the Islamic world. The bombing of Jewish targets outside Israel, like the communal center in Buenos Aires by Hizbollah, indicated that Jews everywhere were considered legitimate targets in the worldwide war of Islam against the Jews. Israel, it appeared, did not deflect the threat of anti-Semitism. It incited it and became, according to Tony Judt, "bad for the Jews." From a Zionist perspective, the appearance of a new virulent anti-Semitism focused on Israel, while it has virtually disappeared from the charts in the United States, is a paradox.

Under normal circumstances, the existence of a common outside enemy should strengthen the bonds between the two communities, but the common threat of anti-Semitism did not still Israeli fears that American Jewish ties to Israel would become weaker. American Jews possess a typical minoritarian defensive persona in sharp contrast with Israel, where the majority of the citizens are Jewish and have a strong sense of belonging. Israelis are secure and comfortable in their skins. Prosperous far beyond the aspiration of their immigrant forbearers, American Jewish identity was shaped by its status as one of many minorities that compose America's ethnic tapestry. Initially not being part of the majority culture translated into a need to prove that they were worthy of belonging. The threat of anti-Semitism is not envisaged as born by an invading Islamic army. It is more ominous for the Diaspora Jew, who has no direct physical means to stay the hand of the anti-Semite and defend himself against his attack. The kind of individual and collective power available to each is quite different. We have noted that while American Jewry may project influence in politics, it commands no divisions. Since it exercises no power directly, as in Israel, it bears no responsibility for its exercise, as do the Israelis. Less aware of the physical threat to the national space and bearing no responsibility for the security of Jewish citizens, American Jews are softer on the security question. They were more likely to advocate pulling out of Gaza and giving up the settlements on the West Bank. For native-born Israelis, anti-Semitism is primarily a force that does not wish Israel well and can be resisted on that basis. For American Jews, it is an age-old danger against which the creation of the Jewish state was to serve as a bulwark. The realization that it does not and may, in fact, provoke it, is not easily reconciled. Their different approach is based on their different circumstances regarding the use of power. A sovereign Jewish state faced with anti-Semitism is unconcerned about the attitude of the majority culture. It is the majority culture.

***

All these factors—American Jewry's special relationship to Israel in the post-Holocaust period, the contrasts of Israel's sovereign power compared to the power of an American ethnic group, the concern about the strength of the bond between the two communities—come to a head in the question of the emigration of Soviet Jewry, in which both communities participated. That incident offers an opportunity to see the different kinds of power in action. In the end, those Jews who wanted to leave the Soviet Union were able to do so, but in the decades of the campaign to win their right to leave, all the tensions generated by different modes of operation and different values were exposed. It tells us a great deal about the play of American Jewish power and what happens when it is combined with the sovereign power of the Jewish state.

We have noted previously that Israel used its state power to build the worldwide Soviet Jewry movement. It dispatched its consuls and sundry embassy workers and members of NGOs to locate and organize the remnants of Russia's far flung Jewry and plant in it the seeds for emigration to Israel. It was probably the knowledge of these activities by Soviet security agencies that contributed to the severing of diplomatic relations and refusing to restore them throughout the sixties, seventies, and eighties. Israel had established a special bureau (Lishka) to promote and facilitate Jewish emigration in its foreign office, which reported directly to the prime minister. Its secret operations were designed to plant the seeds for emigration, while simultaneously awakening interest in the "rescue" of Soviet Jewry among Jews in the Diaspora. These early steps could only have been undertaken by a sovereign power that funded them, supplied the personnel, and assumed the considerable risk of operating in a closed society. The increasing number of Jews who were able to leave did so with an Israeli visa, which could be received from the Dutch embassy acting on Israel's behalf. In the absence of formal diplomatic relations, it would have been difficult for Israel to sustain the operation. Diaspora communities, primarily American Jewry, filled the vacuum.

The operational tandem that developed between the American Jewish organizations and the Jewish Agency serves as an illustration of how formidable a force the meshing of sovereign power and American Jewry's power of advocacy could be. American Jewry could not have taken such an initiative, but its political influence in Washington, coupled with public relations skill, played out in a Cold War context, allowed it to become the enabler of an Israeli initiative. The American-based Soviet Jewry movement first used a bevy of techniques, some borrowed from the civil rights and anti-war movements of the sixties and seventies, to develop the relatively minor Soviet Jewry issue into a nettlesome presence for Moscow's diplomats, who were everywhere followed by activists. A small group of congressional assistants, led by Richard Perle, then Henry Jackson's assistant, conceived of the idea of exchanging credit access and other trade concession in exchange for Soviet Jewish emigration. The Jackson amendment focused interest on the emigration problem and made it a separate issue on the Cold War agenda to be considered apart from the issues of dozens of other aggrieved groups.

At the same time, it also brought to the fore a conflict between Israel and the American movement regarding the resettlement of the Soviet emigrants that illustrates at a glance the problems of meshing two different kinds of power and group interests. We have noted that most of the "drop outs" were secular Jews motivated primarily by a desire to leave the Soviet Union for economic rather than ideological reasons.[13] For Israel, the post-1975 increase in the number of emigrants who chose to "drop out" was a source of dismay, since their presence was a confirmation of the validity of Zionist ideology and, at the same time, a needed biological supplement to keep the Jewish state Jewish in the face of a burgeoning Palestinian birthrate. (It could conceivably also have furnished a demographic argument to retain the West Bank for the Likud party.) Israel resorted to pressure on American Jewry and the Bush administration to direct the emigration stream to Israel.[14]

While the conflict over the drop outs illustrates that being grouped in a category labeled Jewish does not, as the critics of Jewish power in America assume, indicate agreement on a common goal requisite for exerting pressure on policy makers. American Jewry often does not agree with the AIPAC line on what American policy should be. For that matter, there is little agreement with AIPAC's positions by a sizable portion of Israeli voters. While desiring to rescue a beleaguered Jewry, Israel's goals were at the same time tied to serving its national interest. Israel desired that Soviet emigrants help to balance the demographic shortfall she faced in the face of a burgeoning Palestinian birthrate. It saw no conflict between rescuing Soviet Jews and rescuing the Jewish state by compelling Jews to settle there. The American Jewish focus on emigration was more individual and human rights oriented. The right to emigrate was a human right exercised by their grandparents that could not very well be denied to Jews wanting to emigrate today. One could not argue for the right of Soviet Jews to emigrate and then deny them the freedom to settle where they want. Yet it would be an oversimplification to view the conflict as one in which American Jews were on one side and Israelis on the other. Many American Jews who were Zionists shared the view that the Soviet emigrants were not refugees and should settle in Israel. There were Israelis, like Anatoly Sharansky, the well known leader of the *refuseniks*, who opposed pressuring people to settle in the "promised land." On the ground, Israel's sovereign power did not mix well with the human rights approach implemented by the American Jewish help agencies, JDC and HIAS. In the end, a combination of circumstances led to changes in America's refugee policy, these included the budgetary expense of welcoming a growing number of refugees that stemmed from Southeast Asia, the Caribbean, as well as the Soviet Union, and Israel's argument that given the existence of a welcoming Israel, Soviet Jewish emigrants could not legally be considered refugees. The result of the change in American refugee policy was that after the stage was set for a massive outflow from the Soviet Union in 1989. Over 1,200,000 Soviet Jews were eventually resettled in Israel, compared to the approximately 200,000 that settled there between 1960 and 1980.[15] A change in American refugee policy totally altered Israel's security situation and deeply affected the unresolved conflict with the Palestinians. The success in extricating Soviet Jewry increased Israel's population so that its growing demographic shortfall vis-à-vis the Palestinian population was solved, at least for the moment. That biological gain may prove more important to Israel's security than all its victories on the field of battle.

Predictably, the Jewish voice heard in Washington on the Soviet emigration matter became unclear. Israel as a sovereign friendly state used its access to the corridors of U.S. power to make its case, often louder than American Jewish leaders. As long as there was a Jewish state eager to welcome them, the Soviet emigrants did not fit the definition of political refugees. Members of the Union of Councils for Soviet Jewry (UCSJ) argued just as passionately that they met the definition of refugees under the Universal Declaration of Human Rights and therefore had the "freedom of choice" to settle anyplace that would have them. The two communities entered the arena with irreconcilable differences and, in the final disposition of the "drop out" case, it was Israel that prevailed, but only partly. Almost 750,000 Soviet Jews eventually settled in the United States.

* * *

Our task at the outset was to examine the problems encountered when the power of American Jewry, based on its secure position as a well established American subculture, is compelled by historical circumstance to mesh with the sovereign state power of Israel. In most instances, the relationship has enhanced both sides. American Jewish identity and its political voice have been strengthened and its political influence maximized by the obligations it has assumed in relation to Israel. Israel, in turn, can count on the political clout of American Jewry, which has in its arsenal all the resources to use its power to the maximum. Still to calculate precisely how much enhancement has occurred is problematic, since much of what Washington does in the Middle East rests not on a need to comply with the demands of American Jewry, but on a confluence of shared interests and values. Moreover there is no longer an assurance of agreement on where the Jewish interest lies. As is illustrated by the recent case of the effort to gain the right of emigration for Soviet Jewry, the integration of American Jewish and Israeli power does not always strengthen the political voice of American Jewry. The American Jewish-Israel power linkage had sufficient power to place a comparatively minor issue on the agenda of the Cold War. But the "drop out" conflict illustrates that the integration of the power of a sovereign state with that of an American ethnic group creates an unequal contest where the interest of the state inevitably emerges victorious. American Jewry remains an important asset for Israel, but Israel's leverage in Washington rests on strategic factors having little to do with American Jewish power. American Jewry is a condition affecting policy, not a cause.

*   *   *

The assumption that there exists a monolithic Jewish power nexus working its will in the corridors of American power contains the failing of all conspiracy theories. It attributes a cohesiveness and satanic ability to Jews that is able to get government to abandon its interest in order to do its bidding. The case of the emigration of Soviet Jewry notes that the reality is quite different. Israel and American Jewry initially shared a desire to extricate Soviet Jewry, but on the question of their resettlement, rather than unifying them, ideology and interest acted to separate them. The addition of a sovereign state to the Jewish power equation undoubtedly sharpened the political focus of American Jewry. But it also increased the number of alternatives that had to be reconciled to serve the needs of their separate communities. The complexity of American Jewish political culture and its relation to American Jewish political power are the subjects of the following chapters that deal with an aspect of Jewish power in America related to its supposedly inordinate influence on shaping American values and thinking.

Notes

1.   The term Israel lobby refers primarily to the activities of the American Israel Public Affairs Committee (AIPAC), which is registered as a lobby. Few would argue that AIPAC is a communal voice. Opposition to AIPAC originated within the community when the Tikkun group challenged its role. More recently, George Soros, the billionaire Holocaust survivor, has announced the establishment of a new foundation to counteract "the influence" of AIPAC.

2.   There have been alternative images. The establishment of the state marks the return of the Jewish people to an organization rooted in space rather than time. It views exilic Jewry as held together by history, memory, and faith, which are operative

anywhere and do not require physical cohesion in one territory. They view Jews as the first world people. Not all considered the post-Holocaust Jewish reversion to space as a boon. Marxists, in particular, extolled the Jewish ability to leapfrog over the onerous bourgeois national stage. The ultra-religious, like Agudath, also viewed the Zionist return to statehood without the coming of the Messiah as a form of idolatry and remain opposed to the Jewish state to this day.

3. See Zvi Ganin, *An Uneasy Relationship: American Jewish Leadership and Israel, 1948-1957* (Syracuse, NY: Syracuse University Press, 2005), 107-148.

4. There exists peace treaties with Egypt and Jordan and a *modus vivendi* with Saudi Arabia, but they produce only a "cold" peace.

5. Until recently, Israel was the recipient of the highest amount of grants and loans extended by the American government to any nation. Egypt has recently become a close second. It is likely that budgetary politics might yield a more realistic picture of the relationship between Israel and the United States. Few of the dollars that flow to Israel are for welfare or economic development. The overwhelming portion of American aid is for the purchase of advanced military equipment such as fighter aircraft, in a word for matters of security.

6. See Cyrus Adler and Aaron Margalith, *With Firmness in the Right: American Diplomatic Action Affecting Jews, 1840-1945,* (New York: Arno Press, 1977). It catalogues such intercessions.

7. Quoted in Kenton J. Klymer, "Anti-Semitism in the late Nineteenth Century: The Case of John Hay," *Publications of the American Jewish Historical Society*, LX, (June 1971), 349.

8. Google: Soviet Jewry, Israel Hasbara Committee, "Correspondence Re: The Israel Lobby," from *Middle East Quarterly*.

9. The spending of the real estate interests, pharmaceuticals industry, and the legal profession make AIPAC look like minor leaguers in the lobbying business.

10. In fairness, Mearsheimer argues not that there is Jewish control of policy, but an unwholesome, one-sided influence. But there are Jewish scholars, like Tony Judt and others, who have argued that the creation of Israel was a mistake. Even among the neocons, the initial support of the Iraq war soon gave way to an unhappiness with the way the war was being managed, and a reversion to their original preference for nation-building in Iran rather than Iraq. It was, after all, Iran that would soon possess the WMDs vainly sought in Iraq.

11. Tony Kushner and Alisa Solomon, eds., *Wrestling with Zion: Progressive Jewish-American Responses to the Israeli-Palestinian Conflict* (New York: Grove Press, 2003) contains essays by Noam Chomsky, Ora Wise, and Norman Finkelstein, among others, who advocate the end of the Jewish state, or at least some modification of its Jewishness.

12. "Hunker Down with History," *Washington Post*, July 18, 2006. Professor Tony Judt's article, "Israel: The Alternative," in the *New York Review of Books*, October 23, 2003 is less certain about what Israel's ultimate fate should be, but is similarly uncertain of its right to exist in its present form.

13. "Drop out" was the term that came to describe Soviet emigrants who were enabled to leave the Soviet Union with an Israeli visa, ostensibly to reunify their families. Once outside the country, they dropped out of the process that would have resettled them in Israel, and awaited documentation that would bring them to the United States as political refugees.

14. See Fred Lazin, *The Struggle for Soviet Jewry in American Politics: Israel versus the American Jewish Establishment* (New York: Lexington Books, 2005).

15.   By June 2004, one-sixth of Israel's 6,802,000 citizens stemmed from the Soviet Union. It altered Israel's political culture and strengthened its economy. The Soviet emigrants became the largest ethnic group and the best educated. Sixty-two percent had at least thirteen years of formal schooling.

V

American Jewish Political Culture
and the Left

The most interesting development regarding the charge that Jewish lobbyists exercise undue control in the shaping of American foreign policy is its departure from the norm. In traditional classic anti-Semitism, such charges are usually fashioned in tandem with the image of Jews as radicals or communists. Yet, in the case of the neoconservatives, the charge is made against a newly minted conservative group of supposedly Jewish origins. The aim of the discussion that follows is to clarify the relationship of American Jewry to the left, particularly its role in the greater engagement and activism that have come to characterize American Jewish political behavior.

* * *

Not all immigrant Jews were socialists, but a good portion of those who had embarked on the long journey of becoming "modern" were.[1] Socialism was packaged as being scientific and science was becoming the rage among immigrant Jews and their children. For most, the attraction to socialism was more direct. It meant simply that government would seek remediation of the existing economic inequities, it would seek social justice. Traditionally, a righteous Jew was called a *tzadik*, but when that passion was secularized and politicized, the people drawn to it were referred to in Yiddish as *brenendiger* or a *farbrenter*, which suggested an unswerving commitment to the cause, but also contained a subtle warning that such passion could lead to self-immolation.[2] Such modernizing Jews turned naturally to the left, where the quest for social justice was translated into such things as the demand for better working conditions and the panoply of government programs that later composed the welfare state.

The overwhelming majority of Jewish voters supported Roosevelt's welfare state as a kind of American version of socialism. But there was a small group that were true believers in the "new world" that socialism would surely bring. They were identifiable by the passion and sense of mission they brought to politics. Drawn to the mélange of left-wing socialist organizations that would formally coalesce into the Communist party in 1919, they were the most politically engaged. The *farbrenter roiter* or *linker* became a familiar type in Jewish literature and humor. Comparatively few Jews followed this extreme political path. Most positioned themselves slightly left of center, but for many reasons the parties of the extreme left were able to play a role in Jewish communal politics out of all proportion to their small number.[3] In a sense, Jewish party members were as dissident in the Jewish political arena as the Communist party would become in national politics. They became known for their slavish adherence to the party line, which changed with distressing frequency in the interwar years. Like their pious Jewish ancestors, they possessed a penchant for observance. What remained recognizably Jewish about those who affiliated with the nascent party in the early twenties was that they preferred Yiddish, and would have little to do with the study of Hebrew that had become popular for learned Jews of the Zionist persuasion. The terms of the Jewish engagement with American politics, especially its activism, cannot be fully understood without understanding the impact of the various stripes of socialism on the immigrant mentality.

* * *

At the turn of the twentieth century, the Jewish left was composed of a mélange of factions and parties that ranged from the disciplined party-like extremists of various socialist stripes to the anarchists whose weekly, the *Freie Arbeiter Shtime,* endured longer than most Yiddish newspapers. Radical intellectuals, like Abraham Cahan, drifted easily from the socialists to the anarchists. But the number of Jews who actually joined the newly organized party remained comparatively small. Radicalized Jews were uncomfortable with the party's instrumentalist strategy, which sought to use Jewish organizations for a special "vanguard" role. After its establishment in 1919, the party tried to infiltrate the rich Jewish network of fraternal and cultural organizations. When it found that it could not take them over, it simply duplicated them. Laboring under the misperception that American Jewry was all-powerful, the Communist International (Comintern), established in 1919, targeted the American Jewish labor movement as the best available instrument to penetrate the American labor movement.

With the exception of Finnish Americans, Jewish political culture was, in fact, further to the left than that of other immigrant communities. Still, there were also clear alarms from Social Democrats that socialism had gone awry in the Soviet Union. In 1921, the Bundist leader Vladimir Medem issued the first of several warnings regarding the anti-democratic tendencies of the communist regime in Moscow. That year too, the Democratic Socialist *Farband* broke away from the mélange of factions in which the Yiddish-speaking communist party was incubated. Having observed first-hand the abuse of the Bolshevik regime, the anarchist Emma Goldmann was trying desperately to leave the Soviet Union. By 1923, even Abraham Cahan, the editor of the *Forward*, who at first disregarded Medem's warning, recognized that the new regime in Moscow was no friend of socialism or of the Jews.[4]

Bundists and Labor Zionist may have come in conflict with the party, but other factions were not yet prepared to cut themselves off from the "socialist motherland." They remained convinced that Russian Jewry, like the Jews of the West, was finally undergoing its emancipation. After all, Lenin had spoken out against anti-Semitism. Promising better working conditions, the party was making strides in penetrating the garment unions. Before the disastrous communist-led strike of 1926 and the dual unionism campaign that followed, the communists nearly won control of the crucial garment workers unions and were within striking distance of gaining total control of the Jewish labor movement itself. It took the International Ladies Garment Workers Union (ILGWU) years to recover from the strike, and had it not been for the factionalism that tore the party apart after 1928, the communist hold on the Jewish left might have been consolidated. Less successful in withstanding infiltration was the American Labor Party, which was rested from the control of the International Garment Workers Union as the war approached. By 1944 there was sufficient confidence that social democratic forces could hold their own against the party's onslaught. Alex Rose, president of the Hatters union, established the Liberal Party, which threw its support to Harry Truman in the crucial campaign of 1948.[5]

It is difficult to pinpoint the precise historical moment when the party was compelled to exit the Jewish political arena. By December 1957, the party's membership, which stood at 22,663 in 1955, had declined to about 3,500 and the *Frayhayt* had lost 75 percent of its readership.[6] With the decline in Jewish party members, the influence of the party on Jewish politics became marginal. The Jewish left would move in a different direction.

During the thirty-year campaign to extricate Soviet Jewry, which began in the early sixties, no American Jewish comrades railed against the Zionist conspiracy, as was formally their habit. The party did not raise thousands of dollars, as it once did, to support resettlement of Jews in Birohbidzahn, the "Red Zion." The final blow may have come with the suppression of the uprising in Hungary. But Khrushchev's confessional speech to the 20th party congress in June 1956 was a mortal blow from which the Yiddish-speaking branch of the party could not recover. Leaked to the West, the four-hour speech confirmed most of the charges that had been leveled against the Soviet system, but contained not a word regarding the mistreatment of Jews during the years between 1948 and 1953, which culminated in the infamous "Doctors Plot." Once the residual influence of the party on Jewish politics was broken, an unfettered political culture free of Moscow's influence was free to develop. Some aspect of the street style of the New Left and the activism of Jewish young people in every movement for change and liberation are in some way linked to that unfettering.

Few things disappear into the past without leaving some trace. Our discussion here focuses on examining what happened to the Jewish left after the bonds of the old left were loosened. Jewish radicalism did not disappear, but its character changed. We note later that the New Left of the Vietnam years positioned itself still further from the democratic socialism or welfare state liberalism that most Jews had come to favor. The neoconservatives, convinced that socialist ideology had been pre-empted and perverted by the Soviet Union, abandoned the socialist fold altogether. In the following chapters, we learn that though very different in approach both grew out of the malaise of the old Jewish left.

* * *

The perpetual political conflicts within the immigrant generation hardly interfered with their attraction to the various brands of socialism and anarchism. What drew them was not the complex Marxist dialectics, which some have theorized attracted Jews because of its similarity to Talmudic disputation. Few working-class Jews had the inclination or time to study either Marx or Talmud. More important in projecting the influence of the organizations and propaganda of the left was the rich network of social and cultural organizations that they developed. Once affiliated, an immigrant Jew never needed to feel alone. What appealed to these socially isolated overworked immigrants was the continuous round of activities, which included everything from picketing a "gouging" landlord, usually also Jewish, to the omnipresent balalaika or mandolin ensemble, to a cheap summer camp where one could escape the oppressive summer heat of the city. The party's organized rent strikes offered an added dividend by demonstrating its militancy in search of justice. The party's Yiddish brochures offered a clear, simple explanation of their often dire economic circumstance and allowed the immigrant to feel that he was involved in the heady enterprise of making history. For many, the affiliation with a justice-seeking socialist movement went far to counteract the self-abnegating effects of assimilation that most Jews were undergoing. Socialism permitted tradition-minded observant Jews to make the transition to modernity in a meaningful way. Thousands of Jews were thus drawn into the socialist orbit hardly sensing the change in the way their lives would now be lived. In the Brooklyn Jewish ghetto of Brownsville, recalls the literary critic Alfred Kazin, "Socialism was a way of life" a kind of secular religion, much the way Christianity was to Americans. Jews attended their Sunday morning meetings on the streets of Brownsville the way native-born Americans attended church and baseball games. It was a sport of words, rather than balls and strikes, in which all could participate. The preference for verbal explanation and argumentation persists. To this day Jews are more likely to write to the editor of a newspaper, more likely to petition their representative in Congress, and increasingly more likely to become candidates for office. A high degree of political engagement became a hallmark of Jewish political culture.

The progressive justice-seeking organizations so attractive to the immigrant rarely openly identified themselves as being under the party's tutelage. They were "front" organizations, sometimes sporting a name related to the struggle against fascism in Spain or other causes of the moment. That concealment behind labels like "progressive" makes it difficult to estimate how much influence the party actually exercised in Jewish communal affairs, but it can be assumed that its influence went far beyond the limited number of actual Jewish card-carrying party members.

We shall note later that perpetual strife within the world socialist movement, especially within the communist world, worked to loosen the party's hold in many individual cases. But membership increased again in the thirties, when a renewed sense that the wave of the future lay with the Soviet Union *was* triggered by the collapse of the economy, followed by the Great Depression of the thirties. The Depression gave the party's *pronuncimientos* regarding the inevitable collapse of capitalism a prophetic ring. The reality that the avenues of social mobility were closed by the Depression radicalized many young Jews, and made some more receptive to party preachments. Compelled to abandon their aspirations for climbing out of poverty on the basis of their own talents and energy, the fashion among young Jews now was to rise with their class, rather than above it. Stimulated by rent strikes and other demonstrative forms of militancy, Jewish party membership grew so rapidly during the thirties that a party directive requested that Jewish comrades Americanize their family names. But the overwhelming majority of Jews continued to hold to their moderately left of center political position. It was Roosevelt they loved, not Stalin. American Jews it was observed had "*drei velten, die velt, yenne velt and Roosevelt.*"[7] Yet, to some degree, the Communist Party of the USA, working through its sizable Jewish membership and its general influence on the socialist left, was able to partially deflect Jewish radicalism from the more American reformist path it might have taken.

That deflection was made easier by the fact that the socialism of the Jewish immigrants never felt fully at home with the indigenous radicalism of the Industrial Workers of the World (IWW) variety or the ameliorative reformism of the Wisconsin Progressives. It retained a distinct "hot" eastern European flavor well into the second generation. Incubated in a pervasive and commanding religious culture, Jewish radicalism retained its messianic fervor, even while abandoning the Judaism that was its source. To the dismay of newly minted radicals who had just recently left the religious fold, Jewish anarchists sponsored Yom Kippur balls on the holiest fast day of the Jewish religious calendar. Revolution was revolution, but the need to chant *Kaddish* for the dead was not easily abandoned.[8] The more radical Jewish communists had less inclination to keep one foot in the tribal tent. Instead, the Party sought to capture center stage by preempting issues through which the newly minted Jewish voter would normally connect with the American political arena. A special case that concerned social justice or the path of progress, such as the Sacco

Vanzetti case or the Scopes Monkey Trial, allowed many to overlook the brutal Leninist contest for power in the Soviet Union. Sometimes, as in the case of the Scottsboro Boys, it was able to almost single-handedly exploit an injustice and effectively campaign to place an issue, such as lynching, on the national agenda. By projecting itself as being on the side of justice and progress, precisely where modernizing Jews wanted to be, the party gained support among "progressive" Jews.

* * *

For our purposes, it is important to understand that American Jewry's early attraction to the left also gave it a special vantage to observe that the socialism developed under Soviet tutelage had gone awry. Rather than producing a new humanitarian social order, it was developing a tyranny of unprecedented proportions. It was that basic reality that led to the ferment on the left that produced the neoconservative mindset that, as its first order of business, warned about the ominous developments in Stalinist Russia.

We have noted that the imagined link between Judaism and communism became standard fare in the anti-Semitic rhetoric of the interwar period. It makes the contemporary apprehensiveness of a right-wing neoconservative conspiracy seem strange. The National Socialists spoke incessantly of *Judeobolshevism*, just as the earlier term *Zydkomuna* was formerly used by the White anti-Revolutionary forces in Russia. It was echoed in the halls of Congress and in the Oval Office. As late as 1970, Richard Nixon, whose political career was based on his prowess as a communist spy hunter, observed that the only two non-Jews ever caught in his net were Alger Hiss and Whitaker Chambers. "Every other one was a Jew and it raised hell with us."[9] The immigrant Jewish ghetto dweller who attended party-sponsored dances and lectures had none of the dread of the Russian Revolution that was so prevalent among American political leaders, like Attorney General A. Mitchell Palmer, who in 1919 arrested hundreds of radicals, whether they were anarchists or socialists, and deported them to Europe on the "Red Ark." The disproportionate number of Jews among the deportees was taken for granted. In the American public mind the image of the Jew as a political radical was almost as common as the image of the Italian immigrant as criminal.

The pairing of Judaism with communism caused endless problems for Jewish defense agencies. In 1921 the American Jewish Committee sponsored extensive research into the background of the Soviet leadership in order to present evidence that there was little actual Jewish representation in Soviet governance. But the attempt to prove that it wasn't so was of little avail. Jewish writers, journalists and sundry pundits were too prominent in defending the social and production system developing in the Soviet Union. Jewish representation in the peace commission that Lenin sent to Brest-Litovsk in 1918 to negotiate a separate peace with the Germans was overwhelming. During the devastating purges of the thirties, the foreign affairs department and the security branches of the Soviet government continued to be viewed as Jewish bailiwicks. Of the leadership core of the Raeter republic in Bavaria (November 1918), which sought to bring communism to Bavaria, seven commissioners, including Ernst Toller and Gustaf Landauer, had Jewish ancestry. Similarly, the Spartacist League uprising in Berlin in the final months of 1918 was linked to the names of two well known Jewish radicals, Rosa Luxembourg and Karl Liebknecht. How could one explain away the fact that twenty of the twenty-six new commissars in Bela Kun's communist regime in Hungary, established in March 1919, were Jews?[10] In Romania, Ana Pauker's regime was called "little Jerusalem." Few Americans were aware that social democrats, especially Jewish Bundists and Labor Zionists, were among the first to feel the lash of the newly established Soviet regime. In America, where any political radical, whether he held a bomb or a sign protesting bad working conditions, was fair game, the difference between Bolsheviks and social democrats was not fathomed. For some cold warriors, communism was again seen as part of a Jewish conspiracy. They sought confirmation when Senator McCarthy's House Un-American Activities Committee investigated "Jewish Hollywood" in 1951.

* * *

Yet during the Depression years, left-leaning Jews were hardly alone in harboring doubts about the viability of the capitalist system. But for the overwhelming majority of Jews, their democratic socialist ideology brought them within striking distance of the emerging welfare state. The attraction to the Democrats was increased with Al Smith's administration in New York and became fully blown during the Roosevelt New Deal years. The preference for the left of center position partly accounts for the strong support given to the New Deal by the Jewish voter. At least on domestic matters, the Jewish "love affair" with Roosevelt was reciprocal. The New Deal programs for public housing and social security borrowed heavily from programs first advocated by Jewish social workers and later implemented by the Jewish labor movement. For some left-leaning Jewish voters, who still retained the feeling that Moscow was on the right track, Roosevelt's diplomatic recognition of the Soviet Union in 1933 was especially welcome. If the government in Washington and the Ford Motor Company maintained friendly relations with Moscow, they argued, surely the continuing interest of Jewish socialists could be defended. Few foresaw the purge trials, which raised new doubts about the Soviet experiment.

But buoyed by the Soviet role in defeating Nazism, the party regained some influence among Jewish left-wingers in the immediate post-war years. That may partly account for the comparatively large vote given to Wallace in 1948. The Progressive party platform advocated American-Soviet reconciliation as a central plank in American foreign policy. But the party's influence was a minor factor in the changes in the postwar Jewish political posture. In the immediate years after World War II, Jews were the nation's least enthusiastic Cold War supporters. After the founding of the state in 1948, the primary interest of the Jewish voter and leadership became focused on the security and well-being of Israel. The mobilization of the communal effort to wring diplomatic recognition of the Jewish state from a reluctant Truman administration was the earliest evidence that a more confident Jewish electorate and leadership had emerged, and would play an active role in trying to shape the nation's foreign policy in the Middle East. That early American Jewish response to the Holocaust serves as the seedbed of Jewish activism in foreign policy and it is also at the heart of the charges it faces today.

In the decades following the establishment of the Jewish state, it became clear that Moscow's opposition to Israel was implacable and went far beyond the threat such a small state could pose to a superpower. That was the context in which the Jewish aspect of the neoconservative sensibility, spurred by the intellectuals around *Commentary* magazine, challenged the Jewish affinity for the left. It gained considerable support from Jewish voters who gave the security of Israel high priority. Jewish voters found themselves in consonance with the growing feeling that the Soviet Union posed the major threat to world peace. The party left the Jewish political stage with great reluctance and was helped by the unfolding events of the early fifties. Almost simultaneously with the Korean War, the party, seizing upon an injustice issue, organized a worldwide public relations campaign to halt the executions of Julius and Ethel

Rosenberg, party members implicated in the massive Soviet espionage effort to steal the "secret" of the atomic bomb. Many conservative Jews shared the feeling that the death sentence was too severe, since the Soviet Union had been an ally when the espionage occurred.

But the Rosenberg case hardly put a crimp in the march of the Jewish voter to a more centrist political position. The goodwill Moscow earned among some Jewish voters could not sustain itself. The war accelerated acculturation and narrowed the gap between the political culture of American Jewry and the more conservative orientation of the American voter. The prosperity of the fifties did the rest.

* * *

Furnished with this brief background in American Jewish political history, we are better prepared to understand the political behavior of American Jews in recent years. While organized communist activity exited the Jewish stage in the mid-fifties, its actual influence among Jews declined sharply in the late twenties and early thirties. We have noted that American Jewish socialists were among the first to perceive that the humanistic socialism that gained their support had been perverted by Soviet authorities and turned into a massive tyranny. Some of that animosity was rooted in the murderous treatment of leaders of the Jewish Labor Bund at the turn of the century and during the war. By the thirties, many socialist-oriented Jews viewed the party with great suspicion. Heralded in novels and the English-language Jewish press in the thirties, the informed Jewish reader could not have remained unaware of Stalin's campaign to liquidate the "kulaks" and the thousands disappearing into the *Gulag*. In addition, informed Jews had to confront the destruction of Jewish communal life and institutions and the distressing frequency of Jewish names in the purge trials of the thirties.[11] Soviet propaganda organs threw their support behind the Arabs in the bloody Arab riots of 1929. But the picture remained unclear since these negatives could be balanced by news of the rapid social mobility of Soviet Jews and their integration into Soviet managerial strata during the twenties. Soviet Jews were welcomed into the party, becoming its largest other-than-Russian national minority. Secularized Jews who had little use for religion reasoned that the destruction of synagogues and religious schools was part of government policy to limit the influence of all organized religion. Churches were also considered the "opiate of the people" subject to destruction in the name of freeing the masses.

At the same time, the Soviet Union was the only state willing to send arms and troops to defend the beleaguered Spanish Republic, which had the overwhelming support of the Jewish electorate, much to the dismay of American Catholics. When we add up the number of Jews fighting Franco in the International Brigade, it may have formed the largest Jewish military contingent since the biblical times of Bar Kochba. When Moscow and Berlin signed the Non-Aggression Pact (August 1939) with its infamous secret clause, Jewish communists were wont to argue that the division of Poland had in fact saved over a million Polish Jews and allowed time for the Red Army to prepare itself for the attack that was coming. Despite enormous losses, the Red Army became the only organized military force with sufficient depth to absorb the Nazi blitzkrieg and fight another day. For many Jews, the Soviet Union became the only hope that something might still be redeemed from the slaughterhouse that Europe had become. It was a classic dilemma resolved only by acting as if "the enemy of my enemy is my friend."

At the grassroots level, Jewish sympathy for the resistance mounted by the Red Army was fostered by a bevy of skilled propagandists, like Howard Fast, who did not deny that there were excesses, but argued that a revolution "like an omelet" could not be made "without breaking eggs." Much depended on whose eggs were broken and the twists and turns in the party line. Jewish support ebbed during the ultra-radical period of factional conflict when party membership fell from 28,000 in 1928 to 6,000 four years later. In a demonstration of resiliency, the party recouped during the popular front period (1935-1939), when it sought to unify all left-wing forces against fascism. But after Moscow's signing of the Non-Aggression Pact in 1939, party membership plunged to less than 4,000 from a high of 75,000 in 1937. After the Wehrmacht poured across the new Soviet borders in June 1941, most Jews welcomed the "strange alliance" with the Soviet Union and favored sending Lend-Lease aid through the treacherous Archangel route. The party, now in its patriotic guise, loudly supported Franklin Roosevelt for reelection for an unprecedented third term in 1940 and went as far as urging the prosecution of its rival, the Trotskyite Socialist Workers Party, under the Smith Act.

After its victory in Stalingrad, which many viewed as the turning point of the war, Jews shared the conviction that Russia deserved major credit for defeating the Nazi juggernaut at enormous cost of blood and treasure. When the party officially dissolved itself in 1944, to be replaced by a Communist Political Association, it helped dissipate the wariness regarding the Soviet leadership that had accumulated during the interwar years. In the Jewish ghettos of New York, the starred flag indicating a son in service was sometimes accompanied by a party decal urging the opening of a second front.

*   *   *

We note in the following chapter that the earliest manifestation of what became the neoconservative mindset grew out of the conflict between Stalin and Trotsky within the world communist movement. That conflict contained an unmistakable sign that anti-Semitism was rampant in the Kremlin. If one carefully examined the accusation against the supporters of Trotsky, they appear to be the mirror image of the contemporary accusations against the neoconservatives. Rather than Jews being accused of controlling American foreign policy, they were being accused of trying to control Soviet foreign policy. In short, the same image of an all-powerful Jewish power nexus haunted Soviet decision makers. We see additional evidence of it in the mobilization of the Jewish Anti-Fascist Committee (1943), headed by the renowned actor Michael Mikhoels, which was charged with the mission to mobilize Jewish support abroad for the Soviet war effort. Clearly the Kremlin retained an exaggerated notion of Jewish power that it now sought to mobilize. Just as the prohibitions against organized religion were abandoned by the CPSU during the war, so the idea that "international Jewry," normally a major nemesis in Kremlin demonology, could be used to help win the war became part of Moscow's political strategy. The Mikhoels visit in 1943 marked a high point of Soviet influence in the Jewish community during the war. Only after the Yalta and Potsdam conferences in 1945 did it become apparent that the "strange alliance" could not survive the tensions that had developed during the war and would come to a close. In the Cold War period that followed, Soviet Jews would be among the first to be ensnared by Stalin's paranoia regarding the Jews, especially after Golda Meier's jubilant reception in Moscow in September 1948.

The years between 1948 and Stalin's death in 1953 are called the "black years." They begin with a violent reaction to the fact that, despite its socialist-oriented kibbutzim and its powerful Histadrut, Israel would not align itself with the Soviet bloc as Stalin had hoped. That triggered the campaign to root out "rootless Cosmopolitans," a euphemism for Jews. By the time of the 1953 Doctor's Plot, even the most ardent American Jewish party member might have suspected that something had gone awry in the socialist motherland. As evidence of a pervasive anti-Semitism in the party leadership became undeniable, arguments were developed by party spokesmen to disprove the charge. They claimed that following Lenin's earlier precedent the Constitution of 1936 had made anti-Semitism illegal, which effectively eliminated its propagation. The comparatively high position in Soviet academic, managerial, and even party circles was submitted as evidence that Jewish life in the Soviet Union was unfettered. Occasionally, there was a slip up, as when Khrushchev was asked at a news conference about the denial of access to Jewish students and faculty to the highest ranked universities and party schools. He replied that the Soviet Union had its own "cadres" now. Jews clearly were not considered Russia's own. Sometimes the denials assumed a comical tone. Defenders of the openness of the Soviet life were wont to point out that some leading Politburo members, like Molotov, had Jewish wives. The "some of our best wives are Jewish" ploy only brought knowing smiles in the West where the "best friends" refrain was familiar currency.

As the worldwide campaign to "save" the Rosenbergs indicates, the party's influence continued to be strong in the Jewish community, but by mid-decade it was on the wane. Known and even suspected party members were increasingly denied access to Jewish communal organizations like the American Jewish Congress. It was not an easy task. Party members were frequently the most militant of the activists, the most dedicated strugglers for a better world, but that did not prevent them from concealing rather than proudly proclaiming their party affiliation.

* * *

What happened to the Jewish communists? We have already noted how the party lost its little remaining influence in the Jewish polity during the fifties. The reason for the decline may have as much to do with the change in generations as to the threatening atmosphere of McCarthyism. The political profile of the generation that reached adulthood after the Second World War bore greater similarity to the general American which was distancing itself from its wartime friendship with the Soviet Union as the Cold War got underway. When the Soviets obtained the A-bomb in 1949, followed by the Korean War, which could not have been fought without Soviet support, admiration of the Soviets' contribution to the defeat of Germany was replaced by fear and foreboding. Even without the actual outbreak of the Cold War, it is likely that the political temperament of American Jewry would have lost some of its "radical" flavor. The rising educational level of American Jewry, combined with the growth of the economy, made the new generation less susceptible to the politics of passionate causes, the customary fare of the extreme left. A rudimentary Marxism gleaned from communist pamphlets could make the immigrant believe that he now understood what made the world go round. A few catchphrases could satiate the Jewish immigrant's craving to be educated. But for a generation that had fought in far-off places and lived for the first time in close contact with other Americans of their age, that ideology, based partly on immigrant alienation, no longer sufficed. In some measure, burdening normal political transactions with the objective of changing the world was a manifestation of an Eastern European style. In the immigrant context, changing abusive government by force if necessary was a requisite first step to establishing democracy. That assumption of the justifiable use of force, of revolution, to bring change was a far cry from the assumptions prevalent in the American political arena, where despite weaknesses and corruption, change could still be achieved through the political process. The rapid social mobility experienced by Jews in the post-war years provided evidence that it was possible to improve one's personal circumstance and rise above one's class, rather than with it, as prescribed in the socialist model.

*   *   *

The post-war "Red Diaper" generation rebelled against the Eastern European Jewish political style of their parents, who built their lives on the assumption that class and ethnic lines were immutable and that the socialism prevalent in the Soviet Union held out a better model of a worthwhile life. During the years of the Depression, it was possible to imagine that such was the case. Though on a far lower level, Soviet Jewry experienced social mobility at least comparable to that of American Jewry during the "Roarin' Twenties." The Yiddish-speaking immigrant generation also witnessed a blossoming of Yiddish culture in the Soviet Union, or at least a Stalinist version of it. Yiddish had been made the official national language of Soviet Jewry and its literature, theater, and press outpaced those of Yiddish culture in America, which by 1927 showed clear evidence of decline. That cultural flowering was eliminated at one blow in 1952 with the liquidation of the Jewish literary elite and the closing of its institutions. But what was a terrible blow to the old Yiddish-speaking communists from the foreign language federations who remained in the party fold was barely noted by the "Red Diaper" generation. Yiddish was no longer a binding generational tie. The offspring had ample evidence of the Kremlin's lethal strategic goals regarding Jewish culture, but did not mourn its demise. The failure of the Soviet dream was but one reason for the total denial of anything that could be related to their parents. One chronicler saw the split between the Old and the New left as a classic case of "Oedipal rage."

The trial of the Rosenbergs for espionage gave the party an unforeseen opportunity to recoup lost ground among Jews as a result of the Kremlin's "rootless cosmopolitan" campaign. Many Jews were convinced of the innocence of the Rosenbergs, at least of Ethel Rosenberg, and more thought the death penalty too harsh. That sense of injustice and the suspicion that anti-Semitism was involved, offered an opportunity for the party to use the case for its own purposes. In November 1952, one year after the trial, the handful who sounded the alarm about the Kremlin's motives witnessed how the communist regime in Prague placed its own "Jewish spies," including its trade minister, Rudolf Slansky, on trial. Moscow had ample experience in staging show trials, but signaling out Jews on espionage charges was relatively new.

The Rosenberg case highlighted Moscow's penchant for using Jewish party members, like the Rosenbergs, to do its intelligence work.[12] The suborning of Jewish party members for intelligence work carried a heavy price for American Jewry when they were apprehended. But defending Jews against American anti-Semitism during the Black Years, which would soon treat the world to the Jewish Doctor's Plot, proved too much for many American Jews to bear. It was primarily the accumulation of evidence of the brutality of the Soviet system and its specific anti-Semitism that helped break the influence of the party among "progressive" left-leaning Jews.

Fortunately, the party's preoccupation with Jews diminished as it turned its full attention on the nation's simmering race problem. Anxious to establish his credentials as a Marxist thinker on the nationality question, Stalin had early discovered that American Negroes qualified as a separate national entity. A strict follower of the Kremlin line, the CPUSA entered the civil rights struggle relatively early. That spurred a special party interest in the welfare of African Americans and with it a deeper engagement in American life. It was behind its efforts in the Scottsboro Boys case, which earned the Party kudos from the left and some gratitude from black activists anxious to receive support wherever they could find it. American Jews were one of several political constituencies that evinced a special sympathy for the plight of the American Negro. It was based on the sense that Jewish historical victimization and that of the American Negro were analogous. But the ameliorative approach proposed by such groups as the American Jewish Congress and the American Jewish Committee based on a long-range strategy of bringing the Negro fully into American society as an equal led to general Jewish communal support for integration. That was not what Communist Party policy had in mind. At Stalin's behest, it took a long-range separationist position calling for black empowerment, even while remaining active on the integrationist front. The tension between integration and separation would come up again in the seventies when the SDS reached out to the Black Panthers.

* * *

Few can have failed to notice the prominent leadership role Jewish "baby boomers" play today in every variety of liberation movement that dot the American social and political landscape. American Jewry's political persona is characterized by intense political engagement and the incubation of a disproportionate number of the activists that energize the American political dialogue. Some of the deep engagement and activism of Jews may be linked to the fact that Judaism is primarily a religion of deeds. Yet strangely, contemporary Jews identify themselves as being more Jewish in the secular ethnic sense than in the Judaic religious one. Yet Jewish activism, as any local politician is aware, is more evident than ever on the American political scene. This discussion finds the new source of activism in the Jewish turn of the twentieth century attraction to socialism, which preached as one of its basic tenets the unity of theory and action and in addition provided a morality-based ideology, which was particularly attractive for young Jews seeking to improve the human condition.

On any given day during the sixties and seventies, one could not escape the nightly news footage of the limp bodies of young protesters carried away by the local police for causes as sundry as the right to smoke marijuana to the need to stop the war in Vietnam. The confrontational tactics of the civil rights struggle and the anti-war movement have become a mainstay of American political culture. A disproportionate number of activists continue to be young Jews making a statement for some real or imagined social injustice. Unlike their immigrant ancestors, they seem utterly at home in America and address American problems.

We have earlier observed that the Jewish left, from social democrats to anarchists, understood the importance of making their voices heard. That stemmed from a value adapted from Leninism, rather than Marxism, that preached *praxis*, the "unity of theory and action." It demanded that believers act out their beliefs. The difference between moralizers and those who are authentically moral is that the latter struggle in their daily lives to achieve being moral. Today *praxis* has morphed into simply being "proactive," which means following the mandate inherent in your personal belief. If one believes that continued defilement of the natural environment threatens the welfare of future generations, then one is dutybound to do something about it. To some undeterminable degree, the confrontational tactics we witnessed in the civil rights and peace movements and in the Soviet Jewry movement of the sixties, seventies, and eighties stemmed from the imperative to act embedded in the left-wing tradition of putting dearly held principles into practice. Protest rallies, marches, physical confrontation with authorities, picketing, and the use of poster art, lilting songs, were tactics honed to a fine edge by the Communist party and its front organizations and within the Jewish socialist left generally during the interwar period. Activism enabled a comparatively small group to amplify its impact. During the thirties, when normal politics seemed in a condition of stasis brought on by the isolationist logjam, the refrain often heard from Jewish activists alarmed at the collapse of the will to resist Nazi machinations at Munich was, "at least the communists are doing something."

In the interwar years, public protest and meetings ranging from rent strikes to May Day rallies and parades had only a modicum of communal support. But it was sufficient to allow the Communist Party of the USA to choose the issues, to conceive the slogans, to compose the songs, to organize the rallies and generate the image that theirs was the wave of the future. Often the party's program and tactics were first tried out in the Jewish ghettos of New York and Philadelphia where a mass following could be mobilized. A lynching, a gouging landlord, a municipal agency too slow in distributing federal welfare, innocent black youths accused of rape was sufficient to bring Jews to the street in protest. Similar tactics, including "spit brigades," were deployed with good effect in the pitched street battles to control the Jewish unions. The party used these causes to keep the community in constant turmoil, but in the end Jewish activism goes beyond the legacy of the left. Only a handful of Jews subjected themselves to party discipline. A lingering communal memory when Jews could not act politically fed into the intensity of early Jewish political engagement, especially in liberation causes. Secularizing Jews not yet far removed from the religious tradition may still have been influenced by a faith that gives the highest priority to the deed or act rather than merely the profession of it.

If the parents were traumatized by the Depression, the Jewish "baby boomers" were haunted by the death camps of the Holocaust. When activists for the cause of Soviet Jewry came to center stage during the sixties and seventies, the imagined silence of the American Jewish witness during the Holocaust played a central role in fueling the movement. But the historical memory of contemporary activists was selective. All but forgotten were the giant rallies organized by the American Jewish Congress and the Jewish labor movement during the thirties.

*   *   *

So what happened to our *brenendige*? The simplest answer may be that an unforgiving history happened that, among other things, revealed the yawning chasm between Jewish radicals and radical Jews. The former seek their roots (that's what radical refers to), in a quest of universal brotherhood or what the first-generation immigrant called *weltlichkeit*. (worldliness). They wanted to be part of the universal human brotherhood. The religious tradition was not totally discarded, but became an accident of birth and a source of sentimental songs about Jewish mothers. The radical Jew, on the other hand, begins his search for roots together with other Jews in a secularized Jewish context. Like the Jewish radical he too seeks social justice, but chooses a Jewish conduit, which he may find in the kibbutz or the Jewish labor movement, for the quest to "repair the world" emphasized in the Reform and Reconstructionist movements. They are most likely to be found in the ranks of Jewish social democrats, like Bundists and Labor Zionists, or the Reform rabbinate. The great difference between radical Jews and Jewish radicals is in the fate of they assign to Jewish communal survival. Carried to its logical conclusion, the Jewish radical, like Trotsky, would meld the Jews into the human fraternity, while a radical Jew, like Ben-Gurion, seeks to establish a socialist-oriented Jewish state.

The Holocaust is a great divide in Jewish political culture because it undermined the underlying assumption of Jewish radicals of the old left, which assumed that entry into the human fraternity that undergirds all human society would result in access and security. Jews would finally become an accepted part of the human family. Jews in the Western democracies that had experienced virtually complete emancipation truly believed that they had become part of the universe of obligation, only to discover that the destruction of European Jewry occurred amidst an eerie silence among the witnessing nations. On a smaller scale, a similar experience in the United States by left-wing Jewish activists who learned that they were unwelcome in the struggle for civil rights came as a shocking surprise. It encouraged some Jewish radicals to return to the Jewish fold to become activists in the Soviet Jewry movement. But of all the grievances the old left harbored about their radical children, their lack of Jewishness was not one of them. The relationship to Judaism had always been a problem for the old left and continued to be one for the new. Both generations were ready to "abandon" tribal loyalties in favor of joining the larger human family.

*　*　*

Our aim was to discover what happened to our Jewish radicals who were part of the Jewish left. Did they simply abandon the historical stage and disappear into the past? There is some evidence that American Jewry continues to produce such activist types, but they are more individuated and marching to the beat of an internal drummer, rather than a party commissar. There are few professing communists to be found in the Jewish community, but it does not require a forensic examination to locate the fingerprints Jewish radicals have left on Jewish political culture. Today, the intensity of American Jewish political engagement is deeper than that of comparable ethnic constituencies in America. Everywhere we look, we find Jewish men and women in the forefront of those agencies that push for change. They were conspicuously prominent in the civil rights movement and the movement for women's liberation. There are a disproportionate number of committed Jews working for human improvement from the protest against genocide in Darfur to the campaign against secondary smoke. But there is a difference in what attracts contemporary Jews to activism. American Jewish political culture changed when the influence of Jewish radicals on the communal stage diminished. The Jewish left today seems to have reverted to the more humanistic social democratic position before Lenin summoned the socialist left to form a communist party in 1919. The socialism, which once prevailed, has been meshed with New Deal welfare statism, which was in acceptable striking distance of the socialism of the immigrant generation. The decline of the extreme left explains much of the normalization of American Jewish political behavior, which is more centrist than that of the immigrant generation. Socialism no longer acts like a lodestone pulling American Jewry to the left. But a closer look reveals that the signs of its once formidable influence are still there. Its legacy is felt primarily in the activism that has become a permanent part of American Jewish political culture.

We have noted that the continual ideological tensions within the Jewish community served as the original spawning ground that, in later generations, gave rise to the neoconservatives and later to the New Left. Their respective roles are the subject of the following chapters. In different ways, both are part of a heightened ideological passion associated with Jewish political culture. But clearly something beyond political passions is involved, at least for the neoconservative phenomenon. Whatever else happens, they will be held to account for the role they played in shaping the intellectual dialogue requisite for fashioning the strategy of a world power. The danger is not in their ideas, which they now argue were misunderstood and mismanaged by the Bush administration. It lies in the weakness of countervailing opinions to challenge their assumptions regarding the world order.

Similarly, we note in the following chapters that in 1968 it appeared that a young draft-prone generation led by the New Left would tear apart the social system. But the nation did not become a "Woodstock nation" as some feared. The New Left was a minor blip on the historical monitor that played a role in bringing the Vietnam War to an end. That generation is now reaching retirement age and seeks security from the very world they sought to shake to its foundations. That influence, if it can be categorized as Jewish at all, is based on the impact a distinct college youth cohort had on the American political scene. There is really nothing like it in American political history.

Notes

1.   In the election of 1920, a whopping 24 percent of the Jewish vote went to the Socialist candidate, Eugene V. Debs. In the election of 1924, the merely Progressive candidate, Robert LaFollette, received 17 percent—almost as high as in his Wisconsin home state.

2.   An imprecise translation would be a burning one or an enflamed one. The term *farbrente* or a *brenendige roite* was commonly used by Yiddish speakers to describe those totally consumed by left-wing political ideology. It translates from the Yiddish as passionately, literally burning, communists. But one could be a *farbrenter tsionist* as well.

3.   If there was a discernable political center of gravity in the Jewish electorate during the interwar years, it was probably its support of Zionism of the labor variety, slightly left of center.

4.   Yet others like Paul Novick, editor of the party organ, *Frayhait*, even after Khrushchev's secret confessional speech before the 20th Party Congress in 1956 was fully published in the *Daily Worker*, would not accept that all was lost. He favored changing the name of the paper to *Amerikaner Yidishe Folks-Tsaytung* to prioritize Yiddish culture, rather than the idea of class struggle. The paper now aspired to be "an independent progressive Jewish labor and people's newspaper."

5.   That was the same year that Henry Wallace's bid for the presidency on the ticket of a newly organized Progressive Party. Generally acknowledged today to have been a largely communist party enterprise, it received fifteen percent of the Jewish vote in 1948. Like most third parties in the history of American politics, the Progressive party proved to be a bee that stung once and died. Thereafter it was the Liberal party that played the role of balancer in New York State politics, even as Jewish voting support returned to the Democrats.

6.   An indication on how firm was the party's hold on Yiddish-speaking communists is the fact that the *Frayhayt*, founded in 1921, still had 6,000 readers in 1977 and did not finally cease publication until 1988. It outlived most other Yiddish newspapers. *The Daily Worker* halted publication in 1958 and was succeeded by the *People's Daily*, which became a weekly. Progressives were able to keep up by reading the *National Guardian* and the *Monthly Review*.

7.   "This world, the other world and Roseworld (Roosevelt)."

8.   The Day of Atonement (Yom Kippur) is the holiest day on the Jewish religious calendar during which fasting is customary. Kaddish refers to the traditional prayer recited by male mourners at least three times daily for an eleven-month period after the passing and on all religious holidays and the Sabbath.

9.   *Newsweek*, November 18, 1999, p. 30. Quoted from a National Archives release in 1999.

10. In fact, by definition, few communists were affiliated with the Jewish community or considered themselves as Jewish. The term "of Jewish ancestry" more accurately describes their status. Like Karl Marx they considered their Jewishness an unhappy accident of birth.

11. Today there is some doubt that, given the high position Jews attained in government and the party, that Jews were disproportionately victimized during the purges.

12. The names of Jewish agents recruited from party ranks are legendary. It included a "walk in agent" like Jewish congressman, Samuel Dickstein, founder of the HUAC, whose NKVD codename was "the crook." Their prevalence in security agencies went beyond their reliability as "true believers." One branch of the CPUSA had always remained underground after the Palmer Raids of 1919 and predictably fell under the control of the NKVD, the Soviet intelligence agency of the period. Many of its recruits were drawn from the foreign language federations that had joined the newly established party en masse in the twenties. The left-wing Jewish socialists were the largest group among the federations and the federations were the largest group within the newly organized party. During the twenties, only 10 percent of the party members were native English-speakers. During the thirties, the underground section of the party was headed by Sandor Goldberger, alias Josef Peters, and another Jew, Bernard Schuster, the organizational secretary of the New York State District of the CPUSA. Both acted as recruiters for Soviet intelligence. Although the best-known agents apprehended during the fifties, Judith Coplan and Colonel Rudolf Abels, did not come to the espionage game through this domestic channel, the handful of other Jewish agents were recruited in this way. See Joseph Albright and Marcia Kunstel, *Bombshell: The Secret Story of America's Unknown Spy Conspiracy* (New York: Random House, 1997).

VI

Neocons: Do They Represent a Jewish Communal Interest?

We come next to a different kind of power that some attribute to American Jewry. It is embodied in the neoconservatives, the name given to a varied group of public intellectuals who supposedly have exerted a strong influence on American governing elites. Determining the Jewish identity of the neoconservatives is problematic since their aims were couched in national interest terms and the policies advocated did not reflect a consensus within the Jewish community. Neither the neoconservatives nor the New Left, to be discussed in the following chapter, were particularly attached to the Jewish polity or its major organizations. They might best be identified by the great fear they have aroused by would-be defenders of the republic. Those who imagine a Jewish conspiracy to control policy assume that the predominance of Jewish intellectuals, journalists, and sundry pundits in the early stages of the development of the group is sufficient evidence of its Jewishness. They are Jews by accusation.

Yet there is a Jewish fingerprint in both groups that stems from their early incubation in the perennial conflict within the left. We have noted in the previous chapter that the role of the left in shaping the development of a distinct American Jewish political culture was strong. A broad and pervasive Eastern European version of democratic socialist political culture was part of the cultural baggage the immigrants carried to the New World. The Russian Revolution held out the promise of emancipation already in the possession of Western Jewries. Once the socialist mentality was transplanted to the immigrant communities of the eastern seaboard cities, it was adopted in several variations by the newly proletarianized workforce and eventually transmitted to the second and third generation, who, paradoxically, were seeking a way out of the working class. The manifestations of the socialist worldview could be seen in every facet of immigrant Jewish communal life, but most especially in its labor movement. Even as Jews in the 1920s experienced rapid economic and social mobility, many looked favorably at what was happening in the Soviet Union. Often the transition from religious orthodoxy to a socialist secular one was made so quickly that a social vacuum was left in its place. The *esprit de corps* generated by the local *Poalei Zion* or *Arbeiter Ring* group and the dozens of *Landsmanshaftn* affiliated with them gave the uprooted immigrant Jew, who was in the process of giving up his binding religious tradition, something to fill the social vacuum. There was also the perennial balalaika ensemble and chorus, lectures on health and politics, but also matters of "justice" concerning a gouging landlord or kosher butcher. Picketing of such "exploiters" was organized in order to make them see the sinfulness of their ways. Some explain the penchant for the democratic left by noting that observant and deeply conservative Jews were accustomed to having rules to live by. The socialist idea could mean almost anything, but it also proffered new and yet familiar rules of behavior, a socialist *Halacha* (Jewish code of law). That socialization and the politicization of the immigrant Jews occurred simultaneously and reinforced each other. The resultant amalgam between social bonds, called *chavershaft*, and political belief was so durable that it could be passed on to the following generation, and ultimately became a factor in the remarkable political engagement of the Jewish electorate. Jews loved politics, which they first practiced with great passion in their own organizational world.

For the Jewish immigrant, socialism offered a clear, simple explanation of the dire economic circumstances in which he lived. It allowed him to feel that he was involved in the heady process of making history. Becoming a "sozialist" also helped the immigrant to negotiate the wrenching changes, especially in religious observance and greater gender equality, required by the acculturation process in which he was willy-nilly involved. In Jewish neighborhoods in Brooklyn and the Bronx, local parks were the scene of fiery impromptu political discussions. The speeches were sometimes filled with partisan invective, but physical confrontations were a rarity. It was a war of words. The ordinary shophand could, for a precious moment, sound like a rabbi, albeit one of a secular variety.

The Jewish left was characterized by perpetual conflict and fragmentation as new positions and leadership types came to the fore. Card-carrying membership in the nascent ever-changing communist party was never a major phenomenon in the Jewish left, since adherence to the principle of democratic centralism, which was the mainstay of party control, did not come easily for politically committed but also highly individuated Jews.[1] The temptation to question party authority and go one's own way was omnipresent in the free atmosphere of the ghetto. Organizational splits resembling the process of cell mitosis made political life in the Jewish world contentious. That political turmoil formed the nesting ground for the birth of the dissidence that led a generation later to the neoconservative phenomenon, which began with the realization that something was amiss with the Soviet custodianship of the socialist movement. In a sense, the later New Left, which had at its core organizations like the Students for a Democratic Society (SDS) and the Berkley's Free Speech Movement, was part of a continuing response to the malaise within the socialist left.

* * *

Vaguely similar circumstances in their origin and similar problems in establishing their Jewish bona fides allow us momentarily to group these two movements together, but in their political objectives, style, longevity, and vision, neocons and New Leftists are dissimilar. What makes them different from each other is the generational factor. The founding group of neocons was composed of children of the depression and war and the bitter internecine fighting within the left during the twenties and thirties. The New Left was composed of children born of "progressive" parents in the freer, less encumbered post-war years.

Over a two-generation period, the neocons went through several different incarnations. During the thirties they began as a disaffected political faction spun off from the bitter conflict between Stalinists and Trotskyites. The latter faction had early become aware that a new kind of tyranny parading under socialist banners had developed in the Soviet Union. The revolution had been betrayed. Fixated on transmitting the real nature of the Soviet tyranny in the 1950s, they became primarily interested in preventing the foreign policy establishment from succumbing to the siren song regarding "peaceful coexistence" emanating from Moscow. They were part of the mélange of socialist factions whose common ground was that they had lost faith that the model of economic and social organization developing under Stalin in the Soviet Union was appropriate for the United States. They were America's earliest "Cold Warriors" and that was often the extent of their conservatism. Except for Irving Kristol, they spoke little of the traditional conservative fare, smaller government, lower taxes, and balanced budgets. To the chagrin of the paleoconservatives, the traditional guardians of free enterprise, the newly minted conservatives were not churchgoers and seemed mostly interested in foreign affairs. In their support of the civil rights movement they were often as liberal as their fellow Jews. But they were appalled by the ignominious abandonment of South Vietnam and during the seventies they offered the strongest opposition to Kissinger's détente policy, particularly its disarmament program.

Viewed through the prism of the Jewish political culture of the left, neoconservatism is a contemporary resonance of Trotskyism. Trotsky had a peculiar attraction for the American Jewish left. He was at once a man of action, a brilliant military strategist and organizer, and an intellectual of the highest order who could make as well as write history. Before he ran afoul of Stalin, he served as evidence that the Jewish and Russian or any other host culture could be successfully amalgamated. That was the highest aspiration of the Jewish communist. Max Shachtman, who became a supporter of Trotsky in the Communist party split of the twenties, is in a sense the first neoconservative. In his later years he was a supporter of the Vietnam War and a "Scoop" Jackson Democrat. He had gone all the way.[2] In 1972 the Shachtmanites changed their name to the Social Democrats USA (SD/USA) and became in effect the left wing of the neocons. In the early seventies they were mostly registered Democrats, but some began to drift away from the party when they perceived a leftward drift in the party's McGovern wing. When Jackson failed in his second campaign to secure the Democratic presidential nomination in 1976, the drift of neocons to the Republican party quickened. By the 1980s, a former Democrat associated with the labor movement, Jeanne Kirkpatrick, had become Reagan's ambassador to the United Nations.[3]

There was also a distinct difference in the way each group approached the support of the security of Israel, a crucial issue of the Cold War and the Jewish agenda. The New Left was at best indifferent to Israel, and in its extreme form joined with the growing disapproval of the Jewish state prevalent in the European socialist movement. That hostility may account for the trickle of Jewish activists who withdrew from groups such as Congress of Racial Equality (CORE) and Students for a Democratic Society (SDS) to join the Soviet Jewry movement. If there is a central neoconservative assumption aside from their anti-Soviet stance, it relates to their strong support for the security of Israel. It was based not so much on their Jewishness as their appreciation of Israel as a robust democracy that could serve as a model in the Middle East, as well as a proven combat-ready counter to the string of Soviet client states. Today, paleoconservatives cite that support of Israel as evidence that the movement is part of a Jewish conspiracy to use American power as a proxy for a Jewish interests. But neocon support is more easily understood as part of a strategic and ideological position that called for the strengthening of the democratic sphere. We have noted a similar blending of American and Jewish interests in the case of the emigration of Soviet Jews. Some of the younger neoconservatives who worked for Senator Henry "Scoop" Jackson, such as Richard Perle and Morris Amitai, used their influence to open the gates of the Soviet Union for the *refuseniks*. They were involved in designing the Jackson-Vanik amendment, which proposed to deny the Soviets Most Favored Nation treatment and the access to credit which accompanied it if the *refuseniks* continued to be denied the right to emigrate. But their support went beyond the fact that they happened to be Jewish. The emigration issue was a cudgel with which to beat Moscow on the subject of its greatest vulnerability, the denial of basic human rights. Senator Jackson, who was deeply involved in the emigration question and was at the same time the strongest voice for Israel in the Senate, was the personification of the prevailing neoconservative sensibility. Yet comparatively few of his news releases were specifically focused on the travail of Soviet Jewry. They speak rather of human rights for all suppressed groups in the Soviet empire.

Were it not for the shrill cry from conservatives and others that accuse the neocons of being part of a conspiracy to co-opt American power, the question of their Jewishness would be of little account. American Jews are, after all, disproportionately involved in general American politics and neoconservative political positions found little support among Jewish voters, who were the nation's least enthusiastic supporters of the Cold War. Yet in the case of the neocons, the Jewish influence goes beyond their conspicuous presence among the founders. The core ideas of neoconservatism were initially conceived by political thinkers who were at least nominally Jewish. Max Shachtman and his special early insight into the Soviet experiment that had produced the tyranny of a new class, or Leo Strauss, Albert Wohlstetter, Sidney Hook, Lionel Trilling, Irving Kristol, Norman Podhoretz, and others that have given the movement intellectual muscle and propose a strategy for revitalizing democracy do not deny their Jewishness, but are usually not affiliated with the world of Jewish organizations. Yet that predominance of political theorists who happened to be Jewish allows the paleoconservatives to argue that

American foreign policy is now controlled by a small group of Jewish ideologues "with dreams of empire." One right-wing researcher described the neocon group as "a complex interlocking professional and family network centered around Jewish publicists and organizers flexibly deployed to recruit the sympathies of both Jews and non-Jews in harnessing the wealth of the United States in the service of Israel."[4] The talk of the "Israel lobby" is not an innocent scholar's classification, but relates to a classic anti-Semitic image of a power-hungry Jewish cabal anxious to take control of the nation's foreign policy.

That classification, which has everywhere won acceptance, is in fact a contemporary version of the old Tsarist forgery embodied in *The Protocols of the Learned Elders of Zion* which places it outside the purview of rational discussion and confines any response to legitimizing the classification.[5] That leading neoconservative spokesman, like Senators "Scoop" Jackson and Daniel Patrick Moynihan, and political advisors in high positions, like Jeanne Kirkpatrick, William Bennett, and Michael Novak were not Jewish adds fuel to the charge, since they have been shrewdly manipulated into fronting for Jewish causes. If one points out that Jewish political interests are broad and encompass the entire range of the nation's domestic and foreign policy problems, the response would be that it is all held together by the centrality of Israel. Running parallel with the notion of a Jewish effort to control Middle East policy is the feeling that Jews are intruding into the conservative political terrain where they have no roots. The conservative movement, runs the grievance, has been stolen by Jewish ideologues who are not authentically conservative and, by their very nature, cannot be. In some quixotic way, the image of a Jewish lust for power has a life of its own that cannot be refuted, even by a historic event that witnessed two out three European Jews slaughtered by a charismatic dictator who was convinced that an all-powerful Jewry had somehow brought on the First World War.

* * *

Leaving the neocon relationship to Jewish power aside for the moment, it would be useful to learn what power this group actually exercises. Until the Reagan administration, the neoconservative influence was barely perceptible in the actual shaping of policy. The foreign policy of the Nixon, Ford, and, to some extent, Carter administrations was based on détente, the desire to avoid direct confrontation. During Henry Kissinger's tenure as chairman of the National Security Council and secretary of state, which dominated the foreign policy making process for much of the seventies, the war in Vietnam was brought to a close. But the breaking of the Geneva agreement by the movement of the Vietcong into Saigon in 1975 produced an ignominious image of flight by helicopter from the roof of the American embassy that was never forgotten by the neocons. The absence of an "exit strategy" from Iraq haunts the neocon sensibility to this day.

Kissinger adamantly opposed the Jackson-Vanik amendment to the Trade Act of 1974, which would have continued to deny Moscow Most Favored Nation treatment should the emigration of Jews be denied. Neoconservatives also characterized the American response to Soviet thrusts in the Middle East and the Horn of Africa as weak and unfocused. Discouraged by McGovern's soft approach to Moscow, some leading neoconservatives began drifting to the Republican party in 1972, only to become equally unhappy with the détente policy pushed by the Nixon and Ford administrations.[6] Strangely, that a foreign-born Jew exercised far greater control of foreign policy opposing the imagined influence of the neocons is rarely mentioned by those who see a Jewish conspiracy. Kissinger's détente policy was in fact closer to the consensus of the Jewish electorate than the tough anti-Soviet position of the neocons, who today stand accused of spearheading Jewish power on Capitol Hill.

Ultimately, even Reagan's tough Cold War stance, which included his refusal to abandon the visionary "Star Wars" strategy proved insufficient for Norman Podhoretz, a founding member of the group; he was convinced that Reagan's rhetoric about the "Evil Empire" was only talk and did little to check Soviet expansion.[7] Carter had acted more forcefully when, after the Soviet invasion of Afghanistan, he cancelled the SALT II talks and refused to participate in the 1980 Olympic Games. But the perception that Carter was also ineffective in containing the Soviet Union, much less in rolling it back, and a failing response to the new threat of a crusading Islam in Iran, negated any chances that neocons would return to the Democratic fold. Only after 1988, when the Soviet empire showed early symptoms of unraveling, did neoconservative voices agree that Reagan's higher defense spending had stretched the Kremlin's budget beyond its limits.

But aside from the sustained opposition to Soviet expansion and apprising decision makers to consider the possibility of rolling back the Iron Curtain, neoconservative spokesmen said little of their grand vision involving nation-building on a democratic foundation, such as had been successfully done in Germany and Japan after World War II. So focused on winning the Cold War was the neoconservative strategic approach to foreign policy that there seemed little left to do after the collapse of the Soviet Union following the breach of the Berlin Wall in November 1989. It was not until the failure of George H.W. Bush to topple Saddam Hussein after the Gulf War victory in 1991, a betrayal that neocons pointed out led to the death of thousands of Shiites and Kurds, that the new grounding neoconservative principles of democratic nation-building came to the fore.

These principles tapped into a familiar stream in American foreign policy that concerns the American mission to bring the benefits of freedom and democracy to the world. Traces of such thinking are discernable as early as the nineteenth-century belief in Manifest Destiny. Others see its earliest influence in Roosevelt's "Big Stick" policy, projected primarily to assure America's dominance over the weak and corrupt republics of Latin America. When the Dominicans defaulted on their debt in 1904, Roosevelt is purported to have angrily proclaimed that he would teach the Dominicans democracy, even if he had to break every bone in their body. It appears again in different form in Wilson's fourteen points and in the slogan on the lips of American troops sent to Europe in 1917 to "make the world safe for Democracy." The crusade to bring freedom to a blighted world was again sounded in the Atlantic charter (1941) and the post-war Marshall plan and Truman Doctrine, which brought democracy to the frontline of the emerging Cold War. What neoconservatism proposed was hardly new, but rather part of the continuing tension between realism and moralism in American foreign policy. The prevailing theme of the neoconservative approach to foreign policy was to reawaken the nation to its democratic heritage. If it contained a Jewish note, it was the view that American democracy was a wonder drug that could repair the world. It was that militancy that came to the fore as a new polarization pitting Islam against the West developed. Predictably, the struggle was couched in terms reminiscent of the Cold War. In place of the "Evil Empire," there was an "Axis of Evil," the emerging Islamic republics based on the Iranian model, whose binding ideology was referred to as Islamofascism.[8] Neoconservative certainty regarding the identity of evil turned the nation's foreign policy into something resembling a morality tale. It pertained not only to full rights for women, parliamentary institutions, and a free press, but also promotion of a pluralistic, tolerant, and secular public culture to regulate such mundane matters as prohibiting the facial veils worn by observant Moslem women.

In practice, the purity of the morality tale was compelled to give way to reality. The withdrawal of the Soviets from Afghanistan in 1982 was touted as a great victory for democracy in its struggle with communism. But a closer perusal revealed that it was equally undemocratic tribal chieftains—mobilized, subsidized, and armed by the CIA and as opposed to secular democracy as the Kremlin—that forced the Soviets to withdraw. The victory had nothing to do with democracy and it would become clear that Afghanistan would become the training ground for worldwide terrorism. The world was not, as the neocons assumed, "wired" for democracy. It sometimes needed a little push.

The book that sings the praises of democracy, much the way Walt Whitman sang the praises and hope of American democracy in the nineteenth century, was written by a former "prisoner of Zion," Natan Sharansky, whose influence in the Oval Office reached its zenith in the administration of George Bush.[9] Though not confined to the notion of an expansive crusading democracy in the Middle East, the strategic thinking of leading neoconservatives was naturally focused on it, since the region's oil and the potential destabilizing effect of the intractable Arab-Israel conflict made it a dangerous flashpoint. When, in 1991, George H.W. Bush rejected the notion of allowing Operation Desert Storm to culminate in deposing Saddam Hussein, neocons viewed that as a great lost opportunity to begin a kind of falling domino effect for democracy. The invasion of Iraq in 2003 to prevent the use of weapons of mass destruction (WMDs) would easily be seen as a neoconservative and hence a Jewish contrivance. It had won the full support of Richard Perle, Paul Wolfowitz, and most other leading neoconservatives in the government, who, though aware that Iran posed the greater threat, sensed that Iraq was riper for the picking. The easy "slam dunk" victory that was surely in the offing would at once break the logjam in the Middle East and finally bring peace between Palestinians and Israelis and fuel the growth of democracy in the region. The prospect of nation-building in the Middle East seemed more rewarding then the hunt for an elusive Bin Laden in Bora Bora.

The reality proved to be otherwise and among the many consequences of the debacle was an intensification of the notion that American Jewry's neoconservatives had led the nation down the wrong path for the sake of Israel's security.[10] Lost in the shuffle would be the fact that neoconservatives did not operate from a base within the Jewish community, which, in fact, had expressed little enthusiasm about the war. For most

Jewish voters, the idea that redemption could come from the political right, which they associate with anti-Semitism and the Holocaust, made the notion that the American foreign policy making process had been hijacked by a band of Jewish ideologues seem ludicrous. Not only was there little unanimity among neoconservatives supporters regarding the rush to war, the goal of enhancing the security of Israel had little support among Israel's strategists, who were more concerned about the threat posed by Iran. However, such realities had no effect on the conviction, especially strong among Arab opinion leaders, that American Middle East policy was controlled by neoconservatives acting in the name of American Jewry.[11]

Conservatives of the traditional stripe who believed in smaller government, lower taxes, and opposed "foreign adventures," viewed the neoconservatives now occupying key posts in the policy making process as part of a Jewish coup. The fact that the neocons echoed a crusading moral streak that was traditionally present in American foreign policy was alien to them. They understood only that neoconservative advisors, like Richard Perle and Elliot Abrams, had no military experience or training, yet were in positions in the Defense Department to advocate policies that placed "American boys in harms way." There was a mystery attached to the neocons' influence. Unlike the Jewish core of the New Left that co-opted the youth culture of the seventies, neocons lacked a basic currency of American democracy, the power to swing votes. There was no neoconservative party or even a co-opted wing of a party. Neoconservatives were primarily public intellectuals who projected an elitist influence on the making of foreign policy.

Their opposition to the Soviet regime, like their support of Israel, was predicated on the idea that tyrannies had to be suppressed and democracies supported. The post-war restructuring of non-democratic societies, like Germany and Japan, into parliamentary democracies ruled by law strengthened their conviction in the moral rightness of democracy and their zeal for nation-building. Israel was such a beleaguered democracy and the support it received from the neoconservatives became the seedbed of the charge that a Jewish lobby, composed of a chain of related organizations at the head of which stands AIPAC, has captured American foreign policy. They are supposedly supported by a series of think tanks that over the years have either produced or taken over journals such as *Commentary*. Behind it all is a group of public intellectuals composed of well known journalists, political commentators and pundits, and distinguished scholars that are incubated in great abundance in the Jewish community.[12] These, in turn, are often affiliated with the nation's best universities, whose tenured faculty contains some of the best known neoconservative publicists who amplify their position.[13] There are also individual journalists and public intellectuals, such as Norman Podhoretz, Charles Krauthammer, Joshua Muravchik, Midge Decter, David Frum, Max Boot, Lawrence Kaplan, Jonah Goldberg, and Alan Wald, who over the years have developed an audience in the media. In a word, neoconservatives project influence by skillful use of the popular TV, radio, and print media. Paradoxically, if the group had a Jewish fingerprint at all, it was in its penchant for ideological, moral, and strategic thinking. In the absence of a deliverable voting bloc and party affiliation, the neoconserative phenomenon resembles more a special interest group than a political movement. Some refer to it as a cabal, but that too does not capture the wide variety of neocon types.

* * *

The persistence of suspicion that Jews conspire to win power to further a specific Jewish interest remains a mystery whose roots may lie in prehistoric myths and fears. There are, of course, Jews who want to project influence on political leaders to support their interest in Israel and elsewhere. They vigorously exercise their rights as American citizens to influence and shape public policy and find communal support from an unusually politically engaged Jewish electorate whose primary advocacy in domestic politics is focused on human rights and environmental issues. The disproportionate role of Jews involved in the civil rights movement and most progressive endeavors from women's liberation to saving the whales is well known. American Jews compose an important portion of the leadership of the hundreds of general interest groups that are a vital part of the political process in a democracy. But the political engagement of American Jews has been largely in favor of international conciliation and has, since before World War I, favored national self-determination as a general principle. There is little in Jewish political culture to suggest that a strident expansionism, even to strengthen wobbly democratic regimes would long hold the favor of the American Jewish voter. The assumption that a handful of commentators and government officials, some of whom happen to be Jewish, constitutes a Jewish conspiracy to control Middle East policy tells us much more about the paranoid underbelly of the anti-Semitic imagination than it does about the play of Jewish power in America.

In the introductory chapter we noted the similarity of democratic principles and values shared by Jews and Americans that formed the basis of a confluence of interests. Confluence helps explain much of the rationale behind America's protective mantle over Israel and its efforts on behalf of Jewish emigration from the Soviet Union. In the case of Israel, few would take issue with the fact that the national interest is well served by treating a democratic Israel as an ally in the developing conflict with Islamic jihadists, who consider themselves at war with the West. But there are degrees of confluence depending on strategic importance. The case of American support for Soviet Jewish emigration is not as clear cut. The support of the emigration issue stemmed largely from Congress, with an occasional supportive official like George Shultz mixed into the brew. American interest in calling attention to the Soviet inability to maintain accepted standards of human rights was not unusual, but it posed problems when the emigration issue, embodied in the Jackson-Vanik amendment, was used as a lever against the administration's policy of détente by Jacksonian Democrats. As Secretary of State Henry Kissinger pointed out repeatedly, the United States would no more tolerate interference in our right to control our immigration policy than would the Kremlin. In international law, immigration policy is considered an internal matter. Conjuring Jewish control was not confined to Judeophobes. There were American agricultural interests who strongly favored opening the Russian market to American surpluses in wheat and other grains and were prone to argue that the Jews held American trade policy hostage. Sometimes, the play of forces ran against the Jewish interest as in the case of selling AWACS radar planes to Saudi Arabia. Government largess toward Jewish refugees from war-torn Europe was considered against the national interest and was not forthcoming, even when the light of victory was seen at the end of the tunnel and news of the genocide was well known.

In the end, policy does not bend for a cluster of activists who stand alone in their advocacy. The political process requires that there be at least a modicum of public support. Like all interest groups, American Jewry relies on its ability to persuade the American public and the administration in power that supporting Israel serves the national interest. In the context of the Cold War, a generous policy towards Soviet refugees easily won majority support in Congress, and was undoubtedly helped by the fact that it served the political interests of both parties. Even when there is confluence, those interested in calculating the actual play of Jewish power are forced to contend with a "chicken-or-the-egg" problem. Which came first, an American Jewish "cabal" that convinced Congress and the Oval Office that American interests are best served by extending diplomatic and military support to Israel, or a realization by American strategists that the small democracy in the Middle East that shares American values is a dependable regional ally?

Still, when interests and ideological principles are involved, there is bound to be considerable variation in the degree of confluence. There can also be conflicting interests among allies. American Jews, for example, favored Washington moving its embassy to Jerusalem and the recognition of that city as the capital of Israel. But to safeguard Washington's posture as an honest broker such a move has been resisted for years. A similar tension emerges regarding the neoconservative new twist to an old theme in the history of American foreign relations, a more crusading active approach to the defense and expansion of democratic regimes. There are many who absorbed a different lesson distilled from the war in Iraq; that overreaching goals can place a democracy in great peril. When Jewish voices in the Senate are most outspoken in their opposition to the war (Joseph Lieberman excepted) it requires a considerable stretch of the imagination to see it as a policy made for the benefit of Israel by American Jews.

That there exists a Jewish interest, if such an interest can be identified and defined with any precision, that shares a proclivity for democracy, which incidentally helps amplify its domestic political voice, should not come as a surprise. Historically, the Jewish community thrives wherever democracy has developed. It has an interest in keeping the conduits to American power open and its polity stable. The Jewish relationship to government policy is transactional and serves the interests of both partners in the relationship. When that is not so, as it was not during the agonizing years of the Holocaust, when American Jews advocated a more active rescue policy, then no amount of power made a difference until the nation's primary aim of defeating Germany was in sight.

* * *

For Jews, the discovery that Jewish power exists and is in play can never be an innocent exercise. The charge that neocon motives in advocating the Iraq war were related to ensuring the security of Israel, rather than the national interest, has inherent in it the possibility that American Jewry may be asked to pay a price for the misuse of its imagined political power. In that sense, the failure to prevail in Iraq has the possibility of developing into a security threat for American Jewry. The charge of betrayal is well precedented in the history of modern anti-Semitism. It was a mainstay of the anti-Semitic imagination in Germany's Weimar republic. The charge of dual loyalties has been a longstanding bugaboo haunting Jewish communal life. It is not limited to the rhetoric of small anti-Semitic groups who dwell on the margins of the American political landscape. There is resentment among ordinary conservatives that neocons have co-opted their voice. David Keene, chairman of the American Conservative Union, railing against the intellectual arrogance of the new conservatives observes that "it is not so much that they have been wrong. It is that nobody has ever convinced them that they have ever been wrong."[14]

As the debate about the Iraq war enters its fifth year with no solution in sight, the likelihood that right-wing groups anxious to deflect responsibility for the debacle will assign some responsibility for the failure of American arms to American Jewry cannot be ignored. That is bound to happen, despite the fact that a number of American and Israeli leaders who favored war would have preferred waging it against Iran, which they saw as the greater threat to American and Israeli interests in the Middle East. But that made little difference to those anxious to bring these charges into the political arena. Paradoxically, the defense against that charge runs the risk of resurrecting a traditional mainstay of the anti-Semitic imagination, that of insufficient loyalty and patriotism. The accusations against the "Israeli lobby" may indicate that the post-World War II prohibition against the appearance of a Jewish question on the America political agenda may be approaching its end.

If that should happen, the indictment of American Jewry will predictably not be limited to the charge that a Jewish neoconservative cabal maneuvered a hapless nation into a losing war. There will be little probing to explain why a community that has done so well in acting out the American dream should want to foul its nest. Instead the remarkable performance of American Jewry in every area of American life from sports to corporate management, from medicine and law to high culture and popular entertainment, will be challenged. Its effectiveness in using the openness of American society and economy will become part of the indictment against it. Having lived out the American dream under such extreme circumstances can become part of the bill of particulars brought against the Jewish electorate. There are Americans who view the disproportionate success of its Jewish citizens with a jaundiced eye.

In the throes of a virulent outpouring of anti-Semitism in the thirties, the well known social reformer Upton Sinclair penned a popular essay entitled "It Can Happen Here." The essay was aimed at the complacency of the American people and alerted them to the dangers of domestic fascism. It didn't happen here, but there were moments during the Depression when it looked like an American version of what was happening in Germany was occurring. But the apprehension that could then be noted in the American Jewish community, which at the time was 17 percent foreign-born, is not apparent today. Anchored in its American experience, contemporary American Jewry has the confidence that it lacked then. Its response to the rescue crisis of Soviet Jewry easily outmatched the ineffective witness role it played during the thirties and forties. It may learn that it has been premature in abandoning its early warning system earned at a dear price during the Holocaust era. Jews understand that the notion that they form an all-powerful group seeking control is not only foolish, but also dangerous. But at the same time, they are aware of their political skills and their still formidable communal organizational structure. A secure community finds it difficult to foresee an abandonment of that openness and tolerance because it is clearly the only path for remaining functional in an ethnically and racially variegated society. For America's Jews, there exists an additional safeguard that gives some assurance that it will not happen again. In a strange way, it would be difficult to target Jews for their success. The assumption that hard work and mastery deeply embedded in the national value structure are rewarded is a driving force in American life. In acting out the national success ethos, Jews are being quintessentially American. That consonance with what is definitionally American can be taken one step further. In their intense political engagement advocating a broad array of interests, Jews are models of the kind of citizens democracies require to flourish. Even if the paranoid vision of a minority of Jews exercising a controlling influence in the making of the nation's foreign policy prevails, it would tell us more about the failure of our decision making process than about a conspiratorial Jewish cabal. It means, in effect, that the various interests in the political arena who are free to exercise their countervailing power have not done so and allowed a small minority to pull the national interest in a self-serving direction. The failure of the political system to counter the ostensible challenge of the neoconservatives, or any other group that projects influence on policy, suggests a far greater threat to the system than the imagined conspiracy.

* * *

We return finally to the question posed at the outset: "Do the neocon-servatives represent a Jewish communal interest?" The answer to that query is crucial to the calculation of the play of Jewish power in America, which we seek to determine. The contemporary charge that claims that Jews as a community exercise such controlling power cannot stand if the very agency of their supposed control is revealed as unconnected to Jewish communal interests. What we see is that despite the origins of the neoconservative phenomenon in the malaise of the Jewish socialist left and despite the early predominance of Jewish public intellectuals, neither the neocons or AIPAC, or any other group imagined to speak for the Jewish community, has ever had any fiat to do so. That connection is a figment of the fevered imagination of those that see a Jewish conspiracy everywhere. There is no political procedure within the Jewish community to assign such a role to any group and from what we know about the views of the Jewish voter, they were less passionate about the "communist menace" during the Cold War and today are hardly enthusiastic for the democratic crusade of nation-building. The neoconservatives are one of many ideological groupings whose ideas are weighed by a highly edu-cated politically engaged community. That such a broad range of ideas find a good atmosphere to flourish among American Jews is part of a political culture that takes ideas and the possibility of progress seriously. We witness that again in the following chapter, when an informal group of young students, often incubated in a left that was itself on the way out of the Jewish fold, tries to repair the world from the bottom up.

Notes

1.   Democratic centralism meant, in effect, that after a ruling by the leadership cadre was handed down the rank and file was expected to comply and end all debate on the issue. But party discipline was ephemeral and could not contain conflict.
2.   The radicalization of the Jewish New Left by the war in Vietnam can serve to highlight the contrast between the two groups. It pushed the New Left further into its anti-war positions and the neocons further to the right.
3.   Neocons never became a formally organized interest group and there were internal variation in political positions. The drift to the Reagan administration involved key persons, like Jeane Kirkpatrick, who then retained Joshua Muravchik, Kenneth Adelman, and Carl Gershman as her deputies; Richard Perle, who was appointed assistant secretary of defense for international security policy, brought Frank Gaff-ney and Douglas Feith on board. Elliot Abrams, who became assistant secretary of state for human rights, Max Kampelman, who was appointed U.S. ambassador to the Helsinki Human Rights Conference at Madrid, and Paul Wolfowitz, who was appointed assistant secretary of state for East Asian affairs, were also key figures. When Bill Clinton became president, many returned to the Democratic fold to rejoin Ben Wattenberg and Robert Strauss, who had remained Jackson Democrats even after his death in 1982.

4.   Kevin MacDonald, "Neoconservatism as a Jewish Movement," in *Understanding Jewish Influence: A Study in Ethnic Activism* (Augusta, GA: Washington Summit Publishers). See www.WakeUpAmerica.com. The family part refers to the fact that both Norman Podhoretz and Irving Kristol have sons who are publicists and that Elliot Abrams is Podhoretz's son-in-law.

5.   Published by the Tsarist secret police at the turn of the century, the *Protocols* is today widely circulated in the Islamic world. It features a similar cabal or Sanhedrin conspiring to control the world. The widely held belief that 9/11 was part of a wide-ranging Jewish conspiracy can be traced to the *Protocols*.

6.   Some supported Henry Jackson in his failed campaign of 1972 and 1976 and then went on to support Reagan in 1980. The most notable convert was Jeanne Kirkpatrick who became Reagan's favorite neocon and foreign policy advisor.

7.   See Norman Podhoretz, "The Neo-Conservative Anguish Over Reagan's Foreign Policy, *New York Times Sunday Magazine,* May 2, 1982, p. 30.

8.   The current use of the term Islamofascism to describe the violence and political malaise in Islamic countries is reminiscent of the thirties when all who opposed the Moscow line were dubbed "fascists. It became the most frequently used pejorative against the right.

9.   Sharansky's influence preceded the publication of *The Case for Democracy: The Power and Freedom to Overcome Tyranny and Terror* and his friendship with George Bush. He had gained the support of the rank and file of the Soviet Jewry movement and the ear of Sen. Henry Jackson, Dick Cheney, Condoleezza Rice, and Donald Rumsfeld. The idea that democracy had to hit back was partly a product of the dissident movement in the Soviet Union.

10.   Such a suggestion is made by Michael Lind, *How Neoconservatives Conquered Washington and Launched a War*, April 10, 2003. www.antiwar.com/orig/Lind1. html. That neocon defense intellectuals like Paul Wolfowitz (then deputy secretary of defense) Cheney's chief of staff, Lewis "Scooter" Libby, Elliot Abrams, Richard Perle, and others linked to the Israeli lobby foisted a losing war on the nation is especially strong among Arab political thinkers of all stripes.

11.   See, for example, David Brooks, "A War of Narratives," *New York Times*, April 8, 2007, p. 10 (News of the Week in Review).

12.   Sources listed as part of the neocon press are varied and often confused with agencies associated with Israel, such as the American Israel Public Affairs Committee (AIPAC). Others are think tanks and organizations in which prominent neocons have served, such as the Jewish Institute for National Security Affairs (JINSA), Washington Institute for Near East Policy (WINEP), American Enterprise Institute (AEI), the Center for Security Policy (CSP), Middle East Forum (MEF), Project for the New American Century (PNAC) and Washington Institute for Near East Policy (WINEP). These NGOs are not necessarily of the same politics or quality. Social Democrats/USA (SD/USA), for example, is more of the old anti-Stalinist 1930s-vintage party in which someone like Daniel Bell would feel comfortable. The Zionist Organization of America (ZOA), which some include in the neocon camp, has that political coloration today after a bitter internal fight that put it in the Likud camp. Some of these agencies publish their own journals, but the amplification of the neocon view rests on coverage in major newspapers or magazines such as *The Wall Street Journal, The Jerusalem Post, The Weekly Standard, The Sun*, and such conservative publications as *National Review*, and occasionally, *The New Republic*. Scholarly magazines such as *The Public Interest* and *Commentary* form yet another phalange, although they are not totally devoted to following a neocon line that has some breadth. There is also amplification through the English-language Jewish press.

13. If the neocons have a university base at all, it would be the University of Chicago of the fifties and sixties. An alternative might be the City College of New York of the thirties and forties, which was the nesting ground for such thinkers as Irving Kristol, Nathan Glazer, Daniel Bell, and others. But as social democrats and Trotskyists, they did not fit into the prevailing left-wing Stalinist spirit.

14. *New York Times*, October 20, 2006, p. 1.

VII

The New Left and the Jews

The New Left is joined at the hip to neoconservatism by its common roots in the malaise of the Jewish left, but it is an entirely different political phenomenon. There is little in the short life of the New Left that would lead one to believe that it is a Jewish "cabal" intent on twisting the national interest to serve a Jewish need. Yet that accusation persists despite the fact that, like the neocons, determining its Jewish identity is beset with problems. For young Jews drawn to what Lenin identified as the "infantile disorder" of left-wing sectarianism, radicalism often served as the means to break the powerful bonds of Jewish ethnicity and religion.

The New Left represented the final phase of a multifaceted conflict within the Jewish left whose fallout lasted two generations. An aspect of that conflict concerned the relationship of socialism to traditional forms of Jewish identity and affiliation. Not only did the New Left find little support among American Jews, the movement eventually attracted many non-Jews, who helped give it a non-sectarian face. In those rare instances when the movement's aspirations were articulated at all, there were few signs of a special interest in the Jewish agenda. Many affiliated Jews considered their style as un-Jewish.

The New Left began as student movement drawing its membership from the disproportionate percentage of Jewish students attending college.[1] Altogether about 60 to 80 percent of student radicals were of Jewish origin in the sixties and an astounding 30 to 50 percent of the core organization, the Students for a Democratic Society (SDS), were Jewish. The same overwhelming predominance was found in related organizations like the Yuppies and Berkeley's Free Speech Movement, five of whose seven leaders were "of Jewish origin." There was no mistaking the Jewish presence among the campus radicals, but determining their Jewish affiliation was not an easy task since taking on the radical mantle served for many as a path for the assumption of a new identity.

125

The members of SDS were often the children of "progressive" Jews nurtured in the political culture of prewar ghettos and further radicalized by the Depression. Most of their parents considered themselves "progressives," were readers of the left-wing *National Guardian,* and perhaps voted for Henry Wallace in the campaign of 1948. Others were merely liberal and a surprising number of SDSers were raised in homes where there was little interest in politics. Nevertheless, despite some variation in their family backgrounds, the term "Red Diaper" babies was collectively applied to them by the media. They were, in fact, Jewish "baby boomers" raised in the prosperous post-war and post-Holocaust years, loosely connected to the Jewish left, but no longer fully of it. The generational disconnect was rooted in the different economic and political circumstances in which the two cohorts, the old and the new left, reached adulthood. "We are people of this generation," stated the introductory sentence of the Port Huron Statement, "bred in at least modest comfort, housed now in universities, looking uncomfortably to the world we inherit."[2]

The New Left entered the mainstream of American politics neither as a voting bloc nor a special interest group. They had little thought of organizing politically, thereby limiting the possibility of projecting their influence beyond their own generation. Its preferred arena of activity was the college campus, followed by the street, and later for some few, the commune. Its influence was particularly strong among those youths eligible for military service in Vietnam. What came to be called the New Left began and ended as a dissident youth movement with its own cultural values, music, parlance, and hair style. Spawned in part by the old left, its persona and aspirations were oddly reminiscent of a type of nineteenth-century romantic anarchism. Freed from the sense of mission and high principle of their parents, the New Left retained elements of both and yet in its political culture it was libertarian.Their militancy first becomes visible as a resonance of the civil rights struggle, especially as it played out against local authorities in the South and then blossomed with the early disquiet felt regarding the war in Vietnam.

* * *

Readers believe that American security was confronting a growing threat from Moscow during the sixties and seventies will be surprised to learn that little evidence exists of the machinations of the world communist movement in the New Left's brief fling at making history. The men in the Kremlin were probably as surprised as American political leaders at what was transpiring in the universities and on the streets of American cities. Some might have hoped that the long-sought revolution had finally arrived, but that was hardly the case. The New Left phenomenon had roots in the turmoil of the sixties and seventies and a generational malaise within the Jewish left.

The left-wing Jewish cohort that reached adulthood after the war, sired by a generation of veterans, bore stronger similarity to their general American neighbors, with whom they shared the war experience, than the immigrant generation. The war accelerated the Americanization process, including its distinctive Jewish political culture. It sent young people out of the all-Jewish neighborhoods and exposed them to the full variety of the American social and geographic landscape. In the postwar decade, economic prosperity replaced the Depression, but after the Soviets developed the A-bomb in 1949, followed by the Korean War, anxiety about foreign problems pressed down on the American psyche as never before. The nation did not assume the mantle of world leadership with ease, and the fear and foreboding about the developing Cold War undermined the spirit of cohesiveness that prevailed during the war, leaving only patriotism as a binding force. Whether the bomb should have been used and how it could be controlled became a preoccupation in the nation's think tanks and universities. But neither the Baruch plan for sharing the development of atomic energy, nor the cry for "peaceful coexistence" emanating from Moscow during the fifties found a way to relieve the anxiety of a possible thermonuclear holocaust. Its prevention preoccupied American Jewry as it did all Americans.

Even without the impact of the Cold War, it is likely that the political temperament of American Jewry would have lost some of its left-wing political shading. The rising educational level of American Jewry made them less susceptible to the politics of passionate causes, the customary fare of the left. Communist propaganda catchphrases and simple explanations could satiate the Jewish immigrant's unquestioning craving for anything that appeared to be educational, including party *agitprop*. In some measure, burdening normal political transactions with the objective of improving the world was a reflection of the Eastern European political style that prevailed among the first-generation immigrants. In the Eastern European context, changing abusive government by force if necessary was a justified first step to establish a normal democratic political process. It was a necessary step forward to achieve the much-desired social justice they sought. But the assumption of the justifiable use of force to bring change was a far cry from the rules prevailing in the American political arena where, despite many weaknesses, change could still be achieved through the political process.

Awareness that change was possible from within the system went far to steal the thunder of the more extreme forms of radicalism. The rapid social mobility experienced by Jews in the post-war years provided evidence that it was possible to improve one's personal circumstance and rise above one's class, rather than with it, as the socialist model prescribed. American Jewry began its climb to achieving the nation's fastest rate of professionalization and highest per capita income during the prosperous post-war decades. Many former Jewish socialists enjoyed the affluence that defied all that they had been taught about the failings of the capitalist system. Predictably, Marxist exhortations about class struggle increasingly fell on deaf ears. Compared to the twenties and thirties there was a mellowing during the fifties. American Jewish political culture retained its need for engagement, but gave up its innocence and much of its idealism. That was also the decade during which the New Left was incubated.

Their parents had experienced three decades of party members and extremists in their ranks slavishly following the Moscow party line. That served as fertile soil for a new generation to reject the exhortations of their parents, much less the commands from a distant, increasingly alien Soviet-dominated world communist movement. The Jewish left of the "boomer" generation spoke more of their personal emotional needs, of their feeling of alienation, and less of Karl Marx and his nineteenth-century analysis of the pending failure of the capitalist system. They were drawn to the social psychology of Antonio Gramsci and the Freudian Marxism of the Frankfurt School, rather than Lenin's politics of gaining and holding political control. Almost without realizing it, the post-war Jewish generation turned to the quintessentially American aspiration for self-realization. In their politics, it was accompanied by something similar to the reform ideology of the American Progressive movement, albeit of a more militant variety. Unresolved problems in the social system were resolvable by a dose of more democracy at the grassroots level.

That was not as sharp a departure as it appears, since SDS founders like Mark Rudd, Al Haber, Robb Ross, Steve Max, Mile Spiegel, Mike Klonsky, and Todd Gitlin stemmed from middle-class, permissive homes, usually recently transplanted to the suburbs, where their left-wing parents had found comfortable havens. Sometimes it was difficult to distinguish whether the militant rhetoric of the New Left was directed against the parents who had settled for bourgeois comfort, or whether the real source of their vitriol was triggered by the blandness of suburban life.[3]

Discomfort with the ambiance of the left was not unprecedented. The immigrant socialists did not fit easily into the normal socialist class configuration. They had been artisans and craftsmen in Eastern Europe with little contact with the industrial worker who was to lead the revolution. Their idealism and quest for social justice seems to have had greater drawing power among Jews than the ideology of class struggle culminating in violent revolution. Despite the Marxist glorification of the working class as the true source of value, their sojourn in the working class was temporary. The parents of the SDS and Jewish student radicals generally were neither the children of workers nor would they produce sons and daughters who were. By World War II and the decades after, Jews were energetically establishing themselves in the middle class, thus they were hardly suitable material to become the "vanguard of the working class." Yet neither were they fully comfortable in their new middle-class station. Normal notions of class-consciousness did not seem to apply to the political behavior of American Jews who in the words of one commentator "earned like Episcopalians but voted like Puerto Ricans."[4]

The post-war "Red Diaper" generation rebelled against the Eastern European Jewish political style of their parents, especially the assumption that socialism offered the only model for living a meaningful life. During the years of the Depression, when the economic system collapsed with drastic consequences, doubt about the viability of capitalism was not uncommon among leftists. Among party members, it was reinforced by awareness that Soviet Jewry seemed economically secure and experienced social mobility at least comparable to that of American Jewry during the "Roarin' Twenties." Communist propaganda endlessly proclaimed that there were no breadlines in the Soviet Union. The Yiddish-speaking immigrant generation took considerable pride in the blossoming of Yiddish culture in the Soviet Union, or at least a Stalinist version of it. Yiddish had been made the official language of Soviet Jewry and its literature, theater, and press outpaced those of Yiddish culture in America, which by 1927 showed clear evidence of decline. That cultural flowering was eliminated at one blow in 1952 with the liquidation of the Jewish literary elite and the closing of its institutions.

But while the decline of Yiddish was a terrible blow to the old Yiddish-speaking communists from the foreign language federations who
remained in the party fold, it was a matter of indifference to the "Red
Diaper" generation. Yiddish was no longer a binding generational tie and
had in fact become a sign of the disconnect between the generations of
the Jewish left. Instead the offspring received additional evidence of the
Kremlin's lethal goals regarding Jewish culture and the blindness and
culpability of the parent generation regarding Soviet excesses. That loss
of confidence in the "peace camp" was not confined to the Jewish left.
The sense that the Soviet Union could not serve as a world center for a
proletarian revolution first arose when the long-awaited revolution occurred in backward peasant-ridden Russia, rather than in a nation with an
industrial proletariat, like Germany. Now it was again heard in France in
May 1968 and in the "Prague Spring," which called for "Socialism with
a human face." But the "Prague Spring" was crushed by the invasion
of the Warsaw Pact and in the United States, the SDS fragmented into
several groups after their demonstration of street power at the Chicago
Democratic convention in 1968. Paradoxically, at the historical juncture
when the intractable war in Vietnam would supplement civil rights as an
issue that could win nationwide attention, internecine strife, which had
been the bugaboo of the old left, also became manifest in the new. But
there was also something new, a growing conviction within the left that
under Soviet tutelage the socialist camp had somehow lost its way.

Yet there remained one problem that the old and the New Left continued to hold in common. Both experienced problems with their ethnic
identity as Jews that showed signs of inability to withstand the siren song
of an absorbent benevolent majority culture. As the children became
more American and less Jewish, the divide between themselves and
their parents became deeper. The dilemma was most manifest in their
relationship to Israel for which American Jewry felt a pervasive sense
of concern based partly on kinship. Except for Jewish communists,
concern for Israel was manifest in the full spectrum of Jewish politics.
Moscow's adamant opposition to Israel, whose welfare and security had
the highest priority on the American Jewish agenda, became the heaviest
cross Jewish radicals had to bear. In Marxist doctrine, Zionism, which
gained some influence among Jewish thinkers during the twenties and
thirties, was depicted as a retrogressive form of bourgeois nationalism.
The fortunate historic circumstances of Jews being organized in time,
rather than space, would enable them to skip over that stage represented

by Zionism. While European socialists may have lost confidence in the leadership of Moscow, they continued to condemn Israel as an agent of Western colonialism.

It would be in the Jewish arena from whose confines they desired to escape that the identity conflict of Jewish old and new leftists would come to a head. As noted previously, the issue of the merit system for attaining civil service positions as teachers, for which Jews had struggled, was accompanied by a virulent outpouring of anti-Semitic rhetoric. By supporting the abandonment of the merit system in Ocean Hill-Brownsville, the Jewish radicals separated themselves from their Jewish community base, but found little support for the leadership role they wanted to play in the African American community. It was a moment of truth for the Jewish left, which sought to play such a role. Finding a bridge for Jewish radicals to somehow reconcile their dilemma, which also involved their failing support of Israel fell to the B'reira movement established by Michael Lerner, a rabbi affiliated with the liberal Reform branch. But only a generation after the Holocaust, such an endeavor had little chance of success. It seemed that neither the left nor the right could be entrusted with matters of Jewish survival.

*   *   *

In the end, it was the accumulation of evidence of the brutality of the Soviet system and its specific anti-Semitism that helped break the influence of the party among progressive Jews. The party's claim that it deserved the credit for its long-standing efforts to focus the nation's interest on the problem of race and the related issue of civil rights went far to reestablish the party's bona fides among progressive Jews. The unresolved race problem had a special resonance among Jews. The party's early exploitation of the civil rights or race problem had inherent in it what party members were wont to identify as an "internal contradiction." Its earliest view of the race problem following Stalin's teaching on the nationalities question, classified the American Negro as belonging to a separate nation. The party's separatist approach to the race question actually created a split from Progressive liberals, who were integrationists from the outset. For Jews there was an additional reason for sympathy beyond Stalin's contribution to Marxist gospel. Many Jewish thinkers assumed that the Jewish historical circumstance of victimization and that of the condition of the American Negro were analogous. That assumption generated a special sympathy for the civil rights struggle.

*   *   *

Like the neoconservatives, the Jewish New Left was incubated within the Jewish old left but ultimately rejected its parentage. But many "Red Diaper" offspring continued to harbor a proclivity for activism in their cultural baggage. It was what parents and grandparents had done in the numerous "struggles" of the thirties and forties. That a Jewish background was the single most important predictor of participation in campus protest activity might have been foretold. Overlooked is the fact that the overwhelming majority of Jewish students had little to do with the SDS, whose members often stemmed from progressive families. The number of Jewish pre-med or pre-law students vastly outnumbered Jewish radicals on campus and, in the long run, had a far greater impact on the American Jewish condition. The failure by the Johnson and Nixon administrations to end the war created an opportunity for an activist minority to seize the leadership of what was basically an anti-war movement.

With the exception of an occasional non-Jewish student leader like Tom Hayden, Jewish representation in Students for a Democratic Society (SDS), the primary organizational expression of the New Left, was overwhelming. The surfacing of a pervasive dissidence among Jewish students came to more than acting out a revolutionary scenario. They understood that they were privileged children of the middle class. Their movement represented the first small bump in the otherwise smooth post-war path of American Jewry to the middle class. Once the principle grievance of the war is removed finding a common ideological thread was problematic. Within the SDS, there existed considerable differences in the degree of radicalism, which was reflected in differences concerning the confrontational tactics employed on campus. The coherence of party-sponsored protest was nowhere to be found. There were also early signs that the New Left would not be a permanent feature on the American political landscape.

What passed for a formal statement of the ideological creed of the New Left was the publication of the Port Huron statement promulgated by leaders of the SDS in 1962. What is interesting about the statement is that, unlike the socialist model of the parent generation, the dissatisfaction of the promulgators was concerned with the direction the society was taking on the racial question, on the Cold War, and on the danger of thermonuclear war. Many of its themes became part of the ongoing political dialogue. They complained about "the sapping of the earth's natural resources." They condemned the failure of an over-bureaucratized education system. They were convinced that the political party system was dysfunctional and corrupt. Together with former President Eisenhower, they worried about the power of the military-industrial complex and the concentration of wealth and power in the hands of a few, rather than the many. The growing inequities, they became convinced, was attributable partly to the failure of organized labor, which in the words of the Port Huron statement, allows "hard core poverty to exist just beyond the neon lights of affluence." Predictably, it decried colonialism, which had become a catchall for a multitude of capitalist sins. While many SDSers understood the devastation that party membership had wrought on a personal family level and cautioned against the human rights excesses of the communist world, they nevertheless condemned the American government for pillaring the tiny American Communist Party and spoke of "an unreasoning anti communism [having] become a major social problem for those who want to construct a more democratic America."

The Port Huron statement presented a fairly complete catalogue of what went wrong with the promise of America viewed from the perspective of the disaffected children of the left. But unlike their parents, they were far less certain on what might be done about it. What was espoused was not a solution but a process. Borrowed from the platform of the Student League for Industrial Democracy (SLID) the answer was participatory democracy. In practice that meant all kinds of things from allowing students to run the university to community control of the schools. Experimentation with new forms of social organization would be the order of the day. The answer to the systemic problems of democracy was not revolution, but more democracy.[5] The Huron statement closed with a ringing proclamation that "modern complexity" must be transformed into issues that can be "understood and felt close-up" by every human being. But the last sentence of the statement ended on a note of uncertainty: "if we appear to seek the unattainable, ... Then let it be known that we do so too avoid the unimaginable." The statement came years before the Vietnam War came to an end. The war would subsume the noble sentiments of the declaration and threaten with military service the generation it addressed. It was that circumstance, perhaps more than the noble sentiments penned by Tom Hayden, that opened an opportunity to impact public policy.

*   *   *

The New Left's sharpest departure from the old was not its antiauthoritarian principles. We shall note that in practice that was not the case. It came in the area of cultural style, their penchant for free living and discarding the restraints of societal rules. The older generation of Jewish radicals idealized the notion of struggle as experienced in the physical confrontation of the labor wars in the garment industry. The political theater played by Abbie Hoffman and Jerry Rubin and the yippies was perplexing. Using the media to draw attention to the issue was not struggle as they understood it. For the older generation, reality shaped the image, but now the reverse seemed to be the case—shaping reality could be achieved by manipulating the media. The master of such manipulation was Jerry Rubin, the founder and leader of the Yippies. He once explained his tactics to a disappointed activist by noting that if the coverage of a given story was inadequate, the answer is to go out and make your own news. But for old leftists, raising mayhem in a Chicago court was incomprehensible and lacked authenticity. The old left understood the need to draw attention to the cause. They performed brilliantly in the case of the Scottsboro Boys and traces of that talent might still be detected in bringing the Rosenberg case to world attention. But it was the New Left that moved the heavy-handed practice of *agitprop* to the art of public relations.

Intergenerational tensions are perennial, but rarely are they as intense as the gulf in values and behavior between the brave generation that defeated a murderous enemy and the "boomer" generation determined to live their lives to the fullest without the fetters that bound their parents. Though far from prudish, the open sexuality and freeness the Jewish New Left seemed irresponsible to the parent generation, who viewed random sexuality as a form of male exploitation. The boomers of the left preferred free living, sometimes in communes, to centralized command structures whether it took the form of *pater familias* or the democratic centralism of the party. However, the distaste for authority remained personal and did not rule out favoring dictators from a distance. Cuba, whose racial and class upheaval made it a favorite model of the New Left, posed no dilemma despite the fact that Castro clearly fit the mold of the Latin American *caudillo* (dictator). Similarly, New Left favorites, such as North Vietnam's Ho Chi Minh and China's Mao Zedong, ruled tightly controlled authoritarian regimes, hardly suitable models for the libertarian New Left.

Also nettlesome was the seeming abandonment of the traditional concerns of the left for amelioration of the evil consequences of unregulated industrial capitalism. The quest was now for individual emotional wholeness. They spoke of the pain of anomie, alienation, and anxiety, thought to be the byproducts of modern and postmodern society. If the New Left added anything to traditional socialist doctrine, it was that the idea of societal well-being was emotional as well as economic. The truths of psychotherapy, which had become a common practice in the suburban homes of the Jewish middle class, combined with the buzzwords of the liberal arts, particularly social psychology, seemed to swallow up traditional socialist and Judaic precepts, which were centered on building a society based on social justice. In separating its quest for happiness and self-realization from the traditional struggle for social justice, the New Left had a distinct American flavor.

Except for the common heritage of activism, there was little recognizable that the old left of the interwar years shared with the new. Often possessing an overweening confidence rooted in their certainty that they were on the side of progress, most old leftists and progressives saw little to admire in the headline seeking histrionics of the younger generation. Their socialism carried with it a code of civility and a sobriety that was requisite for the grueling, often dangerous task of organizing the unorganized. One can only speculate about how such a sharp generational disconnect developed. It may be related to the travail of the "boomer" generation, which was born largely when the veterans returned, rather than being staggered over the war years. The first post-war generation subsequently overwhelmed every social institution with which it came in contact. In the schools, Johnny couldn't read, in college, chemistry was irrelevant, as was the Selective Service obligation. He smoked marijuana and when the commitment of marriage was made at all, it became serial monogamy. The honor of labor, so cherished by the parents, became a necessity from which, if successful, one could altogether avoid working or plan an early retirement.

* * *

The Jewish "boomers" of the New Left carried an additional burden into the political arena. They wanted to speak to the nation with an American voice, rather than the voice of a marginalized ethnic subculture. In manners and clothes and song they set out to mimic the semi-rural America of the heartland, which most had never experienced. There may have been a more mundane explanation for the unshaven, unwashed, raucous street fighter image they sought to project. Brought up in protective Jewish homes they simply had to reach further out to discover the critical line where parental custodianship ceased and their own lives could begin. Reinforced by families with demanding values and a strong sense of mission, the parental hold was not easily broken. During the troubles at Columbia University in 1961, Mark Rudd, who led the SDS chapter in organizing campus disruption, sometimes had his parents bring him food, which they consumed together in the family car parked on Amsterdam Avenue. Rudd's mother "kwelling" about her son's leadership was quoted in *The New York Times*: "My revolutionary who helped me plant these tulips last November, my rebel."[6] Some radicals possessed loving parents, sometimes overbearingly so.

Unlike the old Jewish left that had been shaped and tested in the bitter intracommunal battles for control of the Jewish labor movement, the New Left was reared in the free, privileged atmosphere of the universities. That the authority targeted first would be the administration of the university was predictable, as was the accommodating response of these cultural surrogates. But the willingness to dialogue usually availed little, since the object of the campus protest was to rail against authority figures and the "system," and to do so before the cameras of the media. If the solution proposed was to create a "counterculture" that would solve the real problems of modern life, such as alienation and abuse of power, then no conciliation with the parent generation was conceivable.

Oddly, the New Left had little inclination to turn to the Marxist analyses favored by the old left to account for the failure of the system. The intellectual fathers of the movement, like Paul Goodman and C. Wright Mills, were radical intellectuals, not Marxists, and even at their most extreme never counseled that the system was hopeless and must be destroyed. They observed rather that the old focus on labor as the principle agent of change was obsolete and the creation of a new counterculture to address the ills inherent in an affluent society must be created anew. Before the war furnished a major issue on which to cut one's activist teeth, a local neighborhood issue such as a plan to build a gym on sacred community territory proved sufficient to bring the activities of the university to a halt. The budding civil rights struggle and later the war in Vietnam offered an opportunity for expansion beyond generational and geographical boundaries.

The amplification of the influence of the New Left came when the protracted war in Vietnam presented an issue that they could claim as peculiarly their own. It featured a bungling older generation of leaders that called upon the new generation to put their lives on the line in Southeast

Asia. In the years that followed, much of their passion and energy was subsumed by the expanding war. It gave rise to the defiant slogan "Hell no—we won't go," which, when combined with the burning of their draft cards, had a deep impact on the TV watching public. If the New Left had some influence in shaping foreign policy, it would be in the role it played in bringing pressure on the Johnson and Nixon administration to bring the war in Vietnam to a close. For the protesters, the burning of the draft card, even if it was in many cases a risk-free action, symbolized at once an act that freed them from the fetters of a government that sought to sacrifice them in an unjust war, and, at the same time, it was an act of defiance of a free-spirited generation. But for their parents, who had served in World War II, the burning of draft cards was often seen as posturing rather than a revolutionary act. Clearly, such a generation of Jewish radicals would never accept a party command, like the one in the early fifties that requested the comrades to get closer to the working class by "going into industry." Unlike their parents' generation, this new breed of activists could not be commanded.

Ideology was not a passion of the New Left, as it was of the old. It was free in spirit and cast off much of the discipline demanded of the old left. But we have seen that while it rejected the authoritarianism of the old left, that hardly prevented it from placing left-wing dictators into a heroic pantheon for celebration. Yet by beginning its radical journey with a quest for personal liberation, it turned the universalist image of the left on its head. It also purged itself of its East European collectivist roots and became fully American. One hears little talk of class struggle and the "dictatorship of the proletariat" from these radicals. Rather each radical seeks his own path to nirvana. Under its tutelage, the legacy of the old left became almost the opposite of what it once aspired to be, a disciplined instrument to hasten necessary social change.

Almost completely absent from the political dialogue was the voice of the Communist party. It would in any case have been difficult for the "boomers" to join its ranks, even in the unlikely case that they were so inclined. During the McCarthy years, the party faced difficult times in America. In 1952, the Supreme Court upheld the conviction of eleven second-rank party officials indicted in 1949 under the Smith Act. In 1951, the party again went underground and disbanded many of its affiliated organizations. A young recruit joining the party would have had to think twice about membership. Not until after a Supreme Court decision in *Yates vs. United States* (1957) curtailed prosecution under the Smith Act did the party dare to resurface. It never recouped its influence.

Ironically, the university, which served as the first testing ground of the New Left and whose academic integrity it sought to compromise, ultimately became a refuge for the survivors of the movement. There was an irony in the fact that the very academic citadels they had sought to trash would, for a handful of radicals, become the base for a continuation of "the struggle for justice" and also for a comfortable realization of self. After Reagan's victory in 1980, noting the disproportionate number of former student radicals now becoming tenured professors, a journalist observed that conservatives ran the government while the former student radicals seemed content to run the university's English and sociology departments. It may be that it was ultimately in the college classroom that the New Left had its most enduring influence.

The accelerated fragmentation within the SDS after 1970 demonstrated that contempt for organizational discipline exacted a price. When the war in Vietnam finally came to an end in 1975, the peace movement, which acted as a mainstay of the New Left, found itself without a cause and without recruits. The tendency to fragment into factions within the SDS could be observed as early as 1969, a year after the violent street battles at the Chicago convention of the Democratic party. Some, like the Weathermen, turned to violence; others disappeared into communes or simply vanished from the historical stage. Some Jewish SDSers reverted to the secure, tenured, comfortable lives their parents favored. The New Left disappeared into the past as all movements must. But it left its fingerprint on American and Jewish political culture in the disproportionate number of activist Jewish young people involved in advocating change in government, law, and policy, and in challenging the validity of majority values.

The contrast between the old and the New Left developed on the issue of civil rights, the preferred academic euphemism for the unresolved American race problem. During the thirties the Communist Party USA focused upon the simmering race problem as an opportunity to raise the "political consciousness" of the nation. Black liberation became the backbone of its domestic political program, but the solution that emerged led to a rift between the merely liberal/progressive left-wingers who favored "integration" and the party, whose early position viewed the American Negro as composing a separate nation with its own language, culture, and homeland centered in six southern states. That notion was derived partly from Stalin's writing on the national question. Paradoxically, by favoring "Black Power" over integration and linking itself to the Black

Panthers, the New Left seemed to be moving closer to the party's original position on race. It became an important factor distancing the New Left from the liberal Jewish community, which had become committed to racial integration.

What remained of a decade of youthful "sturm und drang" was the habit of social activism, which had become well ingrained in a new generation of young Jews. Viewed from a historical perspective, the decline of the party's influence opened the door for the Jewish left to revert fully to the "human face" socialism never abandoned by the social democrats. In some way, their apprehensiveness regarding overweening bureaucracy gave the New Left an opportunity to touch base with the neoconservatives and other groups who earlier sensed that Soviet socialism, with its goals of creating a "new Soviet man," had gone awry. But that is where the resemblance ended. The roots of the New Left go back to the pre-1919, the year party was established. The final commune phase to which the remnants of the movement retreated bears some resemblance to the turn-of-the-century Am Olam movement, which claimed the allegiance of Abraham Cahan among others. But commune living, which marked the final phase of the New Left, was not cut from the same ideological cloth. These were not hard-working farmers who gloried in the soil and nature, as in the kibbutz or New Harmony. Nor could they ever be a conspiratorial "cabal," such as the neoconservatives were accused of being. That required organization and discipline, which are precisely what they sought to escape. The New Left reacted to unjust conditions, such as the war in Vietnam. It never proposed a totalistic solution as did their parents.

* * *

The growth of the New Left also revealed a deepening chasm between Jewish radicals and radical Jews. The former seek their roots, (that's what radical refers to) in universal brotherhood or what the immigrant generation called *weltlichkeit*.[7] It proved to be a powerful solvent for the Jewish post-war "boomers." They came to consider their Jewishness an accident of birth and aspired to belong to the fraternity of man, not merely a tribe within it. The radical Jew, on the other hand, begins his search for roots from within the Jewish fold, usually a highly secularized segment of it. Like the Jewish radical, he too seeks human brotherhood and social justice, which he may lead him to the kibbutz or the labor union or simply to becoming a staunch supporter of the dozens of government and private welfare programs. Politically, radical Jews are most likely to be identified with the Jewish social democrats, like Bundists and Labor Zionists, or the Reform rabbinate. The great difference between them is that carried to its logical conclusion, the Jewish radical would meld the Jews into the human fraternity, while a radical Jew, like Rabbi Michael Lerner, the publisher of *Tikkun*, seeks to express his ideals within and through Jewish text and communal agencies, including the possibility of a socialist-oriented Jewish state. Jewish radicals seek to break down the tribal walls that separate. Radical Jews seek justice and fraternity from within the Jewish fold. They do not seek to crawl out of their religious or cultural skins.

In practice, the gulf between the two was usually unbridgeable. The position of a radical Jewish organization, like B'reira or Meretz or the Peace Now organization, advocates change in Israel's foreign and domestic policy, but strongly upholds Israel's right to exist. Jewish radicals, like former party members or SDSers, on the other hand, if they thought of the Jewish state at all, viewed Zionism as a form of racism and Israel as a theocracy that need not exist. Like European socialists, they often condemned Israel as an agent of Western colonialism. That proved to be a moment of truth for the Jewish New Left, which barely thirty years after the Holocaust, found itself supporting a war of national liberation, a "people's war" against the Jewish state. For Jewish radicals, even a residual sense of identity had to be denied. The difference between radical Jews and Jewish radicals comes into clearer focus on the domestic scene. The Ocean Hill-Brownsville conflict pitted an almost all Jewish union, which upheld the merit system of appointment, against black activists who insisted something new was called for to give the black community greater voice in the education of its children. The trouble concerned the merit system for attaining civil service positions, which had been bitterly contested by Irish Americans after it was used by Jewish women to win licenses as teachers. Predictably, it continued to command strong support in the Jewish community. The confrontation was accompanied by an outpouring of virulent anti-Semitic rhetoric. By condemning Israel as beachhead of colonialism in the Middle East and supporting the abandonment of the merit system in Ocean Hill-Brownsville, the Jewish radicals cut themselves off from their Jewish base, only to discover little support in the American community. Even more than the old left, the Jewish New Left was isolated and now unable to build bridges to the majority culture. There was no place for the New Left to go accept to "armed struggle," actual physical resistance that was advocated by the "Weathermen," the most extreme faction of the SDS. Realizing that their position had become untenable and that their moment in the sun had passed, other Jewish radicals drifted back to the Jewish fold. A handful became activists in the Soviet Jewry movement.

The lack of Jewishness was not among the several grievances that the old left had about its radical children. Rather, the primary complaints of the older generation about their offspring concerned the denial of the heroic dimensions of the "struggle" that had preceded their arrival in the world, as well as their lack of socialist civility and morality. In the end, neither the old nor the new Jewish radicals of the left could escape being linked to the very Jewish world they sought to escape. That much the current preoccupation with a supposedly conspiratorial Jewish power seeking to pull public policy in the direction of a Jewish interest can tell us.

* * *

Calculating the impact of the New Left ought not to be confined to the activist element it added to American political culture. It was a movement that impacted the general culture through its free cultural style, which included everything from hair length to smoking marijuana. The new raucous American popular culture, which came into its own in the early sixties, was in some measure developed and carried into the public arena by the New Left, especially its open attitude regarding matters of race and sex. Its impact was the more telling because it was made at the juncture where the general culture translates into politics. One can question whether the New Left created the counterculture or whether it only exploited a change that was already in the wind. Whatever the case, the practice and style of grassroots American politics was altered, sometimes beyond recognition. Aspiring new politicians affected the style of informality as much as possible. It went beyond the denim trousers and the omnipresent guitar to a new kind of populist folksiness.

How much of that is related to the Jewish origins of the New Left cannot be easily determined. It was part of the mix of elements that altered popular and political culture. The general rural American style became very popular among urban Jewish "boomers." But millennia of city living could not be easily changed. Everywhere we look we find Jewish men and women in the forefront of those agencies that push for change. The intensity of Jewish political engagement is not new, but the leadership role it assumes is. It is that intensity, which can take us from the troubles on the college campus and the Woodstock happening, that differentiates American Jewry from other ethnics. There are many reasons for the disproportionate Jewish input into what used to be called the counterculture that today is part of the general culture. A great deal is related to the raucous Jewish communal politics of the interwar period, which generated a many-sided leftist political culture. The Jewish "New Left" of the sixties and seventies is in some respects reminiscent of that culture. It gives us some idea of what the Jewish left might have been, had it been better able to withstand the rigid dogmatism coupled with intense activism of the small minority that was drawn to the extreme left, including the communist party. In some sense, the Jewish New Left served as an important corrective to the old when it stood at almost opposite poles of its parent generation.

It cast off not only the discipline, but also the devotional commitment of the old left. Gone were the remnants of the collectivist roots stemming back to Eastern Europe. Its *sine qua non* was its anti-authoritarianism in any form, whether it stemmed from the university provost or the policeman on the beat. Yet at the same time, it chose as its heroes the most authoritarian figures available, Fidel Castro, Ho Chi Minh, and Mao Zedong. Above all else, by beginning its radical journey with a quest for personal liberation, it turned the traditionalist universalistic image that fueled leftist ideology on its head. Each radical would seek his own path to Nirvana. It was a kind of free enterprise messianism. That is what the legacy of the old left had become.

Unlike the neoconservatives, its power lay not in the analysis and strategies submitted to decision-making elites. It eschewed the political process, which included such mundane matters as voter mobilization, campaigning, and fund raising. The legacy of the New Left is primarily in the activism that has become a permanent part of American Jewish political culture. Three decades later, the New Left has morphed into an alert, well-informed voting constituency that remains deeply involved in the political process and furnishes leadership for much that is new and on the cutting edge of American politics.

* * *

Our quest to find and assess the play of Jewish power in American politics becomes problematic when focused on the New Left, which was a cultural and generational movement that entered the political arena at the university and student movement level. Whether the New Left can be classified as a political movement, in the sense of dealing with power and power holders, remains elusive. There seems nothing new about it and little that is recognizably of the left. There are some commonalities with neoconservatism. Both grow out of the ferment of the Jewish left. Both do not relate to their tribal ties, though neocons, in the end, are consistent advocates of what they believe serves Israel's interest, which they view as consistent with the national interest, while those affiliated with the New Left usually hold the negative attitude of European socialists.

There is also the question of the reality of that power. Can the neoconservative influence long endure outside the context of the Cold War and the so-called "war between civilizations" that followed? Can it survive the Iraq debacle with which it has become associated? Would the New Left have reached so deeply into the national culture if the popular consensus against the war in Vietnam had not reached its zenith in the early seventies? In a word, is there an American Jewish power nexus that stands independent of its confluence with the American national interest and outside the political process by which communal interests are sought? Those, who for whatever reasons, are obsessed with Jewish power can surely find some evidence of its existence in the New Left phenomenon. Yet that power remains difficult to locate with any certainty. Its ties to the American Jewish community are uncertain at best. Its influence seems more related to its response to the war crisis than a planned conspiracy to reshape the nation in its own image.

Notes

1. It is estimated that 75 to 80 percent of Jewish high school students are enrolled in college upon graduation, comprising about 5 percent of the total U.S. college population. Of these, about 27 percent identified themselves as "far left" compared to 4 percent for Protestants and 2 percent for Catholic students.
2. The Port Huron Statement (1962) was written primarily by Tom Hayden for the SDS convention, which met from June 11 to 15 at Port Huron, Michigan to hammer out a platform for the SDS, the core student organization of the New Left.
3. The term New Left, as distinguished from Old Left, was conceived by the sociologist C. Wright Mills in his "Letters to the New Left," *New Left Review,* No. 5, September-October 1960.
4. Milton Himmelfarb, the Jewish house intellectual of the American Jewish Committee, who made the observation, did not get it completely right, since today Jews earn more than Episcopalians and consistently maintain the nation's highest voting rate, in contrast to Puerto Ricans, who, together with other Hispanics, are just emerging from political somnolescence.
5. A response similar to the "Wisconsin idea" proposed by the Progressives who proposed such new political mechanisms as the initiative, the recall of judges, referendums, and the party primaries to lubricate the machinery of democracy.

6.   *The New York Times*, May 19, 1968, p. 1. See also http://markrudd.com/home/why-were-there-so-many-Jews-in-SDS/.

7.   The English translation of this term is worldliness or universalism.

VIII

Epilogue

The classic anti-Semitic paradigm concerns the question of power. Jews are imagined to have too much of it, which they intend to use for evil purposes. The cases examined here demonstrate how problematic such a proposition is, especially when applied to a people that historically has been more vulnerable than most. Nevertheless, like all living things, Jews do have a modicum of power that, in the context of the American democratic system, they use effectively, so much so that sometimes it appears greater than it is. The foregoing chapters demonstrate that in the American political context, identifying the wielders of power and calculating their influence and aspirations is at best an uncertain exercise. In the hands of Judeophobes, it culminates in an indictment of Jews for wielding a power that they do not, in fact, possess or exercise only within the permissible parameters of the American system of governance.

History is full of examples where the misperception of power has led to catastrophe for its wielders as well as its victims. Before the invasion of the Soviet Union in June 1941, the balance of forces so heavily favored the Axis that the odds of an Allied victory were virtually nil. But two strategic errors, which brought the Soviet Union and the United States to the Allied side so radically changed that balance that, in theory at least, the Axis defeat was only a matter of time. Similarly, after years of talk of missile gaps, the Soviet empire collapsed despite the fact that the Warsaw Pact fielded the largest army in Europe and the Soviet Union possessed a full arsenal of weapons of mass destruction. Despite the formidable power of the American military, Washington did not have its way in Vietnam or Iraq. Clearly, even when the military accoutrements of power are overwhelming, so many tanks and so many guns, it does not fully encompass what power entails. Strategic errors and weapons of the spirit can undo superior numbers. There are also non-military factors, such as national morale, the quality of a nation's education system,

145

the productivity of its labor force, the extensiveness of its transportation network, and, above all, the quality of mind of its leaders and the spirit of its people to consider. There is special ingredient that must be added to the factors that today affect the relationship of Jews to power. The will of a people to recoup and go forward after suffering radical losses is also a manifestation of a kind of power. Its weight cannot be calculated, but it is nonetheless real. It is that will to survive that is a silent witness to the history we have probed for answers in these pages.

*   *   *

What conclusions can be drawn from the cases here used to illustrate the play of American Jewish power? When all else is peeled away, Jewish power is revealed as a tenuous force unable by itself to control the events that impact on Jewish life. When its presence is identifiably Jewish, it is usually in the realm of moral ideas whose impact is difficult to measure and is unreliable against an immediate physical threat. At the most critical juncture in Jewish history in the twentieth century, when American Jewry was called upon to mobilize all its political influence to rescue its European brethren it found its power insufficient to convince Allied leadership that the rescue of Europe's Jews should be part of the nation's war aims. That failure has ever since haunted Jewish leaders, especially those who personally experienced the fact that Jews were not considered part of the universe of obligation during World War II. Yet what one researcher has called "the abandonment of the Jews" hardly diminished the apprehension of those who see inordinate political power held by American Jewry. It is that fear that we discern in the recent cluster of complaints about the Israel lobby.

With all the problems that tracing the play of power poses in the American polity, there are some generalities that can be drawn from the foregoing historic examples. We note that Jewish power seemed most conspicuously in play when its objectives and interests were consonant with the perceived national interest. Two instances are cited: American diplomatic support and military aid to Israel, which in the context of the Cold War and common adherence to democratic values had a strategic rationale, and American support of the Soviet Jewry movement, which in the context of the Cold War allowed a human rights issue, the freedom of movement, to be used as a cudgel to beat the Soviet Union. There is always a debate inherent in a democratically conceived foreign policy regarding what best serves the national interest. Convinced that the tactics of the Soviet Jewry movement on the floor of Congress worked against détente, which many felt was the surest road for peace, Henry Kissinger, then secretary of state, took issue with Senator Henry Jackson and his Jewish supporters regarding the Jackson-Vanik amendment. To this day, the question of which policy best served the national interest remains unresolved. More puzzling still is the fact that Kissinger, who at the time was considered the most powerful Jew in the nation, adamantly opposed the amendment, which most American Jews thought served the Jewish interest.

Viewed through the lens of confluence between American and Jewish interests, what appears as Jewish control of policy is in reality part of a more complex transaction. For Israel, its victory in 1967 went beyond the enhancement of its strategic position. At one blow its self-confidence and sense of security was immeasurably enhanced. Viewed through Washington's Cold War prism, Israel's decisive defeat of Soviet client states vastly improved the American power position in the Middle East. Some assumed that the Soviet foothold in the area had been all but eliminated. Israel's importance as a strategic asset was apparent when Nixon did not hesitate to call upon Israel to display its formidable air power to keep Syria in line in 1970. It was not a one-way street. Israel relied on Washington for a crucial resupply in the '73 war and for diplomatic support in the international arena. The unspoken alliance was based on more than mutual strategic interests. It is rooted in a mutual affinity for parliamentary democratic government practices and the rule of law. But contrary to the Judeophobic imagination, it does not proffer an absolute access to American power. During the protracted debate over the Jackson-Vanik amendment, a countervailing power represented by grain interests and others involved in trade with the Soviet Union made its weight felt, and often succeeded in circumventing trade and credit restrictions. Similarly, the military and economic support of Israel today does not go unchallenged. It is compelled to live side by side with aid extended to Arab nations. Today, the aid package extended to Islamic nations in the Middle East easily matches that given to Israel.

* * *

We have noted that in the American democracy, what might be identified as the normal exercise of ethnic power seems amplified. American Jews are notably successful in finding the levers of power and using them. Jews quickly learn how to maximize their influence within the bounds of the system. It is not risking hyperbole to note that the American Jewish citizenry contains the ideal human material to make democracy work. The community maintains an interior communal polity which, though often raucous in atmosphere, acts as a kind of training ground for teaching the art of politics. Someone once jokingly observed that American Jewry's real contribution to the political process is the manifold uses it has developed for the disruptive uses of parliamentary procedure, especially in the use of "points of order" in their fiery discussions. Their voting rate remains among the highest in the national electorate and it is enhanced by the strategic locations of Jewish voters in pivotal states. Their larger incomes and a tradition of giving make for disproportionately larger contributions to political campaigns that are at the heart of American politics. As a rule, American Jews are more engaged in and better informed about political issues than other voting blocs. They are more likely to maintain contact with their congressman and write letters to the editor of the local newspaper. What critics see as domination of the process is, in fact, a fully involved citizenry using the system the way it is designed to be used. Most Jewish political energy is, in fact, invested in non-sectarian political issues, such as zoning regulations, education, and health issues. The security of Israel is an important issue, but it is far from being an exclusive one.

The high level of Jewish political involvement is partially explained by the perennial insecurity seemingly inherent in the Jewish historic situation. There seems always to be a Jewish community somewhere pleading for help on the basis of kinship and religion. Jewish organizations and individual citizens feel a need to seek government support that exceeds other ethnics voting blocs who have found place and a modicum of acceptance in the world order. Religiously committed Jews are commanded to help their brethren as a first order of business. We have seen that, after the Holocaust, the need to help such Jews remains the *sine qua non* of Jewish life. The imagined failure to do so effectively during the Holocaust has strengthened that need. It is the most identifiable characteristic of an otherwise widely varied Jewish political agenda.

The more intensive Jewish use of the political process is only partly explained by their historic circumstance or religious command. Those who fear that Jews seek to control American foreign policy are baffled by the fact that the evidence they use to demonstrate the political dominance of American Jewry applies equally to non-Jewish sections of the nation's operational and educational elite. What is remarkable is how much Jewish political behavior and voting patterns resemble holders of higher degrees of education especially in the liberal arts. Jewish political behavior is comparable to that of the professoriate, social workers, writers, people in the communications industry, or cultural institutions, employees of philanthropic foundations, only more so. There is, in fact, little, aside from its special concern about Israel, that differentiates Jewish interests from the university-trained elites that govern America. In a sense, what those who find a Jewish conspiracy to rule may really have discovered is that the Jews have become an integral part of the nation's operational elite. There is nothing particularly Jewish about the aspiration of the Jewish voter that is not also shared by other educated voters. Once that is established, then the next logical target for Judeophobes would naturally be the American university that produces these elites. Some are convinced that that is already underway.

That naturally brings us to the question of determining what is identifiably Jewish about Jewish power, other than that Jews exercise it. The anxious guardians of the national interest hear a specific Jewish voice ostensibly advocating a Jewish interest in the political arena. They are convinced that those who claim to speak for the Jewish community actually have a mandate to do so. What we have seen, in the examples here drawn from American Jewish history, is that the case is often otherwise. As much as some organizations, like AIPAC or the Conference of Presidents of Major Jewish Organizations, may claim to represent the Jewish communal interest, in fact, no such mandate representing all American Jewry, the majority of whom are no longer organizationally affiliated, can be given. It is an aspiration rather than a legal datum. While a particular administration may unofficially select certain people to speak for the Jewish communal interest, no American ethnic group is constituted as a political corporation. Jews invited to the Oval Office are not automatically considered to be communal leaders. They may possess added political weight because they can act as a bridge to the administration, but legally they speak only for a particular special interest or themselves. To have it otherwise would give the president power to preempt communal leadership. That accounts for the persistent lack of coherence and the cooption of the communal voice by organizations, like AIPAC, or individuals, like Rabbi Stephen Wise, whom Roosevelt once called "the Pope of the Jews."[1]

In virtually every case, the bona fides of Jewish communal representatives to speak to power was challenged. If there exists a Jewish conspiracy, it certainly lacks requisite unity and popular support. The fingerprint of Jewish organizational life is not cohesiveness, but variability, which reflects the wide variations of interests, culture, and faith within the community. Given the inexorable progress of the assimilation process, the idea that there exists a community with a single coherent interest articulated by its leaders is a false picture of how American Jewry governs itself. There are many Jewish interests and they are often in bitter conflict with each other.

In the case of the neoconservatives and New Left, both groups have common roots in the malaise of the Jewish left in the twenties and thirties. But we have noted that other than the accident of birth, the substance of their Jewish identity remains unclear. The Jewish left was universalist in its political culture and often provided a path out of the tribal fold. In the case of the Jewish communists, that process went so far that, in some rare cases, Jews were lured to becoming agents of the Soviet Union when it was clearly detrimental to the Jewish interest. Throughout the early years of the Cold War, Jewish party apologists denied that Soviet policy was infused with anti-Semitism. Beyond the fact that they often bore the onus of being Jewish within the party, it is difficult to identify anything particularly Jewish about them. Neoconservatism began as an anti-Stalinist sensibility and concluded with the assumption that the American national interest would be enhanced by the active expansion of democracy. The support of Israel is reinforced by that conception, but that has led to the charge that the neocons place Israel's national interest ahead of the American. As the war in Iraq turns sour, the accusation grows shriller. When neocons are transmuted into a thinly disguised Jewish group acting for the welfare of Israel, it raises the charge of dual loyalty, which has long been a source of apprehension in American Jewish history. It hardly mattered that Jewish support of the neoconservative position on the Iraq war was far from monolithic and that many neocons counseled that a war on Iran was the more winning strategy. That support for the war stemmed from an amorphous grouping that reached to the highest echelons of the Bush administration also mattered little. The charge that the war was somehow a Jewish war was on the table. When the Iraq war is viewed as a conspiracy to strengthen Israel's position in the Middle East, it contains the potential of a public relations anti-Semitic onslaught against American Jewry. At the time of this writing there are signs that it has begun with the accusations that Iraq was a Jewish war to further a Jewish interests.[2]

The New Left was incubated within an old left whose sons and daughters had turned against much of their parents' left-wing ideology and culture. All that remained to share with their parents was a mutual ambivalence regarding their Jewishness. The universalism of the left served to conceal the self-abnegating effects of the assimilation process they were undergoing. The movement focused not on Israel or some goal especially close to Jewish interests, but on domestic issues, like the civil rights struggle or bringing the Vietnam War to an end, that were part of the nation's political agenda, to which Jewish citizens were also drawn. The New Left seemed more attuned to the student uprising in France of May '68 and the model of leadership presented by Kohn Bendit than they were to the exhilaration most Jews felt after Israel's victory in the 1967 war. When expressed at all, it shares the "post-Zionist" view of the European socialist left, which viewed Israel as an unwelcome residue of a dying colonial enterprise.

It is the central position occupied by the claims and needs of Israel in American Middle East policy that is at the heart of the emerging indictment of Jewish political power in America. The addition of the sovereign power of Israel enhanced American Jewry's pride and self-confidence, which needed shoring up after its ineffective role during the Holocaust. American Jewry's sense of self was never higher than in the years following the establishment of the state in 1948. It was further enhanced by Israel's victory in 1967, but that war again brought home the reality of the unacceptability of Israel in the Islamic neighborhood of the Middle East. From the beginning Israel's need for American Jewish resources and political advocacy was balanced by the emotional asset Israel had become for American Jewry. We have noted that concern for the security and welfare of Israel is a crucial factor accounting in some measure for the intense political engagement of the Jewish electorate. It encouraged American Jews to learn the art of politics and how to use their power. Israel gave the American Jewish polity the focus it did not have before World War II. The nurture of the Jewish state became the consensus in a community that otherwise could find little to hold it together. The nature of American Jewish political culture is incomprehensible without an appreciation of the role and position of Israel in it. When that support is criticized as undermining loyalty to the nation it hits upon a very sensitive point in the political experience of American Jewry. Before World War II, American Jewry's greatest fear concerned the charge of dual loyalty, a mainstay of classic anti-Semitism.

When the reality of the deep divisions within the Jewish polity is juxtaposed with the obsessional quality in the thinking of those who imagine inordinate Jewish power, there is reason for being apprehensive. Such a riven polity is, after all, hardly an appropriate staging ground for the kinds of elaborate conspiracies of which American Jewry stands accused. The interests of Israel and those of an American Jewry are often at odds, so that the UJA slogan "We Are One" has become a source of humor.[3] The story of those conflicts in the Soviet Jewry case and in others is told in the preceding chapters. Even the cohesiveness stemming from concern for Israel, the central building block of Jewish unity, cannot be taken for granted. As Jews become more American and less ethnically Jewish, the bonds that have tied American Jewry to Israel may grow weaker. The nervous monitoring for signs that the communities are growing apart, based on such things as tabulations of visits to Israel or philanthropic giving to Israeli institutions, is rooted in the fear of weakening ties. The "drop out" debacle in the Soviet Jewry case was the source of much concern among communal leaders. The fear goes beyond the waning of the attachment that hyphenates feel for the "mother country." Most American Jews have never visited Israel and have little sense for the land. But they know from their recent historic experience that there is great danger when one is compelled to live in a threatening world without having one's own space. That is attributable to the memory of the Holocaust and sustained by Arab hostility to Israel's existence.

If recent surveys are correct, those Judeophobes who believe that they have found the locus of the secret Jewish power in their communalism may have reason to rejoice. The surveys find a continued willingness to be counted as Jews, but little affiliation with its organizational or congregational structure. A growing number of Jews respond to questions about their affiliation with "just Jewish." The tribe is but one of several things that claims their loyalty and perhaps not even the most important. Not only is the Jewish communal base to mount an evil conspiracy nonexistent, the day may be approaching when they will no longer be able to "conspire" about their communal survival.

* * *

Alarums warning of the danger of power in Jewish hands are not new in the Jewish experience. They are in conflict with the Jewish perspective that finds that there never seems to be sufficient power to do all that is necessary to nurture a threatened Jewish community abroad. Such communities seem to exist in almost every period of Jewish history. The American Jewish agenda is continually overextended in relations to the power available. It may be that Jews simply have a greater need to find and use power. For most of their exilic history, Jews were bereft of the normal accoutrements of power in a world that was at best indifferent to their fate and at worst murderously hostile. The Jewish people would not have survived for millennia in an often-hostile world without some kind of power at play that stemmed either from a crucial craft or commercial skill or the protective mantle of a friendly sovereign. The Holocaust partly undermined that comfortable belief based on the assumption that they were part of the universe of obligation embodied in emancipation. Had the National Socialist regime emerged from the war as victors, few Jews would have survived. There is no other historic "grouping" in the world that is compelled to live with that reality.

By the end of World War II, American Jewry had ample additional evidence of what the absence of power could mean for individual and communal survival. Had there been a Jewish state or had American Jewry been able to convince the Roosevelt administration to include the rescue of European Jewry in its war aims, it would have been possible to rescue many more of their kin. It was that realization that led all Jews, including anti- and non-Zionists, to support the establishment of the Jewish state, which did not become an agreed upon goal of the world Zionist movement until the Biltmore Conference in May 1942. Only six months later, Richard Lichtheim, the Jewish Agency executive agent in Geneva, together with Gerhard Riegner, the agent of the World Jewish Congress, were able to confirm the unbelievable fact that a modern nation-state was implementing its master plan to exterminate the Jews of Europe.

* * *

What these case studies are intended to show is not that Jews are bereft of power. A people that have survived for millennia, while other civilizations are in ashes, cannot have done so without some kind of power. Our challenge is to discover its substance and to confront the assumption that it is inordinate and exercised conspiratorially. That quest is fueled, in turn, by the fact that the normal accoutrements of power, armies, national sovereignty, cannot be found in the American Jewish arsenal. What kind of power is this that is invisible yet everyone has felt its lash?

Our discussion here is confined to the United States, whose democracy makes it a special case. The control of American foreign policy is merely one of several power conspiracies of which Jews stand accused. There was the case of Jews being charged retroactively with the crime of dominating the slave trade.[4] There is much talk of the exploitive role Jews and other groups played in former colonial nations as middleman minorities. We have noted that the accusation that Jews possess inordinate power appears repeatedly in Jewish history. Ironically, democracy itself is a great amplifier of the myth of Jewish power, since it allows Jews the full play of their abundant energy.

It is the accusation, that Jews possess inordinate power and exercise it with satanic fervor, that lies behind the accusation that Jews control American foreign policy. It takes its place with past overarching explanations regarding Jewish power, such as control of currency and credit banking or Judeobolshevism, relentlessly propagated by the political right. Today, it builds its case around the fiction that Jews seek to control the sole superpower, the United States, to ensure the security of Israel. What links the current case to the overarching conspiracy theories of the past identified with classic anti-Semitism is its preoccupation with secret Jewish power and the assumption that Jews want to harm or control the world. The power that arouses such fear cannot be found in divisions and battalions or in political legerdemain. I have variously called it ideational or moral power. If the Jews trespass at all, it is in using their historically vulnerable position to remind the world to be better than it wants to be, perhaps than it can be. It reminds them of the moral grammar at the base of all societies that, like ours, stem from the Judeo-Christian tradition.[5]

From a Jewish perspective, the danger from this latest foreboding regarding Jewish power that focuses on the role played by the neoconservatives in bringing on the Iraq war is that it may become part of the conventional wisdom. Studies show that it is well on the way to becoming so in the Islamic world, where it is propagated in the mosque and the schoolroom. If that happens, it is not inconceivable that at some future time, American Jewry, together with the communities and institutions that compose world Jewry, may be compelled to answer charges regarding the misuse of its power. What surprises is that less than seventy years after the Holocaust, little has changed. Jewry remains a beleaguered vulnerable people whose very existence conjures visions of great power.

Jews undoubtedly have their share of greedy lobbyists and those who otherwise feed off the system, but such types are not conspicuously common among Jewish officeholders. The most recent accusations concerning Jews and power reinforce their sense that little has been learned since the destruction of the Jews of Europe during World War II. It is a charge that is strangely disembodied. In their engagement with politics and their activism, the nation's Jewish citizens are probably closer to the model citizen that assures that the American democracy remains viable.

The American political system encourages special interest groups to mobilize their resources and Jews have done so in several ways. They exercise the franchise perhaps more fully then other voting blocs. Their practice of public relations to support Israel and to highlight issues like racial tolerance, civil rights, and emigration of Soviet Jewry has had a profound influence on the way the American political dialogue is framed. They are unusually generous in helping their favored candidates to fund their political campaigns. Yet, while Jewish organizations have used the available instruments to their maximum in the past, a weaker communal affiliation may translate into less common ground for unified action in the future. Endemic disunity continues to be the fingerprint of Jewish communal life, undermining the strength of its advocacy. There are deep divisions within the Jewish electorate, even on such sacred issues as the security of Israel. Like all voting constituencies, Jews have full access to the public square, only to discover that their vision of the future is becoming more American Jewish and less Jewish American. If, indeed, such special lines of influence to power are in the Jewish arsenal, they no longer know, if they ever did, what to conspire about.

To become aware that some portion of Jewish power is ideational still leaves us a distance from our goal of discovering the substance of Jewish power, which so exercises the anti-Semitic imagination. Ideational or moral power casts no shadow, yet there is evidence of its play in international affairs. Recent events allow hope that whether it is the Czechs communist head of state, Alexander Dubzek, speaking of "socialism with a human face" or Chinese students raising a *papier mâché* icon of the Statue of Liberty in Tiananmen Square, or the outcry against the genocide in Darfur, there is, since the eighteenth-century Enlightenment, a basic sense that the road to a better world is not in the direction of gulags or suicide bombers. The content of these ideas is not the possession of any single ideology or religion. They are universally known and supported. One version was stated in the Universal Declaration of Human Rights (1948) and repeated in Basket III of the Helsinki Accords (1974). But the problem of whether they can be mobilized in time to save threatened peoples, who, like the Jews, are compelled to live outside the universe of obligation remains unresolved.

It is from within this sub-stratum, which somehow survives in the most brutalized of societies, that these "civilizing ideas" are incubated. Throughout their exilic history, it was the absence of power that compelled Jews to call upon the world for succor. That is the reason that the view of a Jewish power grandiose enough to rule the world, or at least the American foreign policy making corner of it, has in it a bitter irony. From the Jewish historic perspective, the kind of power it possesses has proven insufficient to assure their security, much less the fulfillment of the mission to repair the world, with which some Jews feel they are charged.

The existence of Jewish power is a given. It is the second part of the accusation, that it is inordinate and exercised with satanic intent, that makes the image so threatening. Those who submit these accusations to the listening world are unable to show an arsenal of normal accouterments of power or great motives for wanting to harm the world. The paradox is that while its foes fear the lash of an imagined Jewish power, the evidence of the play of such a force in American politics is slight and its evil intent nowhere in sight.

*   *   *

No examination of American Jewish political culture, in which the power question is embedded, can be considered as complete without some comment on its current status. There is no easy way to calculate the extent of Jewish power exercised in America today. That may be a primary reason why the overestimation of its play is so common. There are few examples of the direct communal use of Jewish power in the American experience. It is in the nature of power that when it is not used, but known to exist, that its impact is maximized. Once power is committed, its limitations become apparent. Witness the failing role of American armed forces in Vietnam or more recently in Iraq, or the failure of the Soviet military in Afghanistan. But that concerns physical power, which American Jewry does not possess.

We have noted in the foregoing pages that the use of that power is indirect in that it seeks to persuade the administration to use its power to help realize Jewish goals. It is most effective when those goals correspond to the American national interest. Judging from people of Jewish origin who have the ear of the Bush administration, it is today at a high point, but only if those who claim to speak for American Jewish interests possess some kind of communal sanction. We note that no such political mechanism exists and therefore the claim to speak for America Jewry need not, and often does not, represent a Jewish consensus. Yet in no prior period of American history have strategies proposed by Jews been held in such a high regard and Jewish communal life lived with such confidence and self-assurance.

We note two separate dimensions of American Jewish power. There is the actual exercise of Jewish power on the ward or grassroots level, composed of such factors as voting rate, the effective use of public relations, and the dozens of special skills associated with the profession of politics that extend from poll taking to campaign planning. The second dimension is far more difficult to identify and calibrate. We have characterized it as "soft," moral or ideational and it is here where the mystique of Jewish political power is rooted. Jews not only bring to the public square life affirming ideas drawn from the sub-stratum that exists in all societies, but communally it possesses a highly developed ability to market them.

Yet if the Jewish experience in the twentieth century shows anything, it is that the hope of survival based solely on such moral suasion is insufficient. There has occurred a change in the Jewish political mentality that acknowledges that survival requires sovereignty and the territorial space and military power that accompanies it. That realization is the primary reason for American Jewry's staunch support of Israel's sovereign power. It will continue to be an anchor point of American Jewish political culture as long as those who witnessed the unwillingness of those who composed the universe of obligation during World War II to act remain alive. It has caused a reshaping of the way American Jews play the political game and a change in the pre-Holocaust assumption of their political culture.

Still, America's Jews are not like other hyphenates that populate the American social and political landscape. The Jewish state did not exist when most American Jews settled here. The trauma of the Holocaust leaves nothing in Jewish political and spiritual life unaffected. Israel is not only homeland; it serves as a back-up for American Jewry, many of whom view it not only as the realization of the biblical promise, but also as a safe haven in case of emergency. The need for such a haven has not been forgotten, even while Israel's victories on the field of battle have done much to build pride and confidence. But the promise of finally living in an unthreatening world has not been fulfilled. Despite the formidable security structure developed in the post-Holocaust decades, the inability to win acceptance in the Middle East and the portents of virulent anti-Semitism that stem partly from the very establishment of the Jewish state pose an ominous threat. Almost as if to prove its Jewish bona fides, Israel has become the lodestone of anti-Semitism. It seems to be as much the despised other in the family of nations as any Jewish community in pre-war Poland.

Her atomic monopoly, which served as the ultimate assurance of security, is on the verge of being broken, so in the years ahead, Israel's possession of atomic weapons will no longer serve as an ultimate guarantee of its security. But this time the playing field between victim and perpetrator is even. The mutual ability to destroy each other makes all equally powerless. That reversion to the condition of powerlessness is not a new experience for Jews, especially the Jews of America, its most successful Diaspora. Bereft of physical power, American Jewry has developed new sources of security and vitality. We learn in these pages of American Jewry's real power, its entrepreneurial courage, its enterprising spirit, its formidable level of education, its participatory sense of citizenship, and especially the role of its young people as change-agents. We have spoken a good deal about the remarkable affinity between America and its Jews. The strongest evidence of that is their sharing of a basic optimism that progress toward a better world can be achieved. It is these shared aspirations, anchored perhaps in common Hebraic roots, which create a confluence between Jewish and American political aspirations so frequently mentioned in these pages. It is the true source of Jewish power in America.

Notes

1.   In 1918, in preparation for the Versailles conference, the Jews held a community-wide election to determine policy and leadership. It was part of Rabbi Stephen Wise's attempt to democratize communal governance. The attempt remained singular and was not repeated, nor was the Jewish example followed by other ethnic groups. "Who leads?" remains a perennial problem in American ethnic politics.

2.   See, for example, James Bamford, *A Pretext for War: 9/11, Iraq, and the Abuse of America's Intelligence Agencies* (New York: Doubleday, 2004), preface and p. 22ff.

3.   For an elaboration of the communal pluralism theme, see Edward S. Shapiro, *We Are Many: Reflections on American Jewish History and Identity* (Syracuse, NY: Syracuse University Press, 2005).

4.   Eli Faber, *Jews, Slaves, and the Slave Trade: Setting the Record Straight* (New York: New York University Press, 1998), is an archival study that proves that such was hardly the case.

5.   That moral grammar may find its original roots in the Judeo-Christian ethic, but it did not become universal or natural until the Enlightenment. There was little concern regarding the rights of the individual in English common law. It took an additional century and a half after the Declaration of Independence and the French Declaration of the Rights of Man (1789) for it finally to be inscribed in the Universal Declaration of Human Rights (1948).

Index

For Paul Tobias,

  I hope your banking
experience in the UP goes
better than mine (at D&N).

  Best of luck! You may
pick up a few pointers in this
book regarding dealing with
people, customers and
employees in the UP.

          Sincerely,
        & Best Wishes,

      George P. Schwartz
          6-10-05

SHAREHOLDER REBELLION

How Investors Are Changing the Way America's Companies Are Run

GEORGE P. SCHWARTZ, CFA

IRWIN
Professional Publishing®
Burr Ridge, Illinois
New York, New York

This publication is designed to provide accurate and authoritative
information in regard to the subject matter covered. It is sold with
the understanding that the author and the publisher are not engaged
in rendering legal, accounting, or other professional service.

ISBN 1-55738-883-0

Printed in the United States of America

BB

1   2   3   4   5   6   7   8   9   0

LK

To Judi—a pearl of a wife,
and the light of my life.

Contents

I <u>am</u> the state.

— Louis XIV
*Addressing the French
Parliament in 1651*

Acknowledgements

Many thanks to the following people for the help and encouragement they provided in researching, writing, and editing this manuscript.

My wife Judi, and children Annie, Mike, Tim, Bob, and Katie provided an enormous amount of encouragement when the research got tedious. I owe a debt to Tom Morrisey, who provided editing and professional writing guidance; Robert L. Fenton, my literary agent, skillfully guided the project to completion. Rick Nelson, Jack Dudley, and Lisa King provided various inputs and expertise. An extra special thanks to longtime colleague and friend Rick Platte, whose idea it was to write this book as a therapeutic exercise after a difficult proxy contest which I ran (and won). Thanks to my staff members Bob Dailey, Cindy Dickenson, George Sertl, Debra Gilbert, and my assistant Joan Kotcher, all of whom had to pick up the slack at the office while I wrote. Thanks to my father Walter G. Schwartz, who taught me the meaning of integrity, whether related to corporate governance or otherwise, and to the memory of my mother Marian V. Schwartz, who taught me independence and almost every other good human trait possible (only a few of which have stuck with me). I owe my brother Gregory J. Schwartz, immeasurably for early instructions in the art of value investing. My gratitude to Ralph Coleman, another Benjamin Graham disciple, who for many years ran the Over-the-Counter Securities Fund which our Schwartz Value Fund attempts to emulate to this day. Thanks to John D. Paul, a mentor who taught me the proper way to run a commercial bank and a public company—simply for the benefit of the owners. To Frank S. Moran, another mentor, who taught me patience, professionalism, and the merits of looking at things from more than one angle.

A Tempest Without a Teacup

It is a story known and cherished by every American schoolchild.

One cold winter evening in 1773, American colonists boarded British merchanteers in Boston Harbor and proceeded to cast the cargo overboard. The cargo was tea, and the action was precipitated by a tax which had been levied on that commodity.

American colonists were British subjects. They were expected to pay the same taxes as English citizens; in fact, the colonists were subject to some taxes from which the citizens of the mother country were exempt. But the tax, *per se*, was not the issue. Rather, it was the lack of representation in the government supported by the tax. Infuriated by a king who took their money but refused to allow them a word in how that money was spent, the colonists reacted, and now history has the Boston Tea Party.

One can only wonder how those colonists would have reacted if they had known that 200 years later, their descendants would again be denied voice in how their money was spent. But this time, the culprits would be corporations, and the autocrats turning deaf ears to the sources of their funding would be corporate directors who simply *behaved* as if they were kings.

It takes capital to start and run businesses. The idea of sharing that financial burden among several parties is by no means new. In fact, it is safe to say that America was literally founded and built on shareholder investment.

All of the original colonies—the Jamestown colony, Williamsburg, Plymouth, and others—were created with capital collected under royal charters. These charters were not dispersals of Crown monies. Rather, they were simply a form of royal permission to collect funds by subscription. Those who invested were generally merchants who wished to import tobacco, furs, and other products from the New World.

Indeed, even the discovery of the New World was indirectly the result of shareholder action. Despite popular belief to the contrary, Queen Isabella of Spain did not contribute a single *real* to Christopher Columbus' voyage of discovery. What she gave him was a piece of parchment— a royal charter—under the aegis of which he was allowed to approach private sources of funding and state his case. Columbus' patrons were all private capitalists who hoped that his voyage would inaugurate a new and faster route to the rich silk and spice markets of the Orient. These would-be merchants banded together and formed a company to sponsor the expedition.

Like modern corporations, these charter companies had their own directors. And to a man—Queen Isabella aside, it was a male-dominated business—these directors were the merchant-capitalists themselves, or members of family-owned businesses, tied by blood to the sources of their capital. The interests of the shareholders and the interests of the directors were identical, so directors worked toward the well-being of all of the shareholders (in the case of Columbus, for instance, they insisted that he take on an experienced captain, since his own credentials as a seaman were decidedly shaky). With family-owned businesses, patronage was a circular situation. No one ever had to speak to a Medici about fiduciary responsibility; if a company under his direction took a bath, he would be the first to get wet.

Directors' relationships with their companies evolved—perhaps the better word would be *de*volved—as companies became larger. Eventually, "family-owned" would be as much a measurement of size as it was of attitude. With the opening of the New York Stock Exchange in 1792, the idea of a publicly held company became common. Background and blood no longer played a part in the matter; shares were purchased by people who would never see a company's facilities, and possibly would never even come in contact with its products. This obviously precipitated a shift in directorial attitude. When the dollars you invested were your own, or your father's, or Uncle Alex's or Cousin Nancy's, you invested those dollars with great care. But when the money came from a nameless, faceless entity—when you weren't even likely to know the stockbroker who handled the transaction, let alone the investor who bought the shares—an entirely new season opened up.

It wasn't the family fortune any longer.

It was Other People's Money.

Call it a canny understanding of human nature or call it cynicism. No matter what you call it, the corporate board of directors is a product of the same channel of thought that created the republican system of government. Just as the executive and legislative branches of government are intended to exert checks and balances upon one another, a board of directors is an entity created to monitor the judgment of the corporation's managers and, principally, its chief executive officer (CEO).

The prevailing idea, of course, is that while an individual may have lapses in ethics, intelligence, or faculty, a collection of individuals will not—stronger fiber will reinforce the weak, and cooler heads will prevail. It is a romantic notion, a solution to the dilemma of choosing between a single-minded monarch and a directionless committee.

When they are working properly, boards represent the interests of shareholders. Some companies go to extremes to present at least the *appearances* of representing stockholders; others strive to make it appear as if they are representing the interests of *everyone*. Look at the traditional board of General Motors, for instance, and you will find a union man, a churchman, a liberal, a woman, and someone who astoundingly never seems to take offense at the implication that he was chosen simply because he is a member of a minority race. Every board that sat for GM from 1975 through 1990 was constructed this way (although the woman and the minority may occasionally be one and the same—a "two-fer"). In recent decades, the GM board of directors has been like Prego Spaghetti Sauce; pick a belief—"it's in there[SM]."

Appearances aside, boards quite often do not work as intended. Most CEOs of large corporations have hand-picked their board members—until very recent years, GM's board was an example of such a practice. Even today, it is common for a Fortune 500 CEO to have power of ratification or veto over the appointment of a director. This cronyism creates, at best, a ticklish situation. How does one vote against awarding a bonus to the fellow who vetted one into one's country club—particularly when it's a choice between supporting good old Charley and considering the interests of a body of nameless, faceless shareholders whom one will never see, let alone meet?

It's human nature to side with a friend, regardless of circumstance. Yet fiduciary responsibility often dictates exactly the opposite course.

There are some boards that will support a CEO adamantly, rubber-stamp every management proposal, and never even have an inkling that they're doing anything wrong. Some directors think the whole idea is to toss their weight behind management.

Unfortunately, we are living in a society where one must pass a test to become a beautician, but no examination exists to determine a person's fitness to function as a director. The position of director has no minimum requirement, not even that of average intelligence, and hundreds of corporate boards stand as evidence to that fact.

Have shareholders stood still for this?

They have not. They have kicked, screamed, and worked themselves into rages. But, outside of elections at general shareholders' meetings, it is absolutely astounding how little voice these owners have in the workings of their own companies.

Consider, for instance, the plight of institutional investors. Mutual funds and pension funds together account for 53 percent of all American stock holdings. Yet this clear majority often must go to extremes—including litigation—in order to even get a hearing on the most basic business of the corporations they own.

In our republican analogy, if the CEO is the executive branch, and the directors are the legislative branch, it stands to reason that there must be some arbiter—a "Supreme Court," to follow the analogy—that mediates between the decisions of the rulers and the wishes of the masses. And there is such an arbiter in the form of the Securities and Exchange Commission (SEC).

Everyone has heard of the SEC. They're the people who move against brokers for misrepresenting stock performance, or apprehend *The Wall Street Journal* columnists for "inside trading"—buying stocks on the basis of material information not available to the general public. With this sort of caped-crusader reputation, it stands to reason that the SEC would come thundering in on any board thathad the audacity to turn deaf ears to its shareholders.

It stands to reason, but like much in the world of finance, reason seemingly has little bearing on the matter.

The fact is, SEC regulations have for years offered some of the most significant roadblocks to shareholders wishing to make their voices heard.

Consider:

- *Shareholders have traditionally been barred from contacting more than 10 of their peers without first filing for permission with the SEC.* The rights to freedom of speech and freedom of assembly are guaranteed by the United States Constitution. Yet, for decades, one had to hold one's hand up before one could speak. And holding one's hand up, of course, waved a red flag to management. Managers and directors could and did speak to one another all the time without ever letting shareholders in on what was going on.

- *Shareholders have traditionally had great difficulty in even identifying their peers.* Look in the minutes of any general stockholders' meeting of years past, and you'd have found a reference to an opening of the shareholders' roster. But just try to get a look at that roster during the meeting; those who've done so have found that they often had but scant minutes in which to examine a document that was hundreds of pages long. This *pro forma* disclosure is like that sea of disclaimer type that appears at the end of a TV commercial—impossible to read, but sufficient to satisfy the requirement.

- *Even though the shareholders are the owners of their companies, they have until very recently been unable to legally determine the total amounts being paid to their top executives.* While base pay is generally a matter of record with publicly held corporations, stock options have traditionally been a closely held secret. In some cases, corporate public-affairs people have used this restriction to distort information: When Lee Iacocca became chairman of Chrysler Corporation, for instance, Chrysler's public affairs office announced that until the automaker had been turned around, Iacocca would accept a salary of only "one dollar a year." What Chrysler did not announce was the value of Iacocca's stock options, which were said to amount to millions.

What we have had, then—and have had for years—was a situation in which people and organizations were legally barred from freely speaking with one another, and in which the employees of a company (albeit the top employees) were allowed to hide the amounts of their total compensation from the very people whose money backed up the checks.

If such an atmosphere prevailed in some third-world Caribbean island, there is little doubt that America would have invaded long ago in the name of freedom.

But it hasn't been happening there.

It's been happening here.

And for far too long, we have accepted it as business-as-usual.

Were I approaching this subject academically, I would no doubt find it fascinating. Unfortunately, I do not have that luxury.

As the head of an investment counsel firm managing more than $200 million in capital, I've confronted the realities of crippled shareholder communication.

My clients are, for the most part, individuals. It is very easy for me to put names and faces to the people whose money goes into our stock purchases, and that has made it very easy for me to become exasperated when I see those same good, upstanding people trampled on and treated like outsiders by the very companies they own. Having accepted the trust of my clients, I have found it unthinkable to violate that trust by remaining silent.

Because of this, I have made noise.

I have, when necessary, taken whatever actions were needed to remind corporate managers that they are the hired *caretakers* of my clients' property, and not nobility placed there through divine right.

It has not been the easiest way to do things.

It has required a more active role than that traditionally taken by an investment counselor.

It has most certainly screwed up my golf game.

But I'm glad that I've done it because, as more and more like-minded people have issued wake-up calls to corporate boards and the offices that regulate them, change has become possible.

Actions like the gaining of board seats by major investor groups—actions inconceivable only a decade ago—have entered the realm of possibility today. With enough effort, they will become common tomorrow.

This book is intended to encourage my peers—the American investment community—to stand up and make the necessary effort.

Chapter 1

Whose Corporation Is It, Anyhow?

"You pay your money and you take your chances. . ."

That old aphorism, originally composed to describe gambling, has become a popular description of modern investment.

I bristle at the comparison. So, I think, do most of the people who make their livings through investment counsel and management. Many, like me, are people who live by moral convictions, who recognize their investments as the foundation of their families' financial security.

No rational person trusts his or her child's education and future to the outcome of a toss of the dice. When it comes to buying interests in businesses, I do not gamble.

This is not to say that I do not take risks.

My philosophy of investment has been labeled "contrarian" by those who must put names on such things. Contrarian investment involves the foresight to see the possibilities in companies that are underachieving and thus are undervalued. It is the philosophy of buying straw hats in January on the assumption that they will sell well in July.

If you can see past the deadwood in a corporation's portfolio, you can sometimes find a straw hat in January. Your job then is to bring that promise to fruition—in a marketing sense, to make it July.

Often this involves management changes, and I need to make one thing clear at the onset—change, even when it involves a corporation's most senior executive officers, is not an evil thing.

Minding the Store

I have a friend—we'll call him Al—who became, through dint of hard work, perseverance, and an intimate understanding of his products and his customers, one of the most successful automobile dealers in metropolitan Detroit, one of America's most active and aggressive automotive markets. Al's success in his first dealership made it possible to open a second dealership in a promising area outside the city, followed shortly thereafter by a third. Contrary to popular opinion, successful auto dealers do not play golf in the mornings and count their money in the afternoons; it is a tough business that calls for attention to detail, and three dealerships means three times as much work. Al soon found it necessary to hire general managers to attend to the details at his establishments.

Now, Al is a caring, compassionate individual who contributes generously to charity and believes in giving a person a break. If one of his general managers makes decisions that reduce revenue at that manager's dealership, Al's first reaction is to meet with the fellow, discuss the situation, and arrive at strategies that will rectify it. But having compassion does not preclude the exercise of common sense. If one of his dealerships consistently performs below the potential of its immediate market, and if a general manager proves unwilling or unable to make the changes that will restore that establishment to an acceptable level of profitability, it is within Al's powers to change management at that dealership.

He has, in fact, done so at one of his "stores" (as they call them in the auto business), and no one thought less of Al for doing so. Quite the contrary, people who knew the business looked at what he'd done and proclaimed Al to be a smart businessman.

Now, why is it that when a shareholder in a corporation tries to make the same sort of change in a company that *he* owns, the shareholder is decried as a rabble-rouser and a rebel?

I think a large part of it lies in the effects of dilution. In Al's business, there's no question as to who's boss. Al is boss. He owns the business, he pays the bills, and it's his name on the sign out front. But give Al a partner, and whoever is looking for the boss at that company might start looking back and forth, like a person at a tennis match. Toss in a third partner, or a fourth, and the business of finding the boss at the company becomes difficult.

Bigger . . . Better?

When the ownership roster starts running into the hundreds, or even the thousands, clear ownership voice becomes rare. In corporate situations, the general manager (or his corporate equivalent, the CEO) is often left as the only clear and audible voice in the company.

To be heard in an environment of diluted ownership, a shareholder must exercise the democratic process. He or she must survey fellow shareholders and arrive at a consensus of opinion. If that consensus is for change, then change should occur. It is not rabble-rousing; in fact, that very term contradicts the action that is taking place.

The people involved are not, after all, *rabble*. They are the owners of the company. They are not being *roused*. They are being asked for their opinions. When they exercise their rights as owners, they are doing nothing more than what my friend Al does when he changes management at an underperforming business location. Like my friend, they deserve to have their wishes taken into account when change must be made.

It's their company.

That's only right, but that's not the way it works. When management and shareholder opinion clash, management often reacts by digging in, ignoring the opinions of the people whose money fuels the corporate ship, or even by spending that money to fight off shareholder-driven change.

Probably no book in recent years has made as big a business stir among everyday people as *Barbarians at the Gate*. It was even made into a TV movie.

The movie tended to dwell, of course, on the corporate excesses that most people remember from the book—the fleets of executive jets, the managers hob-nobbing with athletes and movie stars, the gray-flannel retreats on posh Caribbean islands.

But what I remember most vividly from that book is one brief scene in which the authors describe a Carolinian farmer—a man whose family had worked for R.J. Reynolds for generations—waiting in the CEO's anteroom. That man in overalls had, through decade after decade of buying Reynolds preferred stock, become the largest individual shareholder in the company. Yet the firm's managers left him cooling his heels in the waiting room, never granting him so much as a moment of their time.

After all, they had what they needed from him. They had his money.

That tableau—the executive too busy to give a shareholder the time of day—has become the cliché of American corporate management. Shareholder opinion is ignored because management "knows better." That the shareholders' grasp of the situation might often be better (from a company's standpoint) has apparently rarely, if ever, entered into the equation.

THE ADVENT OF SHAREHOLDER ACTIVISM

The phrase "shareholder activist" speaks volumes about the popular conception of people who lobby for corporate change.

We all know what "activists" are. They're loud-mouthed radicals who rant, rave, get guidance from little red books, and generally make nuisances of themselves.

Forgive me if I don't see myself in that light. Nor do I see myself as the exception. As an example, I'd like to turn the spotlight for a moment on a fellow who has been one of the most celebrated "activists" of recent years, a man named Robert A.G. Monks.

A Call for Change

Robert Monks is a practicing vegetarian. In times of stress, he turns to meditation, seeking an inner calm before returning to the chaos of the outer world.

A textbook radical, right?

Perhaps not.

If you place stock in physiology, you should know that Bob Monks stands 6' 6" (that's as tall as Michael Jordan).

If educational pedigrees impress you, you should know that he is a graduate of Harvard Law School.

Bob Monks is a successful industrialist whose worth is tallied in the tens of millions, and he has held high-ranking positions in the Reagan administration.

In fact, it was while he was head of the Labor Department's pension and welfare benefits program that he experienced an epiphany of sorts. He formed the opinion that pension fund managers (who invest in stocks to propagate their funds) should be doing more than just purchasing and disposing. As he later told *The Wall Street Journal,* "I got the idea that stock ownership was a responsibility. Before that, I just wanted to trade."

This was in 1984. That a shareholder body has a right to correct intransigent managers is an idea that even now is met with only grudging acceptance. In 1984, it was a foreign language. Add to that the idea that the shareholder body not only has the right to make change, but an *obligation* to do so when performance so dictates, and you have nothing short of a revelation.

Bob Monks' revelation took the form of a speech, "The Institutional Investor as a Corporate Citizen." This single document set institutional investment on its ear. It set a Labor Department policy that said that pension fund managers should be doing more than buying promising stocks and selling bad ones. It said that they should be exercising collective strength to rouse mediocre companies to perform to potential.

It was not what corporate managers wanted to hear.

You see, pension funds have become for this country what the Rockefellers and DuPonts used to be. They have become the major participants in the shareholder world, comprising roughly half of all American equity. The vast majority of the General Motors and the IBMs of the world are owned not by wealthy widows, but by organizations that handle the retirement money for factory workers and snowplow drivers. In fact, state pension funds—notably those for such well-populated states as California and New York—are the largest shareholders, and thus have the most potential muscle in most of the large corporations in this country.

The odd thing about state pension funds is that they are largely amorphous. The people paying into them—the highway workers, traffic cops, park rangers, and government clerks—generally think of them only as a sort of very large savings account, an entity that is given money today in hopes that it will return it tomorrow. The managers of these accounts are judged by performance; if they get reasonable return on investment, they're doing the job. That they should be getting that return not by buying and selling alone, but by speaking up when their holdings performed poorly, was a revelation of sorts.

What Bob Monks did with his speech was nothing less than awaken a sleeping giant—or rather, a whole community of them. Moreover, he awoke giants who were disposed to act as he had suggested. Monks' speech struck a chord with those people whose financial constituency was largely union and government workers. Such constituencies carried with them a moral imperative to do the right thing—especially when the right thing involved correcting managers who were ignoring the wishes of the corporate masses. Right and wrong—including management behavior—become elements under this aegis, and Bob Monks' Labor Department policy drew upon this instinct of corporate citizenship. To the old repertoire of buying and selling, pension fund managers added a new action: *changing*.

A Call to Arms

Bob Monks not only awoke the giants. He joined them.

He began, after his government service, by founding Institutional Shareholder Services, or ISS. At the time, few pension funds had the expertise to analyze complicated proxies, so most automatically took the side of company management in any proxy issue. ISS provided, for a $10,000 fee, the analytical expertise. Many funds—spurred on by the Labor Department policy that Monks initiated—began to use that expertise to do their fiduciary duty.

ISS went beyond analysis, often conducting proxy campaigns for its clients. In 1989, working entirely with institutional investors, it waged a one-week bout to block anti-
takeover measures at Honeywell. Shortly thereafter, the
firm helped add three shareholder representatives to the
Lockheed board and enacted measures that prevented a
poison pill (making the company too expensive to buy)
anti-takeover tactic on the part of Lockheed's management.

But the action that received the widest coverage in the
business press was Monks' 1989–1991 effort to win a board
seat at retail giant Sears, Roebuck & Co. In this case, Sears
turned Monks' own tactics on him, pressuring its own
equivalent of institutional shareholders—Sears employee
benefit plan trustees—to vote with management. Since
employee stock accounted for about a quarter of Sears equity, Monks began with the odds stacked heavily against
him. Company management then added to that advantage
by budgeting $5.6 million—22 times Monks' own proxy
budget—to contest the anti-management measures.

In the end, to no one's surprise, Monks failed to win a
board seat. But the size of Sears' opposition to Monks'
initiatives did not go unnoticed at the company's 1991
annual meeting, which turned into an hour-long
miniversion of the Nuremberg trials, as shareholder after
shareholder stood up and took management to task for poor
performance.

Writing afterward in *The Wall Street Journal*, Monks said,
"The problems at Sears were precisely those appropriate
for shareholder involvement. This was not a case where
there was an industrywide slump beyond the control of
management. This was a case where long-term
underperformance was attributable to a poor mix of business and a lack of accountability to owners. Returns from
stronger divisions were being used to mask the problem
in weaker ones, to the detriment of both. The company
had not met its own goal of 15 percent return on equity
once in 10 years. And shareholders were paying the price."

As so often happens in proxy campaigns, Monks lost the battle at Sears, but won the war. While Monks did not gain a board seat, he did exert enough influence to force Sears Chairman and CEO Edward Brennan to shed three of his five titles and thus invite more outside scrutiny of his performance. The company decided to sell off Coldwell Banker, Allstate Insurance, and Dean Witter Reynolds, the financial service and real estate businesses it had acquired in its quest for diversification, and to concentrate on Sears' core business, retail merchandising. That move alone triggered a $1 billion dollar shift upward in Sears' market price on the New York Stock Exchange.

That, I suppose, is just the point. As investors—and particularly institutional investors—discover a third alternative to the buy/sell method of investment management, the "activists'" becomes a very good side to be on. Robert Monks showed investors that they do have the power to force changes in the companies they own, just as Al has the power to control his auto dealerships.

And entrenched management becomes less and less of a viable alternative.

Chapter *2*

The Antithesis of Gambling

Don't bother looking for me in Las Vegas or Atlantic City. I am not a gambler.

It's not that I am averse to risk. Risk is part of business: always there, even in the most solid of enterprises, an element that must be dealt with if one is to see gain.

But gambling is an invitation to loss.

Now, as an investment counselor, it's obviously in my favor to hold such opinions. Who, after all, would trust his or her money to a person whose stated intention is to gamble with it?

Yet I see others in my profession who are gambling every day—every hour of the day. Worse still, they are doing it with other people's money, plunking down the hard-earned cash of their clients in a vain hope that they will prevail against the odds and make a killing.

Oddly enough, you won't see any of *these* folks in Las Vegas or Atlantic City, either.

They do most of their gambling in places like Wall Street.

"I think I'll try playing the market. . ."

"I got a tip on a hot stock. . ."

"XYZ Corp. has been dropping for three weeks straight; if I buy now, I *bet* it'll go up soon. . ."

Much of the parlance of "investment" comes straight from the racetrack. Indeed, the way most people invest, they may as well be *at* a racetrack. They look at widely distributed and limited information (*The Wall Street Journal* or the *Racing Form*), they seek the counsel of others no better informed than they (trackside "railbirds" or other market "players"), and based on this limited information they place a wager on an event (a race or a period of stock performance) in which the outcome is governed largely by chance.

A few years ago, one of the TV news-magazine shows picked a number of stocks by throwing darts at the daily NYSE listings. They then sought the advice of a number of market gurus, tracked *their* picks against the randomly selected stocks, and compared gains and losses at the end of a year.

Guess what? There wasn't a difference to speak of between the dartboard picks and those stocks selected by the "experts."

There's a reason for this. The stock market, in general, is a lot like the weather. You can input data gathered over the decades, track trends, note seasonal changes, and determine the statistical probability of any particular event taking place on any particular day.

Yet, in the end, both the weather and the stock market are chaotic systems. Meteorologists talk about the "butterfly effect"—a butterfly beats its wings in China, the resulting tiny gust of air combines with others from similarly random forces and, two months later, there's a windstorm in Alberta. The business world is full of such fluttering butterflies, and the sum of all these random factors is so over-whelming as to make market performance unpredictable to any extent that would be useful to the average investor.

Mass "Marketing"

Track records show that institutional investors, in particular, tend to behave like lemmings—those ugly little Norwegian rodents that are prone to mass hysterical tendencies and periodically engage in communal migrations for the sole purpose of flinging themselves into the sea. Biologists are not sure why lemmings do this, and likewise, nobody is quite sure why institutional investors act as they do.

Students of the stock market, among which I number myself, have long felt that institutional investors are the lemmings of the financial world. They behave according to a sort of mob psychology. Very little independent thinking takes place, and accordingly their actions are often irrational, particularly at market peaks and troughs.

Often, institutional investors seem to want to buy stocks that have gone up a lot—just because they've gone up a lot. Likewise, they sell off stocks with falling prices, because the price is falling. The mistake they make comes apparently from thinking that the current trend is the one which is going to continue in perpetuity.

Despite the fact that most institutional money managers have gotten good educations at Wharton, Harvard, or other business schools, and they spend a lot of time on Wall Street, they exhibit an almost uniform method of thinking that becomes a sort of self-reinforcing mechanism. Institutional investors seemingly prefer to be like their colleagues in their actions, and therefore, in their investment results, despite their often-stated objectives of beating other investment managers when it comes to investment performance.

Consequently, institutional investors buy "institutional stocks"—those with the largest capitalization, those that are followed by most other analysts, and those that are most liquid and to buy and sell in large quantities. They also diversify broadly and irrationally in their portfolios in the mistaken belief that diversity results in the best investment performance.

The truly great investment managers of the world—I certainly include here Warren Buffett, the sage of Omaha (who popularized value investing)—use a different method. They buy fewer issues in more concentrated positions of really fine companies. It's the difference between buying a wide variety of cheap jug wines and buying select lots of good and perhaps little-known vintages that you feel are underpriced at present.

This is not the norm in the investment world, but having seen its long-term results, it is the course I prefer.

Most managers won't do this. Most have very little incentive to make a really contrarian call. The risk of personal loss seems too great, and they are afraid of looking like idiots. If they lose with an unconventional style or a stock selection that is not in lock step with their peers—if they, heaven forbid, dare to look at pink-sheet stocks or under-owned companies—they recoil at the possibility of being ridiculed. Most institutional investors seem to prefer to fail conventionally and lemming-like, rather than succeed in an unconventional manner.

VALUE INVESTING

So what am I doing in this profession?

I am a real investor; not a speculator. While I read *The Wall Street Journal* and other investment and financial publications on a regular basis, I am not doing so in an attempt to get the jump on short-term trends. My entire investment philosophy is based not on gambling on the next spasm in the stock market, or short-term stock performance, but on *value*—the underlying, economic worth of a business.

Value investing consists of carefully analyzing all of the things of worth in a company, adding them up, subtracting the liabilities, and comparing the result to the price-per-share at which that company is trading in the marketplace. If the company's intrinsic business value is significantly greater than the market price of its shares, then that company is a logical investment candidate.

There are several statistical methods of assessing the intrinsic value of a business. To these methods must be added a nonstatistical estimation of economic goodwill.

Traditional value investors will focus on:

- Liquidation Value (LV): The expected proceeds if a company were to be dissolved and its assets sold and liabilities paid off—"breakup value" is a variation in which the LV is determined at the best price for each component.

- Net Present Value (NPV): The discounted value of all the future cash flows that a business is expected to generate. This is, to my way of thinking, the best single valuation method, and the one I'd use exclusively if it were only possible to make precise estimates of future cash flows.

- Private Market Value (PMV): Multiples of net earnings or annual cash flows paid when similar businesses were bought or sold in their entirety (publishing companies, for instance, may be assigned PMVs of 10 times cash flow).

But, analysts' walls of numbers aside, this is far from an exact science. Each method of valuation carries with it its own flaw or set of flaws.

LV ignores the value of "goodwill." Goodwill is the association or reputation accorded a business by its consumer public. Orville Redenbacher's Popping Corn is viewed as a superior product by popcorn aficionados, and so the value of the company is greater than the stated book value reflected on the company's balance sheet. Nikon, Boeing, and Harley-Davidson are all seen by the public as companies at or near the top of their respective fields.

On the other side of the coin, goodwill can never be valued exactly, and goodwill, when considered, is sometimes overestimated.

NPV is dependent on the appraiser's ability to reliably predict a company's future performance. If a vineyard consistently sells all of the wine it produces each season, and the price the public is willing to pay for that wine has gone up every year for the last two decades, a reasonable analysis might be that future cash flows can be predicted—based, for instance, on the average annual yield in barrels, multiplied by the price, with average annual increases taken into account.

But lots of things can happen to upset this prediction.

Weather can reduce or even wipe out a harvest. A bad crop may produce a mediocre product. Insects or groundwater contamination may ruin all or part of the vines under cultivation. NPV is subject to many of the chaotic forces that wreak havoc with economic and financial predictors in general.

And the problem with PMV is that more often than not, apples are compared, if not to oranges, at least to pears. No two companies are exactly the same, and some within the same field can be entirely different.

If, for instance, you are looking at a publishing company with an annual cash flow of $1 million, you may look at other publishing companies, see that they have sold recently for 10 times cash flow, and think that you have stumbled upon a $10 million company.

However, you note that the market capitalization is $6 million, which leads you to conclude that the company is undervalued by $4 million. Where's the checkbook?

But, the fact is there are many different kinds of publishing companies. Perhaps the firms to which you're making comparisons were all companies that produced trade periodicals while you're looking at a business that publishes community directories.

They're similar, but different. And the difference may easily account for the undervaluation of your subject company.

Given the fallibility of each of these methods of valuation, it's easy to see that each type of investment can produce inferior results if improperly applied.

It takes a lot of hard work, patience, and . . . patience.

Guidelines for Value Investing

Warren Buffett said, "The market, like the Lord, helps those who help themselves. But, unlike the Lord, the market does not forgive those who know not what they do." My firm has developed several principles that have served us well in value investing. They are:

- *Err on the side of conservatism*: Taken literally, this means using the *lowest* of the three value estimation figures; in practice, it usually means using a low average, with emphasis on NPV.

- *Know the field in which you are investing*: Going to Thanksgiving dinner at a friend's house one year, I mentioned I'd bring a couple of bottles of very nice Nouveau Beaujolais. My friend said, "Oh, if it's that nice, can you bring me a case? I'll set some aside." But the fact is Nouveau Beaujolais must be drunk in the year it was bottled—usually by mid-December of that year—or it turns to vinegar. I brought my friend some Cabernet Sauvignon instead. She knew enough about wine to know that some of it improves with age, but she didn't know enough to realize that Nouveau Beaujolais is an exception. People make the same kind of mistakes with investments every day. My firm concentrates investments in several businesses that we think we know well—financial companies (banks, thrifts, and insurance companies), healthcare businesses, auto aftermarket companies, and certain manufacturers of proprietary products—and we have chartered financial analysts who specialize in their own areas. We don't take shots in the dark.

• *Stay in your own backyard*: My investment-counsel firm is headquartered in Bloomfield Hills, Michigan, near Detroit—not far from the Ohio and Indiana borders. A large number of the firms in which we invest are located in Michigan, Ohio, and Indiana. This gives us an opportunity to go out and kick the tires, not only before we buy, but afterward.

Getting to know *management*, and understanding its philosophy, is the most important part of visiting a company. Making an estimation of a management team's skills, ways of thinking, and integrity is critical to identifying superior long-term investments. A management team's attitude toward enhancing shareholder value can be the difference between a mediocre investment and a great one. Investment is buying, and you should never buy blind.

• *Be contrarian*: The old investment adage of "buy low, sell high" has one flaw—how do you know what is low and what is high until they're so far in

the past as to be useless to you? But you can predict future needs. Again, it's like buying straw hats
in January—you can get them cheaply then, yet
know you'll have something of value come July. In
the late 1980s, my firm evaluated a Michigan database company called MEDSTAT Group, Inc., which
does outcomes analysis for healthcare organizations. Knowing healthcare to be an area of growing concern, we realized MEDSTAT would be increasingly important to its customers as time went
on. In addition, our analysis showed MEDSTAT's
principal asset, its database, didn't even appear on
the company's listing of assets. We began buying
shares long before healthcare became a political
campaign issue, and were rewarded nearly five
years later when MEDSTAT stock multiplied in
value as a result of a buyout by a Canadian company that appreciated MEDSTAT's true value and
paid a full and fair price, which was more than four
times our average costs.

- *Be patient*: You'll note in the above example that it
  took nearly half a decade for our MEDSTAT investment to come to fruition. We accumulated a large
  position slowly, without making large purchases
  that would have forced up the price. In the meantime, MEDSTAT was a solid investment in a truly
  superior business. This really is the difference between speculation and value investing: speculation
  is gambling, but value investing is like farming.
  And just as a farmer may have to maintain an or-
  chard for several years before it begins to produce
  fruit, the value investor may have to wait patiently
  for his investment to mature. Some years you just
  plant, and some years you harvest.

I realize that all of this may not sound as sexy as "playing
the market."

Sorry.

The appeal of "playing the market" is the same as the appeal of winning the lottery—you get something for nothing (or nearly nothing), with little work on your part. Unfortunately, that's not the way the investing world works.

That's the reason that I don't mind setting my value-investing "secrets" down in print.

First of all, none of this is really a secret. Value-investing principles are used, day in and day out, by any number of conservative investors around the world, some quite low-profile and others—such as Warren Buffett, Mike Price, Peter Lynch, or Chuck Royce—quite visible. You don't read about others because they don't make the big killings that make headlines. They just make steady, very acceptable, above-average returns.

And secondly, I know that putting these ideas down on paper is not going to make one iota of difference to those people who are determined to get rich quick. Value investing involves work—hard work and lots of it—and speculators haven't the perseverance to make a go of it. In 28 years of managing other people's money, I've found that those who are content to grow rich slowly usually have more to show for it in the end.

Today, it seems that investors who are seeking value often end up in debates over the relative merits of "value" and "growth." These two approaches to selecting stocks are argued endlessly by advocates of each camp, yet I have always felt them to be two sides of the same coin. When real value investors are attempting to determine the intrinsic value of an enterprise, they are simply calculating the discounted present value of the future cash flows of a company. Growth investors are just making a calculation of this determined value by the application of various ratios. The results are pretty much the same.

It goes without saying that in order to diligently perform no fewer than three estimations of value on a candidate business, a value investor is going to do a lot more prepurchase homework than a speculator.

Benefits of Proactive Investing

In addition, for investors who are prone to be proactive, much of the work of investing comes after shares are purchased.

A speculator buys without regard for value and doesn't appreciate the difference between price and value. He just wants a quick score.

Value investors purchase undervalued companies and hold those shares at least until the company is trading at a price closer to full value.

But in the meantime, the proactive investor is not just waiting for a ship to come in. The proactive investor continues to monitor company performance, *continuously assesses value using a variety of different methods,* and if the company is performing below potential, *does something about it.*

A speculator does become a shareholder. But a proactive investor acts like an owner of a company. And, like any business owner who is dissatisfied with performance, a diligent proactive investor is not averse to, as Ross Perot would say, "lift the hood and tinker with it."

This hands-on involvement can be anything from an informal sit-down with the CEO or board to a full-scale campaign to get the proactive investor elected to the board where he or she can effectively champion those changes in practice or policy that will enable the business to perform at full potential.

This is not an argument for micromanagement. Effective managers should have the authority and autonomy to move quickly; to do otherwise is to hamper the business to the point that it cannot grow, or even function.

But occasionally, the reason a company was undervalued to begin with is that its managers were *not* effective. In such a case, the investor has three choices: 1) live with it; 2) sell the stock; or 3) make the necessary changes.

Option 3 is not the easy one. But it is the rational one. And it is, in my view, the course more professional investors should take if we are to avoid going through our entire careers in an abstraction.

The important thing in purchasing any stock is the recognition of the fact that when one buys stock, he is purchasing a share of a business, not just a stock certificate. In *The Intelligent Investor*, Benjamin Graham wrote: "Investing is most intelligent when it is business-like."

Graham's student, Warren Buffett, called these "the nine most important words ever written about investing."

The investor who believes that he owns nothing more than a piece of paper is an investor who is removed from actual corporate developments. On the other hand, owners who truly feel they own a portion of a company are closer to its life blood.

Too often, corporate management teams and boards have likewise taken the popular view that their shareholders were just holders of paper, as opposed to the true owners of the business. And this made it seductively easy for management to breach its fiduciary responsibility to the people who truly owned the company.

That's why it's critically important to recognize that when you purchase shares in a company, you become an owner. Owners have certain responsibilities. Shirking those responsibilities—looking the other way while the managers on your payroll do less than adequate work—does more than reduce your return on investment. It diminishes our economy as a whole.

We must begin to view ourselves as investors and businesspeople, instead of speculators, since investment is actually the antithesis of gambling. I think it's time we reduce the distance we've imposed on the relationships we, as investors, have with the companies we own. We should look closely at what we've bought. When those who manage for us do well, we should applaud and reward them.

And when things break. . .

. . .isn't it obvious that we should fix them?

Chapter *3*

I Am Not a Kook

The general public has (often rightly) a somewhat jaundiced view of those who make a living in finance and investment. To the man who labors on an assembly line, or runs a hardware store, it sometimes seems that investment professionals don't really *do* anything. They don't make a product, don't grow crops, don't fix your roof—they don't fall, generally, into what the average man thinks of as the world of conventional trades or professions. That many in the investment profession seem to generate a great deal of money through this apparent inaction just makes most people look askance even more.

This is partly the result of an industry that does little to police or qualify its participants. In today's parlance, a "financial consultant" is too often an insurance agent who is trying to expand his horizons. While many people do buy and sell stocks, they do so directly through a brokerage house, and they have about the same respect for the broker that a compulsive gambler has for his bookie. They see the person they buy their stocks from as a go-between, a middleman who marks up the price and does very little in return.

I'm happy to say that my clients have a very different point of view. I don't sell stock to my clients. I invest their money in profitable businesses. My clients see the people in my profession as talented and hardworking individuals who do the very extensive legwork and the intricate analysis necessary to determine which of the myriad companies trading publicly today have the potential to reward a prospective owner with good return and solid value.

But my clients—and the clients of similar chartered financial analysts—are in the minority in today's investment scene. Most people, even those who are making a living at it, are either investing their money blindly or operating according to protocols that have little or no worth when it comes to distinguishing investment opportunities that can offer high intrinsic value.

Given the high number of lemming-like trend-followers and out-and-out snake-oil salespeople in today's financial scene, I can't blame people for being skeptical.

When I have called other shareholders on the telephone and asked them for support in altering the management of a company in which we both had ownership (as I have had to do with one of the companies in which I invested— a northern Michigan thrift), I have had some very emotional responses.

Some people just plain hung up. Others got angry with me, saying that they had known the president of the company for years, and that his family had founded the company, and how dare I say that he wasn't doing such a good job?

So, let's make one thing clear from the outset. To paraphrase the late Richard M. Nixon: I am not a kook.

It's important to get that out early, because if you go by what management has to say in their communication with shareholders, dissident shareholders are almost always portrayed as kooks, rabble-rousers, opportunists trying to turn a fast buck, or malcontents who are trying to upset the workings of the company.

But you've got to consider the source of this criticism. After all, the first priority of just about any dissident shareholder—particularly one who has finally resorted to the very expensive and time-consuming measure of a proxy contest—is generally to effect a change in management.

And people will say just about anything to keep their jobs.

But if you listen to both sides of the story, you might find your eyes have been opened.

When I spoke with shareholders about the thrift in which we were invested, their defensiveness faded when I asked, "Are you aware that the president of this thrift has been investing our money in junk bonds and derivatives?"

Suddenly, I was no longer some malcontent wacko. Suddenly, I was somebody with whom they wanted to speak.

Another reason people look askance at dissident shareholders is that it has become very popular in recent years to use the mechanisms of shareholder dissidence to lever radical politics into the inner workings of companies.

For example, shortly before the annual meeting, every corporation sends out proxy statements, and if that company is of any size—and particularly if it is multinational—part of the mailing will be proposals being raised by political groups who've bought token shares so they can use the proxy mailing as a soapbox upon which to declaim the plights of whales, repressed foreign populations, toxic wastes, old-growth forests, the ozone layer, snail darters, and a plethora of other issues, which are near and dear to the hearts of their petitioners but have little to do with getting the company to do what a company is supposed to do—turn a profit.

It's little wonder that a friend of mine refers to those little proxy-issue summary sheet portions of the pre-meeting mailing as "the bomb-thrower pamphlets."

Yet, if you are conducting a campaign to get representation on the board, the company summary of your case is going to land right in the middle of the bomb-thrower pamphlet. And the implication is obvious: dissident shareholders and Ché Guevara—birds of a feather, right?

My principal reason for writing this book is not to explain how to be a dissident shareholder or how to conduct a proxy campaign. Only a handful of investors will have the extensive means necessary to take on a corporation in the proxy arena, and those folks already know how to run a campaign.

Rather, my reason for writing this book is to try to reach those millions of investors whose votes will decide if America is going to insist on excellence in business, or if we'll settle instead for a situation in which mediocre management is more and more the norm.

Rebellion, after all, does not always signal a bloodbath.

I remember sitting in front of Mike Price in April 1994 at the annual shareholder meeting of Michigan National Corporation. MNC operates one of the Midwest's major banks, and at this meeting, Mike—who is manager of the very successful Mutual Series Fund and one of the most talented value investors in the world—stood up and delivered a brief but impassioned injunction against MNC's management, which had delivered poor operational results over a period of several years.

Mike urged his fellow shareholders to support his position—that the company should be sold for the benefit of all of us who owned it.

It was an emotional moment for me. Bob Mylod, Michigan National's CEO, was and is a personal friend, and I likewise was close to several of the board members. Nonetheless, when I looked objectively at the company's results, I had to agree with Mike.

The record of earnings was decidedly substellar, the return on assets and equity poor by any measure, despite the value of MNC's franchise. By my own appraisal, the stock, which was trading at about $55 a share, was going for half of its intrinsic value.

Subsequently, due at least in part to Mike Price's prodding, MNC's board voted to sell the company to National Australia Bank for $110 a share.

The merger was announced in February 1995, less than a year after Mike first presented his case.

Mike Price was, at the time, the largest individual shareholder of MNC. He controlled 8.2 percent of outstanding shares through his mutual funds. Yet he was not being selfish in his demands.

Mike Price saw a great franchise in Michigan National, an underutilized and under-managed asset base, and he justifiably felt that the shareholder value—not just his value, but everyone's—existed far and above the price at which the stock had been selling.

The merger proved him absolutely right. My own analysis had concurred, and even though I was a passive investor in this case, I had been loading up on Michigan National stock before Mike ever spoke up, certain that someone would do so sometime soon, and knowing what the inevitable outcome would be.

No proxy bloodbath was forthcoming in this instance. No one had to hire lawyers and square off with management at 10 paces.

Instead, Mike Price honorably and publicly encouraged management to, in the parlance of our times, "do the right thing"—to maximize shareholder value.

He did threaten a proxy contest, and this no doubt influenced the board heavily, but I later complimented the board for taking actions in the shareholders' interests without having to be pushed into the action by force of vote. I sent a note to my friend Bob Mylod—who would probably be displaced after some period of transition—congratulating him for his courage.

After all, my first concern in this case—and Mike Price's first concern and even Bob Mylod's—had to be for fair treatment of shareholders. I'm grateful to both men, and I'm grateful the system works—even if it took a rebel to get the ball rolling.

A decade or two ago, when politicians talked about a "silent majority," they were referring to people who had fallen into apathy and no longer used their vote.

In corporate politics today, the sad fact of the matter is that a great number of shareholders may not even realize that they *have* a vote. And if they do, they may not be sure how to use it.

This is a plea to shareholders everywhere, to exercise their shareholder franchise with the same care and judgment with which they would exercise their political franchise. Be a participant in corporate democracy. Strong industry is, after all, as important to a country in the long run as strong government.

So listen when you're contacted about corporate governance. The person who's calling or writing may not be a weirdo after all.

In fact, he just might be a prophet.

Chapter *4*

Davids and Goliaths

When it comes to governance in business, democratic action is the cornerstone of shareholder activism. Of course, "one person, one vote," the hallmark of American democracy, does not apply when it comes to corporate politics. People don't vote in annual and special meetings; shares do. If I own one share of XYZ stock, and you own 11,000, your voice counts 11,000 times as much as mine when it comes to making decisions about the company.

Now, let me say right up front that I like this system. I believe in it, support it, and happily defend it. Those utopians who believe that all shareholders should be treated equally are confusing governance with government.

Government decisions—decisions concerning the running of a country—affect all citizens equally. If the government decides that people have to have a license to fish, or cannot receive Social Security until age 55, those laws must be observed by each of us.

But when it comes to corporate governance, the profits or losses created by company decisions are borne by shareholders in direct proportion to the number of shares owned. If, in our example above, XYZ Company stood to lose $100 of value a share, I may be looking at the loss of the price of a pig, but you'd be on the verge of losing the farm. In such a situation, of course your voice should speak the loudest; you have the most to lose.

The downside is that it's easy for smaller shareholders to feel they've gotten lost in the corporate shuffle.

Not all do. There are still those malcontents who buy a single share of Exxon so they can go to the annual meeting and have a shot at dressing down the chairman in public. These people are the antithesis of Teddy Roosevelt's aphorism, "Talk softly, but carry a big stick." They get kicked out in fairly short order, as well they should. A stock certificate is not a license to ridicule someone else, or to subject everyone else at a meeting to piece of performance art.

Nevertheless, minority ownership in a company—even a minority as tiny as a single share—is ownership nonetheless. And when a business you own is not performing to potential because of poor management, you have a right to speak up.

So how do you make yourself heard?

One way is by listening.

If a company is losing money or mismanaging itself to the point that even the smaller shareholders are starting to feel it, it is almost a certainty that the larger shareholders have not only felt it as well, but are raising hellfire and brimstone over the matter. If you own, for example, 300 shares of stock in a pharmaceuticals company, and you've been reading in *The Wall Street Journal* that they're wasting money developing a line of expensive drugs for which there is such low demand that the investment can never be recouped—read on. You'll probably also read about a shareholder (or, more likely, a shareholders' committee) that is in the process of holding management's collective feet to the fire over the fiasco.

If that's the case, offer your support. Write the committee a letter (remember the avalanche of mail on the judge's desk in *Miracle on 34th Street*?), and if it comes to a proxy vote, vote in the best interests of yourself and your fellow shareholders.

I said it was rare for a company to raise the ire of smaller shareholders without likewise angering the big ones. Rare, perhaps, but sometimes it can happen.

In the cases of firms that engage in highly specialized businesses, or firms whose businesses require special analysis to be properly understood, I suppose it is sometimes possible for a smaller shareholder who understands the business intimately to smell something rotten in Denmark before it reaches the noses of the big guys.

This goes against the grain of wise investment; a good investor never puts money in a business that he or she does not understand. But such things happen, nonetheless.

In such a case, my advice to the smaller investor would be to seek out the larger investors, including institutional investors (using the same methods I've outlined elsewhere in this book), and explain to them what you know. If you can make a case for better profits or better value through shareholder pressure, you may well find a willing ally who can champion your cause.

Certainly, in any corporation you will find Davids and Goliaths. But unlike the biblical duo, corporate Davids and Goliaths do not have to be at odds with one another. And in many cases, just as in the ancient story, it will be a David who carries the day.

You may only have a few votes, but it only takes a few to make a difference. Don't remain silent; it's your company, too.

Chapter 5

One Step Away from the Trees

If business ran logically, we would not have situations where shareholders wanted one thing and directors did another. But business does not run logically, and the reason it does not is that even though we dress in suits, talk on cellular phones, hang art on the walls of our offices, and go to the theater on weekends, we are, all of us, still only a step or two out of the trees.

I realize that this will irritate any number of people. But I think it is a mistake to flatly deny our animal nature, particularly since, when you come right down to it, it is that very animal nature that is actually running the show.

Animals in nature congregate for one of two reasons. Herd animals congregate for defense. Most herd animals are herbivores—buffalo, elephants, zebra, and the like. They do not need one another to find food, but they do need one another to avoid becoming food for others. By congregating in sometimes extremely large numbers, herd animals escape death by either confusing predators (the herd is literally so large that the predator has difficulty distinguishing a single victim), or by ganging up to butt or trample an attacker.

Pack animals, on the other hand, congregate in more dis-crete groups for the purpose of locating and obtaining food. Pack animals are carnivores. They are hunters. The more successful use strategy in their hunting (such as taking turns chasing a prey animal until it has literally run itself to death).

The hierarchies of these two animal groups are very dif-ferent. Herds often have two types of dominant animal—a dominant male, who runs the show when it comes to procreation, and a dominant female, who actually governs the group and shepherds it from food source to food source.

Pack animals have one "alpha" individual (almost always a male) who holds sway over both the mating pool and the manner in which the pack hunts and eats.

Both groups have pecking orders—a hierarchy within the group—although the order is much more vague among herd animals.

So where does man fit in?

Man is unusual in that (with apologies to my vegetarian friends. . .), man is an omnivore. Human beings in their primitive state can gather fruits or vegetables from a na-tive habitat, hunt meat in the wild, or harvest both flora and fauna through agriculture.

Primitive man both gathered food and hunted, and for this reason, an unusual group-living structure evolved in which the group behaved both as a herd (defending itself) and as a pack (hunting cooperatively).

Most of what we do in groups today is based on the herd/pack dichotomy. Nations exist for the common defense of their people—but nations also attack other nations in or-der to get their resources. Our gatherings, our cities, see to the well-being of the citizenry, picking up their garbage, providing police protection, and caring for the sick or im-poverished. But our cities are also engines of commerce, competing with other cities for income-producing businesses and waging political battles for tax dollars.

Mankind never abandoned its herd/pack roots. We simply institutionalized them.

LEADER OF THE PACK: CEO, BOARD, OR SHAREHOLDERS?

Unfortunately, in institutionalizing the same social structure that got us along for thousands of years on the Serengeti, we also institutionalized the dilemmas that come with organizing a group of individuals who simultaneously act as both predators and prey.

Chief among these is the role, and purpose, of the group's leadership.

Man is the only group animal that does not have consistent patriarchal or matriarchal tendencies across the globe. Whales, in any ocean you find them, will always be led by a dominant cow. Gorilla groups around the world are led by a dominant male. But different human cultures have different ways of running things. In Samoa, women have the ultimate say in things, while in Japan, a woman may have little say in anything at all.

Our western culture has generally been male-dominated, but even here, there are exceptions. For an example, you need look no further than Queen Elizabeth I, whose authority was unquestioned during her time.

And, male or female, the leader of a human group has always had the conundrum of needing to decide, in any given situation, whether he or she is the chief of a herd or the leader of a pack.

There are profound differences.

Herd chieftains are empowered to act only for the good of the herd; their job is to lead the group to food and water and initiate appropriate actions (defensive grouping or stampede) when the herd is threatened.

Pack leaders, on the other hand, act primarily for their own benefit. They intimidate lesser individuals within the group through sheer size or strength, and through such intimidation ensure that only the best genes (their own) are passed on into future generations of the group.

Because, intellectually, we view self-sacrifice as noble and we abhor violence, we want our leaders to be herd chieftains. And because that is what we want, that is what our leaders purport to be. But it is a very rare individual who does not bring pack-leader tendencies into any position of authority.

The evidence is there, before us, in modern corporations. Social-experiment oddities aside, most companies are set up to lend homage and honor, as well as authority, to their CEOs. They get the largest salaries, the biggest offices, and other signs of respect.

In his book, *On a Clear Day You Can See General Motors*, John DeLorean noted that at one time, you could tell how important a GM executive was by the size of the contingent that was sent to meet him at the airport. The covey of "suits" wasn't there for any practical purpose; they simply showed up to *honor* the executive.

Organization charts, those indispensable who's-on-first documents, are really codified representations of a pack's pecking order. They're blatantly obvious: the alpha-animal is the one at the top of the page.

More enlightened executives realize this and try to edit the charts into a more horizontal sharing of power, but I've yet to see an org-chart that did not show a president, chairman, or CEO at the top of the hill.

And I've never seen an org-chart that depicted shareholders as the ultimate sources of authority.

Followers Pay the Price

The solution to controlling a pack-leader executive is, of course, to use pack tactics. In nature, an animal leads a pack until another animal (or group of animals) intimidates him into backing down. In corporations, an individual runs a company until he or she is demoted or fired.

In straightforward owner/manager relationships, this action can be immediate and direct. If the owner of a private business gets to the office on Monday and discovers that her manager has been operating the company for his own benefit, she discharges him (and perhaps sues him), finds a new manager, and that's the end of it.

But in a corporation in which no individual or institutional investor has sufficient power to take such an action, the lead executive typically finds little real opposition to his pack-leader behavior. Since the executive often has enormous influence (sometimes sole influence) over who gets to sit on the board of directors, the board becomes a reflection of the executive's philosophies. And the tendency is to lend less and less credence and authority to the wishes of the actual owners and more authority to the visible leader—the chief executive.

One Example: The Puritan-Bennett Takeover Attempt

Late in 1994, medical device maker Puritan-Bennett Corporation used a poison pill strategy to fend off a takeover attempt by Thermo Electron Corporation. The takeover attempt was admittedly hostile: Thermo pretty much wanted to swallow Puritan up.

So, was Puritan's success in thwarting the tender offer a happy occasion?

Not if you were a Puritan shareholder.

The evening that the tender offer expired, Puritan was trading at $18.25 on the NASDAQ. Thermo's offer had been $24.50 a share—about a third over trading price.

An overwhelming majority—72 percent—of Puritan share-holders had agreed to sell their stock to Thermo but failed to realize their profit because Puritan's board killed the deal.

Now, tell me: If you were a Puritan shareholder, would this have irritated you?

The Puritan board apparently did nothing illegal. A majority of shares *tendered* is not the same as a majority of shares voted at a company *meeting*. To date, the courts have usually ruled that the decisions concerning takeovers lie with a company's board of directors.

But ethically, it's hard to see such a rebuttal of shareholder wishes as anything less than the board thumbing their noses at the wishes of the true owners of the company.

Why on earth would they do that?

The snide view is that they do it because they can.

Boards can ignore such implicit expressions of shareholder desires and still not suffer under the law. They know that whatever reaction shareholders have to getting the door slammed in their faces is going to take a long time and cost the shareholders money.

The shareholders may want to immediately give the board the boot, but in order to do that, they have to: a) form a committee; b) get their communications with one another "blessed" by the SEC; c) either call for a special company meeting or wait for the next annual shareholders' meeting; d) conduct an expensive and time-consuming proxy campaign; and e) remove the board by electing replacements. From start to finish, it could take a year.

Not quite the same as getting your hand slapped while it's still in the cookie jar.

Another reason that the board might ignore shareholder wishes is because the board feels that, based on proprietary information not released to most shareholders, the proceeds of an alternate plan of action (coming out with a remarkable new product that will allow the company to pay extremely high dividends, selling the company in another deal that has not yet taken form, etc.) will be of greater benefit to shareholders than the one at hand.

My personal feelings are that such an explanation, while frequently offered, is rarely true.

A third reason that boards go deaf, dumb, and blind to shareholder wishes is that the board, in its heart of hearts, thinks the shareholders are—for want of a better word—stupid.

A director might reason, "The tender offer gives the shareholder a margin of $6.25 a share, but based on our past performance, we will pay dividends of $3 a share every year over the next three. That means that in three years' time, we will be giving the shareholders $2.75 *more* than what they would get in this offer—and they would still have their investment. Rebuffing the offer is the better course."

Very considerate. But this reasoning also implies that the shareholders were too dumb to figure this out for themselves, and that is quite a leap.

What's more likely is that the shareholders (individuals and fund managers alike) also did the same math, but came to the conclusion that they'd rather have $6.25 today than $9.00 three years from now. Only they can't, because the board has decided not to let them sell what's rightfully theirs.

If it sounds like shareholders are blameless victims in this scenario, let me assure you that by and large, that is anything but the case.

As individuals within the group, shareholders, too, operate for the most part according to pack or herd principles.

Pack animals—predators—are motivated by greed. Observe a pack of hyenas after a kill and you'll see that they expend about as much energy fighting among themselves as they did in bringing down their prey. Each individual in the group is trying to get a little more for himself or herself, and each is trying to prevent the others in the group from getting the better part of the deal. The snarling and nipping can go on for hours.

Herd animals, on the other hand, are motivated by fear. An impala by itself in the middle of a vast African plain is a very nervous impala, indeed. It has no herd into which to blend and confuse those that hunt it. It has no fellows to watch while it grazes. There is nothing protecting its back.

The ups and downs of the stock market—indeed, the ups and downs of the economy—are almost entirely the result of this herd/pack dichotomy among speculators operating in the guise of investors.

A stock begins to go up in price, and a speculator, hoping the trend will continue, buys in. If it continues to go up, greed may motivate him to buy even more.

But let that stock fall in price and fear may set in. What if it falls even further? What if it never stops falling? What will happen to his capital? The speculator sells out.

Legitimate investors—people who buy into a company for the long run—may not wear their hearts so prominently upon their sleeves, but those deep-rooted animal tendencies are still there. They simply manifest themselves in different forms.

WHY WE FOLLOW OUR INSTINCTS

The one overall abiding rule of herd behavior is obedience to the will of the herd, as expressed by the dominant animal. When the head cow starts walking and leading a herd of buffalo to a new area, the buffalo do not caucus and discuss the matter. The buffalo migrate. Period.

To do otherwise is to produce chaos, and a herd in chaos is vulnerable to attack.

That blind obedience to a dominant will is what produces such phrases as "my country right or wrong" (certainly one of the most stupid utterances ever to fall out of the history books), and it is what allows managers to govern many corporations in pretty much any way they choose.

How many times have you questioned an executive's action and then stopped yourself by saying, "Well, he must know what he's doing. . ." or, "Maybe he knows something I don't. . ."?

That's a herd animal thinking. It is in our nature to want to trust those whom we appoint to positions of leadership. But when they use that leadership to gather their own power (pack behavior) rather than to benefit the group, the result can be counterproductive.

On the other hand, as pack animals, we like to overpower others and make ours the most powerful group. This leads to situations like GM trying to sell more cars and trucks than Ford, or Pepsi trying to get more market share than Coke. The result is price wars, sacrifice of margin, and even cases (this happened in the late 1980s) where car companies were selling entry models at a significant loss just to bolster market share.

In reality, market share doesn't make one iota of difference. It's margins that count, and sales without margins are no better (worse, actually) than no sales at all.

Yet, in a we're-gonna-get-'em fervor, shareholders will too often actually support such suicidal tactics, clinging to the illogical belief that if their company eventually comes out on top in sales, then of course it will somehow wind up making money. That's not the way it works, and the shareholders should realize that, but such thinking is done with the gut rather than the brain, and the outcome is the result of this faulty reasoning. Group greed among shareholders is essentially the same thing as mob action, and mob action produces riots.

Now, I realize this all sounds like I'm saying that organized business is inherently doomed by the primitive being who dwells in each of us. But I don't actually feel that to be true.

Look, instead, at the core of every corporate setback, of every bad series of decisions that was allowed to go unchecked by the shareholders, and what you'll find is a dearth of usable information.

It is the absence of information—a shortfall in communication—that triggers the retreat into our herd/pack animal selves.

What triggers most market panics?

Rumors. Faced with an absence of hard information, we manufacture "soft" knowledge to fill the gap, guessing—and often guessing wrong.

What makes us stand by while bad decisions are made by those we put into power?

Paralysis. Unless we know of a better course of action, we too often do nothing, allowing bad judgment to prevail.

Fortunately, there is a remedy for the information gap, and that remedy is communication.

COMMUNICATION = EVOLUTION

The ancient Greeks elevated themselves above packs or herds by developing democracy. Democracy gave each individual a vote and allowed the true will of the masses to be heard.

The democratic system worked well in Greece, which was a collection of small city-states, each capable of easily assembling its population for a vote when decisions needed to be made.

But when that system was tried on a larger scale, it broke down.

The problem was ineffective communication. When Rome came to power, it admired the Greek system but could not assemble the Roman citizens—who were flung all over what was then the known world—for voting when decisions needed to be made.

The Romans reacted by creating a republican system. Republics work by implied consent. Groups within a given area elect a single representative who presumably knows the will of his constituency, and this representative then does the actual voting.

The republican system is the way we govern today. When the United States has presidential elections, for instance, we may think that we are voting for the candidates who are vying for the office but, in actuality, we are simply tallying support for one representative or another, who will eventually gather as the Electoral College and do the actual electing.

The point to which I'm coming is that this is an antiquated system, and it becomes more antiquated with each passing day.

And yet, it is the system that is used not only to run our government, but our businesses, as well.

As shareholders, we typically get one shot a year at speaking relatively freely with one another and making our wishes known—the annual meeting. At that meeting, we elect representatives—the board—who are then expected to know our wishes and govern the company accordingly.

Of course, it doesn't necessarily work that way. Directors may have different opinions from the majority of shareholders, or directors may have their opinions handed to them by a CEO. And those are the situations that lead to problems.

In a world with faxes, e-mail, and touch-tone dialing, it seems to me ridiculous that we are saddled with a system that assumes a lack of communication and so empowers the few to think on behalf of the many—particularly when it is the money of the many that is fueling the machine.

There are two things shareholders can do to make this system work for them.

The first is to petition both lawmakers and the SEC for a continued loosening of the rules governing shareholder communications. A freer discourse and open dialogue gives voice to the masses and allows a company's true owners to reach a consensus of opinion.

The second is to hand that opinion on to those who are making the actual decisions, so bad choices will not be made in a vacuum.

The important point is that while a change in shareholder communication regulations is a downstream wish, communication with a company's directors is a reality.

It has never been easier for an individual to convey his or her wishes to the people who run our companies. Lick a stamp or push a button on a fax, and you can put your thinking in their hands. If your position in the corporation is substantial, you can probably even reach them on the telephone or fly in for a meeting.

Communication turns the dumb masses into a speaking, sentient entity. It is the first key to making a corporation work for the people who actually own it. And it is the only thing that can truly get us down from the trees and put the law of tooth and nail firmly and finally to rest.

Chapter *6*

The Shark and Its Natural Place in the Universe

Sentimentalists can't stand people like me.

I am not without some sympathy for their point of view. Tradition is a wonderful thing. But in a capitalist society, business—while it should never be heartless—simply cannot afford to be sentimental at the expense of profit. A company that has gone blind to its market must have its eyes opened, or it will stumble sightlessly into oblivion.

That's where "outside" investors such as myself come in. We restore what is necessary within a company. We restore vision.

A BELOVED DINOSAUR

Not long ago, I had visitors from out of town, and we found ourselves at the Dawson Great Lakes Museum in Detroit's Belle Isle Park, killing a half-hour before our dinner reservation in Greektown.

One of the newer parts of this interesting little museum is the entire pilothouse from the ore-carrier *William Clay Ford*. An impressive exhibit, the pilothouse is mounted

49

on a second story on the river side of the museum, giving visitors a perspective very similar to that which was once enjoyed by the old vessel's captain.

As I was walking through the pilothouse, I paused to look at a big mechanical typewriter sitting on a stand across from the chart table. The museum's curator, who was walking with my party, noticed my interest.

"The crew used that to make logbook entries and fill out Coast Guard reports," he told me. "We felt it was important to include it in the exhibit—you know, a lot of kids today have never seen a typewriter."

Now, that gave me pause.

Although typewriters of one sort or another have been around for quite a while (Mark Twain actually used a typewriter to complete some of his later works), I, like most members of my generation, still tended to think of them as an icon of the modern-day office. But when I got to my own offices the next day, I listened and realized that the museum curator had been right.

The staccato tapping of typewriters—a sound which I'd heard for so long that I eventually had learned to ignore it—was now conspicuously absent. What I heard instead were telephones, and the faint, muted clicking of computer keyboards.

I went on a typewriter hunt in the office that morning, and I found. . .one.

It was the kind of typewriter that Buck Rogers might have designed. Not only electric, but *electronic*, with light-emitting diodes, a little liquid-crystal display screen, memory buffers, a self-correcting feature, changeable font wheels, a tractor-feed for form paper, and a little port in the back where one could plug in a cord and use the typewriter as a backup printer for a computer. When I turned it on, it blinked its lights enthusiastically and whirred and beeped at me. Yet even this paragon of typewriters was sitting under a dust cover on a table half-hidden behind a potted fern, with not even a chair before it to suggest that it was occasionally used.

"Oh, *that*," my office assistant said half-apologetically when I asked her about the typewriter. "We used to use it to address envelopes, before we got the envelope feeder for the laser printer."

And that's really what happened to typewriters in general, isn't it? When I went off to college, my father gave me a Smith-Corona in a carrying case. Today, it would be a high-memory laptop, a fax/modem, and a portable printer.

Times have changed.

So what do you do nowadays with a company that's in the business of manufacturing typewriters?

If the company's value far exceeds its price—if the stock is trading at, say, 50 percent of actual value—and if the company has holdings that serve a growth industry (like computers), you might actually want to invest in it. And then you might want to do everything within your power to convince the directors to sell off the division that makes typewriters. . .

. . .Even if the company got its start by making typewriters.

. . .Even if the company *invented* typewriters.

. . .Even if the typewriters they make today have LEDs and LCD screens.

. . .Even if the typewriters they make are widely acknowledged to be the world's very best.

. . .Because typewriters, my friend, are lumbering toward extinction.

Hog Scalders to Haute Fashion

I'd like to balance that typewriter story with another one, this one about a privately held Wisconsin firm called Kohler Company.

If Kohler's name sounds oddly familiar, stand up and walk into your bathroom. Chances are you'll find that name imprinted on most of the stuff in there. Kohler is one of America's finest names in kitchen and bathroom fixtures. The Kohler name is practically synonymous with superior plumbing-fixture quality.

It wasn't always that way.

A century or so ago, Kohler sold agricultural implements. They made horse-powered machinery, special attachments for steam threshing machines: the kind of stuff that you only find in museums today.

Then, one year, the Kohler Company came up with a patented process for coating iron with a ceramic powder and heat-fusing it into a porcelain finish. They used this process to make a porcelain-finished hog scalder—a drainable tub with a slope at one end, which made it easier for a farmer to scald the hair off a freshly killed hog and then easily remove it before starting the butchering process.

But when Kohler salesmen came back from the field, they reported that many of the hog scalders never made it into the barn.

Instead, farmer's wives were appropriating them for their bathrooms. The ceramic finish, it turned out, made them much better for bathing than the unfinished cast-iron tubs of the day. The market seemed to be telling Kohler something.

So, the following year, the Kohler catalog featured cast-iron legs which could be attached to their hog scalder to turn it into a very serviceable bathtub.

A few years after that, bathtub sales were outstripping everything else by such a margin that Kohler pretty much got out of the agricultural component business and began to concentrate almost exclusively on plumbing fixtures.

You see, Kohler saw the writing on the wall. The company's fathers realized that internal combustion engines and tractors would make most of Kohler's horse- and steam-driven equipment obsolete within a few years, so they abandoned that business *before* it had a chance to become unprofitable. They then concentrated their energies on a business that cannot obsolesce—after all, unless humans evolve dramatically, we will always need plumbing fixtures.

That Kohler is successful is self-evident. In addition, the company has shared its success with its workforce, creating a "company town" (Kohler, Wisconsin), which is so picturesque that Kohler operates a secondary industry devoted to serving the needs of the hundreds of thousands of tourists who visit every year. Many visit the company's design center, where they get ideas for their own homes and wind up, eventually, purchasing even more Kohler products.

Incidentally, in deference to their agricultural past, the Kohler family raises show horses to this day.

But they're still realists. Kohler Company also has a division that makes internal-combustion engines.

Where the Sharks Come In

The Kohler story is a wonderful example of a company's managers having the skill and foresight to direct a firm straight from one profitable endeavor into another, without needing a recession or a setback to get the picture. There were probably people who decried the company leadership's decision to get out of the horse-driven agricultural-component business. That Kohler and its home town are alive today is testimony, however, to the wisdom of that decision.

Now, let me make a rather odd confession.

If Kohler had decided years ago to stick with its guns and cling adamantly to the business with which it started—if, for that matter, its president decided *today* to chuck the plumbing-fixture business and go back to making horse-powered grain threshers—I would not have a problem with that decision.

I might think such a re-direction odd. I might even feel sorry for the fellow's family or his workforce. But I would not oppose him.

The reason I would not have a problem with such a course is that the president of Kohler is also the *owner* of Kohler. The company is private. It's his to do with as he, and he alone, sees fit. If he wants to stop making bathtubs and go back to concentrating on hog scalders, he has a right to do so, and I have no right to stop him, because it is—quite literally—none of my business.

But if Kohler goes public, and I buy in—hey, they'd better be concentrating on making bathtubs, or they're going to get a personal visit from yours truly.

For some reason—quite possibly because we tend to coddle them and treat them like princes—senior managers all too often act as if they own the companies under their stewardships.

This is, of course, ridiculous. The CEO of a publicly held company is no more its owner than the CEO's chauffeur is owner of the executive limousine. They are both simply employees entrusted with the care of other people's property.

Yet, in cases where the roster of owners—the shareholders' list—may go on for hundreds of pages, it is very easy for a CEO to decide that in light of such a confused and diffused ownership base, his are the whims that should prevail.

Let the CEO do that long enough, and when part of that base rises up in opposition to unprofitable management policies, it is not at all unusual for the affronted manager to react by belittling these activists—who are actually the company's owners—and calling them names.

"Shark" is one that seems to be particularly popular.

I've been called a shark on occasion and you know what? I don't mind it.

Let me tell you a little about sharks. . .

Ichthyologists (who make a living studying such things) report that the sharks swimming in today's oceans are little changed from fossil sharks recorded in sedimentary rock that is millions of years old.

This is not to say that sharks are primitive. Rather, sharks evolved to such a high degree early on that further evolution was, essentially, unnecessary.

Sharks are among the most hydrodynamically efficient of animals, capable of swimming long distances, or at extremely high speeds, without expending a great deal of energy. A shark has no bones in its body, relying instead on cartilage—which can regenerate when damaged—for its skeletal structure. Likewise, when a shark loses a tooth through trauma, it simply grows a new one in its place. A shark can smell blood in the water up to a quarter-mile away from the source, and hammerhead sharks are believed to be able to detect the tiny electrical charge of the prey's heartbeat—from several feet away. Sharks are amazingly resilient and usually remarkably healthy. They are the only animals on earth that are totally immune to cancer.

If all this gives you a newfound respect for sharks, that's good, but the point I want to make is this: even though the shark is a highly evolved, highly skilled predator, it does not hunt indiscriminately.

Rather, like most predators (such as wolves, lions, or hyenas), sharks generally prey only upon the sick, the wounded, the lame, or the less fit of the underwater world.

To the shark, it is a matter of energy. A dying or weakened animal is easier to chase down, and less likely to fight, than one that is fit and healthy. In choosing the weakest prey, the shark makes the most efficient choice, expending the fewest possible calories while taking on fresh calories in its meal.

In his book, *The Ocean World*, Jacques Cousteau asserts that the shark feeding in the sea is performing an act that is no more despicable than a human sitting down to a plate of bacon at breakfast. To this I would add that while the human's bacon came from a source that was (hopefully) totally healthy at its demise, the shark's breakfast was almost certainly less than healthy, and so the shark performs the greatest service: culling out the weak and leaving a stronger breeding-pool behind. A shark may be frightening and terrible to behold, but were it not for sharks, the seas would be overcrowded with feeble and crippled creatures. That is the shark's natural place in the universe. To paraphrase Darwin, the shark is there to help ensure that only the strong survive.

A Shark That Deserves to Be Heard

Profit-minded shareholder activists, likewise, do not rise up against strong and healthy companies. What would be the point? If a company's management is doing its job, and the company is performing to full potential, there is no reason to change the management of the company or force it to run in any manner other than the one its managers have already chosen. And why would anyone in their right mind want to change a business practice that's producing good results?

But, for a sick or injured business—one that is managed poorly or that is engaging in activities that are no longer as profitable as they should be—a shark might be just what the doctor ordered. Activism can motivate changes that eliminate unprofitable activities, or even rescue shareholder dollars by liquidating a dying company and returning the capital to its owners.

To the uninitiated, it may seem mean-spirited to swoop down upon an injured company and cause its managers further distress with calls for change. But the point that has to be remembered here is that the vocal shareholders are not the force that is killing the company. If things get to the point that shareholders feel forced to rise up, the chances are that competition has already killed the company. The activists are simply trying to see to it that the remains go to good use.

And remember, appearances aside, these are not "outsiders" here. These are people whose dollars are being wasted by the company. All the activists are trying to do is to contain their own losses. They deserve to be heard.

SURVIVING A FEEDING FRENZY

When shareholder activists and management collide and take their cases to the shareholders for a decision, emotions will often run high. But a few pointed questions— questions that will often be answered by the parties' literature—can make it easier for a shareholder to reach a decision:

- What is the *substance* of each party's claim about the other? Ignore such emotionally charged rhetoric as "trying to destroy our corporation" or "meddling in company affairs" (due to SEC regulations, such phrases will more often be found in spoken/ off-the-cuff comments than in position statements). Look for substantiation and evidence.

- When an assertion is made, remember Robert Heinlein's maxim: "If it cannot be expressed in numbers, it's nothing but an opinion." If activists say the company is not performing at par with the industry, they should provide numbers that show this. Likewise, if management claims that margins are at industry standards, they should have evidence to support the statement. Again, the SEC generally requires this in mailings, but statements at shareholder meetings can get fairly vague.

- Ask yourself, "Who stands to gain if either course is adopted? Which course leaves me, and my fellow shareholders, on better financial footing, both now and in the long run?"

- Don't be swayed by glitz. The words on a fancy, highly designed, glossy, four-color brochure are not necessarily better or more true than the words on a photocopied sheet of paper.

- If you're in doubt or confused about *anything* you read, call *both* parties and ask questions.

- Make your decisions as if you were the owner of the company. When it comes right down to it, you *are*.

Disagreements over governance—particularly those disagreements that run all the way and become the basis of proxy contests—are often compared to political campaigns, but I don't think this is an accurate analogy.

For one thing, there is the difference in commitment.

You probably remember the old saw about the difference between involvement and commitment—when you have bacon and eggs for breakfast, the chicken is involved, but the pig is committed.

In the same manner, parties in political campaigns are generally involved—they are trying to win something they do not have—but rarely are they truly committed. A politician losing an election usually pays for his loss with a war-chest of donations and then goes on to some lucrative occupation in private life, none the worse for wear.

In proxy campaigns, on the other hand, the activists are committed. They have money—their money—invested in the company. Otherwise, they would not have the right to raise their voices in protest. If they lose their contest, it is the activists' capital that is at hazard, even if they do get part or all of their expenses back. They still have their investment in the company.

Still, some similarities exist between modern battles for corporate governance and modern campaigns for political office.

One is this: If a party begins to indulge in smear-tactics and name-calling, it's a sure bet that this is because the name-caller has a lack of substantive claims to level against the opponent.

That's another reason I don't mind it when a company's managers sink to the bottom of the barrel and begin to refer to me as a "shark."

It's a pretty good sign that my opposition is just about ready to throw in the towel.

You know, if you study sharks long enough, you may begin to think of them as beautiful.

And if you can maintain that same type of objectivity when you're listening to differences of opinions over corporate governance, you might be surprised at how very much sense a so-called "anti-company" line of thinking might make. After all, when the sharks swim through, whatever is left behind is almost certain to be strong.

Chapter 7

Wooden Nickels

Unless a company's management is truly bottom-line driven—oriented toward the highest possible margins and the best return on the shareholders' investment—even well-intended policies can go awry.

In recent years, divisional accountability has been increasingly emphasized by management gurus following the philosophy that if you mind the pennies, the pounds will take care of themselves.

On the surface, this is not a bad philosophy. When service-oriented divisions of companies (the division that arranges use of corporate planes, for instance) charge other divisions for service, it helps keep those services from being abused, overused, or neglected when reckoning the "big picture" of corporate performance. Some of my friends on the corporate side refer to internal dollars as "wooden nickels."

This is good from a costs standpoint. Using our example of corporate air transportation, an analyst might notice that the people who are designing the newest widget are spending millions of dollars in "wooden nickels" to visit a vendor several states away. This could be a clue that the new widget operation would be more profitable if a local ven-

dor were used (or perhaps even if the new-widget development team was temporarily relocated to the same town
as the vendor).

Well and good. The problem comes when a company starts
believing that the money going into the service division is
not wooden nickels, but income.

It is not. Money spent is money spent. Whether it goes
inside the company or outside is immaterial—either way,
it still cannot go to the bottom line.

I think it was Mark Twain who said that there were three
kinds of lies—lies, damn lies, and statistics. The latter
was the kind in operation one morning when I visited with
the head of the research and development operation for
one of the auto companies and he proudly told me that his
division was the most profitable in his entire corporation.

When I asked him about his division's sales, he looked
puzzled. His division didn't sell anything. They came up
with new ideas, developed new manufacturing techniques,
and solved technical problems.

"But," the manager told me proudly, "when you analyze
the worth of our service as compared to the cost of our
overhead, you'll find that we offer the largest return on
investment of any division in the corporation."

That's great. But it doesn't pay a dividend.

It reminds me of the old story about the farmer who bought
a horse from his neighbor for $50. The next day, the neigh-
bor stopped by and said he realized that he really liked
the horse and shouldn't have sold him—so he bought him
back for $75.

The following week, the original buyer came back and said
his wife was heartbroken. She had really loved the new
horse and was despondent to see him go—would the neighbor consider selling him back for $100? He would.

But the original owner was back the next day. His kid wanted the horse. The price this time was $200.

This went on for a month. Pretty soon, the horse was selling for $1,000.

But when the original owner stopped by one morning to buy the horse, the neighbor told him, "I don't have it. I sold it to some sucker from the city for $1,200."

"Are you out of your mind?" his neighbor screamed. "What'd you do that for? We were both making a good living off that horse!"

A silly story, perhaps, but when middle managers start thinking that the "revenue" gathered by their divisions from elsewhere in the company is really and truly revenue, parochial thinking has taken over. A division that fixes on divisional profitability but ignores the corporate big picture is a division that has lost vision. Internal service organizations—organizations that only sell to other parts of the corporation—cannot generate profit. They can only contain cost.

Fortunately, we have seen some awakenings in this regard in recent years. As I write this, Ford Motor Company is in the middle of a corporate restructuring effort called "Ford 2000." It is an effort geared toward recognition of the fact that Ford is a global corporation, and that all global revenues eventually fall toward a common bottom line. Accordingly, redundant internal service efforts are being consolidated—and if they keep the vision of the effort, and recognize that the purpose of an internal service division is to offer a service more economically than outside sources—it should have a positive effect on Ford's profitability. We'll see.

Of course, a critical difference between Ford and the other auto companies is that the Ford family remains both a substantial shareholder group in the business that carries their name and an active force in the direction of the company.

To them, dollars flowing through the company are not abstracts, but real money, tied to their own personal fortunes.

It's amazing what a reality check can do for corporate governance.

MONOPOLY® MONEY

That simple realization—what one is spending is real, hard-earned money and not the stuff that comes with a Monopoly® game—is probably the most important message that shareholders can deliver to their managers.

I say this because management thinking and action have an influence on actions throughout the corporation—indeed, throughout business in general.

One example I see of the Monopoly®-money syndrome is the inordinate amount of attention that has been given to derivatives in recent years.

The public is generally ignorant of investment terminology, but "derivatives"—like "junk bonds"—have made their way into the common man's vocabulary in recent years, primarily because of related public scandals.

While the common man may have heard of derivatives, in most cases he isn't sure what they are.

That's probably a good thing. A derivative is a piece of a larger transaction. It could be the profit (or loss) in a given period of time, the interest gained by a financial instrument owned by someone else—any of hundreds of possible bits and pieces that can be broken out on a spreadsheet and divided up. For the most part, derivatives are rights to bits and pieces of things that other investors own.

The process is called "slicing and dicing," and traders refer to the people who do the slicing and dicing as "rocket scientists." The big-brain implications are obvious, but it does not take a big brain to realize that if I want to hold onto my savings account, but I'm willing to sell you the interest, it is only because I think I'm going to get the better part of a deal by doing so.

There are exceptions. Some cash-poor companies might very well be willing to hock their interest on certain instruments at a loss, just to get capital in hand at a critical juncture. And, by working those exceptions, some very lucky people have gotten very wealthy through investment in derivatives. Derivatives have also been useful as hedging mechanisms. For instance, an American company that borrows Deutschmarks and has to repay in the same currency may invest in derivatives as a hedge against fluctuations in the dollar.

But there are derivatives, and then there are derivatives.

In general, derivatives are extremely risky investments, a fact that was made abundantly clear when Orange County nearly became the first part of California to fall into the Pacific, following the loss of more than $1.5 billion in the derivatives market.

In the midst of temporary fluctuations, it is easy for a lucky speculator to think that he is a genius. But then the day of reckoning comes.

We saw this over and over again in the Southern California real estate market of the latter 1970s and early 1980s. Exercising Will Rogers' admonition to "buy land—they ain't makin' it no more," speculators drove the price of virtually every kind of California real estate through its own roof.

Going on the assumption that California was the mecca of the latter 20th century, and that, given the coming tele-communications-driven freedom from geographically tied endeavors, people would prefer to live and locate in a balmy climate, speculators snatched up every scrap of land they could find within a three-hour drive from downtown Los Angeles.

Greed soon produced ridiculous scenarios. Depression-era craftsman bungalows, originally built in the L.A. suburbs for less than $8,000, were sometimes going for a quarter of a million dollars, or more. Retirees were forced to sell their homes and move into apartments just to escape property taxes that threatened to outstrip fixed incomes. People bought high on the supposition that the price could only go higher.

When the recession caught up with California and real estate prices plummeted, many self-styled "geniuses" were beside themselves with consternation. Their speculative pyramid scheme was based on the assumption that real estate prices could only continue to go up.

TULIP MANIA

Such widespread departure from common sense is not new. In 1841, Charles Mackay described numerous instances of it in a wonderful tome called *Extraordinary Popular Delusions and the Madness of Crowds*.

Most notable of Mackay's examples was "tulip mania," a 17th-century phenomenon that saw the Dutch tulip-bulb market—an area that should have had interest only to a few horticulturists—explode in a speculative frenzy that permeated virtually every segment of Dutch society.

Very quickly, people who had previously paid scant attention to tulips, other than as decorative garden elements, were vying with one another for the rights to exotic specimens. In some cases, people sold their homes to acquire a single bulb.

When that mania finally collapsed under its own weight, it was easy to look back and see that it was foolish to sell a home to acquire something that, at best, could adorn a window box. Many people in Holland were left with bushels of bulbs and not so much as a box in which to plant them.

Southern California real estate and junk bonds—and lately, derivatives—have become the tulip bulbs of modern times. If we step back and take a clear look, we can see the operative madness.

Unfortunately, many people never take the time to take that step back.

COMPOUND DISINTEREST

The scariest scenario in modern business, however, is the intersection of Monopoly®-money philosophies and speculative trends.

The most jarring (or at least the most public) example of such a collision has to be the March 1995 collapse of Barings Brothers—bankers to the royal family of England and a firm that had weathered wars, plagues, and financial recessions for more than two centuries. That such an institution could fall was alarming. More insidious was the fact that the collapse was caused, not by uncontrollable external forces, but by the speculative investments of a single trader in one of the bank's branch offices.

I'll not go into the now well-known details of how Nicholas William Leeson gambled away Barings' future by losing money on risky derivatives and then attempting to recapture his position through larger gambles in even riskier derivatives. The bottom line was that Britain's oldest bank hemorrhaged money to such an extent that it was eventually forced to sell out to an outside group for the token sum of one British pound. Ironically, that rescuer—ING Group—was based in Holland, the country that gave birth to the original tulip mania.

The critical difference between the tulip investors of the 17th century and Leeson's electronically transacted transgressions more than four centuries later was that, while Dutch investors usually squandered their own funds on tulip bulbs, Leeson was trading with his company's money (in some cases, with loans taken out in his company's name).

Call it a leap, but I think that the reason junior traders in branch offices and county government controllers have found their way into such financial calamities is that many of the people managing businesses today—the people who set the tone for the rest of their companies, and the rest of industry—have promoted Monopoly®-money thinking through their own examples.

And certainly, in the case of Leeson and Barings, where no superior or director stepped in and put a stop to the matter before it ran out of hand—fiduciary responsibility was left somewhere far back on the wayside.

Chapter 8

The Runaway Stagecoach: General Motors

Financial writers like to say that what shareholder activists are after is "management change." But that's only part of the truth. What nonmanagement proxy campaigners are usually after in their efforts is positive management *action*, because change without positive action is virtually the same as no change at all. For proof of that statement, I need to look no further than Detroit, my own backyard. . .

STEMPEL'S RESIGNATION

On October 26, 1992, the shareholders and current-model customers of General Motors Corporation received the company's 1993 product catalog. A slick, 37-page publication, full of morning-in-America product shots set against a background of GM's three world-class North American Proving Grounds, the catalog might logically have been expected to open with a message from the automotive giant's CEO. Instead, it began enigmatically with five short statements from people throughout the corporate hierarchy, the most senior of whom was William E. Hoglund, GM's chief financial officer. Chairman and CEO Robert C. Stempel was nowhere to be seen.

That apparent omission proved to be either a rare case of good planning on GM's part, or simply fortuitous coincidence. By mid-morning of the 26th, virtually every GM shareholder had gotten the news that Stempel, a scant two years and three months into his chairmanship, had tendered his resignation, essentially handing control of the company to a cadre of shareholder-driven outside directors on the General Motors board.

By the dawn of the 1990s, it had become apparent that no corporate bastion was immune to shareholder action. GAF and Sears were just two of the Goliaths who were enduring onslaughts from proxy-wielding Davids. And the Davids were taking their toll. Even in cases where management ostensibly won the contests, change was virtually inevitable. Saxon Industries, Tasco Corporation, Kennecott Corporation, American Bakeries, Pullman, Inc., and (closer to home for me) D&N Financial Corporation were all cases in which the president or CEO submitted a resignation within two years of the completion of a proxy fight.

GM was a double-whammy—a case of CEO resignation shortly after dissidents gained seats on the board. And it bears inspection because it was, very nearly literally, a classic case of change following corporate governance by paternalism.

But He Was So Much Nicer Than Roger. . .

Probably the most unusual thing about Stempel's resignation was the extent to which it upset the employees of GM. White-collar workers, usually close-mouthed about matters of policy, lined up to tell TV reporters what they thought of the situation. Some were moved to the point of tears. Even UAW President Owen Bieber, a man whose organization was traditionally the loudest critic of the "14th Floor"—the executive suite of the GM Building in downtown Detroit—expressed outrage at the news.

Partly this was the result of a favorable comparison of Stempel to his predecessor, Roger Smith. Smith was a man who had been nearly universally despised at GM. Stockholders and unemployed workers picketed his press conferences. *Roger and Me*, a quasi-documentary movie on the disastrous effects of the Smith chairmanship, had become a cult classic during Smith's final year at the helm. His own speechwriter had quit to write a poison-pen assault on Smith's seemingly arrogant indifference to the opinions of workers and shareholders alike.

Stempel, on the other hand, was liked because he was seen by people throughout the corporation as a caring father-figure and a "car guy." An engineer by training, he had come up through the ranks, designing transmissions and functioning as chief engineer on some of the company's most successful products. Blessed with the uncanny ability to recall by name virtually anyone he'd ever met, Stempel brought his people skills and lift-the-hood-and-fix-it attitude to a number of GM trouble spots. Before his ascent to the corporation's executive bastions, he had taken test runs with a number of GM divisions. Under his tutelage, Pontiac Motor Division was guided out of its Beach Boys muscle-car era and put into position to market to the up-and-coming crop of middle-aged baby boomers. He took a sagging Opel AG and made it the most successful automaker in all of Europe. In the early 1980s, Stempel came to Chevrolet, a division suffering enormous quality deficits and image problems, and put it back on its feet with programs that would culminate after his departure in a new positioning of the make as the "Heartbeat of America." And as head of the Buick-Olds-Cadillac Automotive Group, Stempel sowed the seeds that began steering GM's upper divisions away from their retiree-transportation image and back to their intended spots in the hotly contended luxury-car category.

At press conferences, Stempel shunned prepared speeches and spoke instead from sheaves of three-by-five cards, each bearing a topic ("alternative fuels") and the length of time ("two minutes") he felt the subject merited. He followed the Dale Carnegie technique of speaking to one person in his audience, adhering to that method so diligently that he usually addressed the individual by name. He was known for striking out on whatever tangent he liked, a style that gave his cut-and-dried GM handlers fits. At one Chevrolet new-model press preview, court stenographers and a trailer full of typists were brought in so journalists could be given the customary typescripts of general manager's remarks when Stempel left the podium. On factory tours, he'd listen to worker comments about a line problem and offer lucid advice on how to fix it. Customers who wrote to him got personal replies.

The Stage Is Set for Disaster

Yet, as charming and human as Stempel's chairmanship was, it was, in the end, simply another form of we-know-best paternalism. The fact remained—and his critics lost no time in pointing this out—that Stempel had been on the GM board of directors since 1986, and so had approved of, if not authored, many of the least successful policies of the Smith administration. He had been on the board that approved the scuttling of a project to replace GM's aging Camaro and Firebird sports coupes—thus essentially closing the door on what little youth market GM still retained. By the time of Stempel's resignation, when the first advance photos of a new Camaro were just starting to appear, GM's average owner was more than 47 years old. Stempel had similarly stood by when Smith squelched a four-door version of the S-10 Blazer and S-15 Jimmy—GM's entrants in the hot and trendy sport utility vehicle category—even though such vehicles had been designed and ready for production since 1986 (they finally came out five years later, their design already half a decade obsolete, after competitors had gained huge inroads on the market). For four years, Stempel had stood quietly by, apparently unwilling to say anything that might disrupt his career path, as progress essentially ceased at General Motors. This had the short-term effect of allowing Smith to retire on a wave of profitability; with little in the way of development or tooling costs, cash virtually cascaded to the bottom line. But the policies also brought GM to the brink. As Stempel was coming to office, his company was selling such anachronisms as a full-size van (a staple of the commercial truck market) that had gone virtually unchanged since 1969. Union workers were fostering a not-going-to-take-it-anymore attitude, pointing at the cutbacks of the 1980s and sure that the money had to be there somewhere. Even at Saturn Corporation, Smith's pet project and the Tomorrowland of General Motors, UAW hourly employees were ripping up their workers'-Utopia job agreements and asking for their money up front.

Stempel's defenders pointed out that his apparent silence during his four years on the Smith board had been a matter of necessity—in order to get the opportunity to make any repairs at all, he'd had to stand by and wait his turn or take a chance of being booted as a malcontent. But the fact remains that once elevated to power, he passed up several excellent openings for change.

One glaring example was the state of GM's financial dealings with its customers. Like most automakers' captive finance organizations, General Motors Acceptance Corporation had been put together in the dawn of the Depression as a lender of last resort. Yet, when other companies were discovering ways to lure ever greater numbers of desirable credit risks into their folds, GMAC was still losing them by the thousands to conventional lending institutions (in the mid-1980s, a GMAC vice president was still characterizing the GM finance clientele as "the cream of the crap"). As a result, at the time of Stempel's ouster, the typical GMAC customer was still purchasing his vehicle through a conventional financing program, but because of the high cost of vehicles and the customer's usually modest household income, the vehicle was financed on a 60-month payment plan.

Ford Motor Company, on the other hand, had already put more than eight years of training and implementation into a program to attract more affluent white-collar buyers into 24-month leases.

The difference was night and day. In October of 1992, both GM and Ford were losing money. But Ford had light at the end of the tunnel. They knew that better than 85 percent of short-term, captive-lease customers would take their next lease with the same automaker—and usually with the same dealer. This meant that Ford was looking at a future in which the dealers and factory alike could budget overhead against a statistically assured stream of incoming lease renewals. It was like programming customers to come in on 24-month cycles. In two years, little goes wrong on a car; Ford customers remained satisfied with their vehicles, came back for more, and fed the dealers' highly profitable used-car lots with burgeoning fleets of desirable, low-mileage vehicles.

GM customers, on the other hand, were driving their vehicles into the ground. Those who kept up on the value of their vehicles generally found that at some point past the middle of the payment book, they were upside down—owing more than the car was worth on the open market. And at the end of five years, they were driving worn-out clunkers plagued with a variety of mechanical woes and worth little in trade-in. They were ready for a change, and change they did. Customers left GM showrooms in droves. GM was losing market share to competitors and not finding replacements for the customers who had left. Even General Motors' import-fighters—the new Saturn Corporation and the Chevrolet-marketed Geo nameplate—backfired loudly. Both sold well thanks to screwed-down low prices (some Geo models actually lost money with each unit sold). But demographic analysis showed that the buyers were coming not from the ranks of first-time buyers and import owners (as GM had intended), but from longtime customers of other GM divisions. GM was bleeding itself dry—cannibalizing itself.

Throughout this time, Stempel remained faithful to a trust-us-we-know-this-business style of governance, resisting, until it was too late, the advice offered by voices outside the traditional company-bred management circle. By doing so, he fell into the ruts of a number of inbred "fixes," none of which did the job. Division general managers, charged with the responsibility to increase volume, did so by lowering profit, seemingly oblivious to the fact that market share meant nothing without profitability. Huge emphasis was placed on commercial sales, such as sales of vehicles to car rental companies. To do this, however, GM guaranteed residual value with ridiculously generous buy-back plans, saddling the company with hundreds of thousands of overvalued used cars. Rebates, once heralded as the marketing idea of the century, had become little more than a dinner bell—customers simply postponed purchases until a rebate was on—delaying, rather than increasing, business. GM was reorganized twice within a single year despite the fact that a previous "streamlining" effort had taken the unexpected turn of actually increasing the headcount in some already overstaffed divisions. GM launched its own MasterCard with a seemingly innovative frequency-marketing twist; the card paid dividends (like the Discover Card), but these accumulated in a fund that the customer could only use against the purchase of a new GM vehicle. As attractive as this seemed from a long-term marketing stance, the GM Card also sent customers the message that they should delay their new-vehicle purchase until they'd built up a balance in their credit-card war chest.

The bottom line: In the final year of Stempel's GM chairmanship, the trading price of GM common stock plummeted a staggering 33 percent. Shareholders—and particularly institutional shareholders, who had been schooled on the wisdom of benchmarking their funds against the traditionally rock-solid General Motors—were beside themselves with anger and fear.

What angered them even more was that to people outside the automobile industry, General Motors' problems were obvious. Looking at the Big Three in the quarter immediately preceding Stempel's resignation, one could not help but be impressed with the realization that Chrysler was profitable, Ford was slightly unprofitable, and GM was hemorrhaging money. The difference was size; GM had all of the American auto industry's woes, only more so. If Chrysler had high healthcare costs tacked onto the overhead in each car, GM had higher costs. If Chrysler had a big retiree population, GM had a bigger one. If Chrysler was handling the R&D costs for two automotive divisions, GM was handling them for six. If Chrysler had tens of thousands of overcompensated employees, GM had hundreds of thousands. The list went on and on. Compounding it was the roster of firms acquired by GM during the Smith administration; firms like Hughes Aircraft and Lotus Car, which were ideally positioned for profitable sale but instead were being carried as albatrosses around the corporate neck.

Even in years past, when the GM board of directors had been an inbred group composed of the chairman emeritus and a hand-picked selection of both his and the present chairman's cronies, the weight of shareholder opinion might have spelled out a death sentence for Stempel. And this wasn't years past.

Nonemployee Board Seals Stempel's Fate

Stempel was answering to a board that included such nonemployee, outside directors as Procter & Gamble's John Smale, Marriott Corporation's J. Willard Marriott, Ann McLaughlin (former Secretary of Labor), Thomas Wyman (the former chairman of CBS), J.P. Morgan's Dennis Weatherstone, and Charles T. Fisher III, the chairman of NBD Bancorp, parent of the National Bank of Detroit. Faced with the realities of GM profitability, there was only one decision this group could responsibly make.

That decision was quickly ratified throughout corporate America. Speaking the next day in *The Wall Street Journal*, Eckhard Pfeiffer (who himself had replaced the deposed Rod Canion as CEO of Compaq Computer Corp.) said, "GM has muddled along for a long time without taking significant action. Small steps don't do it. It has to be revolutionary—that's what seems to have happened now."

Mesa Inc.'s T. Boone Pickens (also the founder of United Shareholders Association) welcomed the Stempel resignation as a remedy to the closed-minded management doctrines of years past, in which, "Institutions had the attitude, 'If you don't like the management, sell the stock.' I think that was wrong. Now I think most people realize that management works for the investors, and directors represent the stockholders."

The chief lesson taught by the GM experience is that a person needn't be a gruff, cigar-chomping martinet to be an ineffective manager. Compassionate, human, and caring, Bob Stempel was and is anything but an ogre. His peers in the executive suite will tell you how he agonized over job cuts and layoffs. It was hard to find detractors among his workforce, some of whom circulated petitions begging the board to allow him to keep his job. To his people he was, purely and simply, a father figure.

But "father figure" is simply another term for paternalism, and it was just that trait, coupled with a resistance to seeking solutions outside the company, that set things in place for Stempel's downfall. Rather than obeying reason and sound business principles, he attempted to govern from the heart, tying himself to failure with the same emotional strings that bound him to his workforce. In doing so, he committed the cardinal managerial sin of bonding with the wrong group. By thinking in terms of product and workforce, instead of profit and shareholders, he had essentially turned his back on fiduciary responsibility. In the end, he was reminded that it was the *shareholders'* company, and the shareholders were hopping, steaming mad.

THE TREND BEGINS

Industry observers were quick to point out that Stempel was simply a notable example of a homebred, company-line executive being thrust into contrast with competitive market conditions. Goodyear's Tom Barrett and Digital Equipment's Kenneth Olsen were both cited in financial columns as other old-line "company men" who had been turned out of their positions by performance-savvy boards. And the ink had barely dried on Stempel's letter before Sears' Edward Brennan and IBM's John Akers were being measured by the business press as the next chairmen destined to join the ranks of the unemployed.

It was entirely appropriate that Barrett, Olsen, and Stempel all resigned their positions in 1992, an election year. The message sent to managers was simple; they were being asked to come home to their constituency. Their job description was being clarified in one simple sentence: Make the company perform to the satisfaction of the stockholders. Through the resignations of 1992, CEOs everywhere were being taught that they enjoyed rights of custody rather than the rights of kings.

For some, it was a very difficult lesson to learn.

Chapter *9*

Sticks and Carrots

I recently saw a special on western military actions during Operation Desert Storm, and one commentator made an interesting point.

The commentator was talking about armored (tank) combat in the desert. Western firepower was so superior to that of the obsolete T-34 Russian tanks used by Iraqi forces that our tank commanders could safely sit back, a mile or more out of Iraqi gun range and, using laser-guided and wire-guided fire, completely obliterate opposing forces.

Like the pilots who were unleashing smart-bomb raids on Iraqi military installations, our tank forces were, by and large, able to conduct combat over such extreme distances that they were able to remain detached from most horrors of battle throughout much of the campaign.

Later, however, when American forces were closing in on troops retreating to Baghdad, they ran directly through positions that they had struck just hours before and were appalled at the carnage. American firepower was so superior that literally nothing survived. For as far as the eye could see, the desert was littered with smoking hulks of tanks and bits of bodies. Tank commanders radioed in and asked that the hot pursuit be discontinued—the slaughter was too horrible, and impossible to further justify.

"Yet what they were seeing," the commentator said, "was literally nothing more than the face of war . . . they'd just been too far away to see it before."

When managers blithely carry on in spite of the detrimental effects of their actions on their companies, I often think that's what's taking place—they're too distant from the action to see the results of their decisions.

There are a couple of ways of narrowing the gap.

BLUE-LIGHT SPECIAL

One way is the path taken by Kmart shareholders in March 1995.

Kmart had been led, in one form or another since 1986, by Joseph Antonini, a generally cheerful and garrulous man and an unorthodox manager. He did not, for instance, like to make appointments, preferring to keep his days open so anything that needed to make its way into his office could get there.

Kmart's official biography on Antonini said that he'd started there in 1964 as an assistant store manager, but Antonini liked to tell visitors that his first position was as a janitor.

His was a shop-rags-to-riches story. Twenty years after his assistant-store-manager appointment, Antonini was president of the firm's apparel division. Two years after that, he was president and CEO. In 1987, Kmart named him chairman.

But two years into Antonini's chairmanship, Kmart was straying out of its core business sector. The company, which already owned Payless drug stores (a sort of Kmart in miniature, popular on the West Coast) bought into Pace, a warehouse-club retail operation. By 1990, Kmart had begun acquisition of OfficeMax (a discount office-supply chain) and the Sports Authority discount sporting-goods chain.

The train had begun to come off the track. While Wal-Mart and even Meijer (a midwestern discounter headquartered across the state from Troy-based Kmart in Grand Rapids, Michigan) were computerizing and concentrating on more personable sales approaches, Kmart was redecorating stores but not doing enough in analysts' eyes to refurbish an antiquated inventory tracking system. Oddly enough, one of the biggest aspects of the business to suffer was apparel—Antonini's old stomping-ground.

In 1992, Kmart bought the Borders bookstore chain, and expanded Builders' Square (its home and hardware warehouse division).

Shareholders began screaming as Kmart earnings ran contrary to those of its industry. The company, they said, was concentrating capital in areas where it had no expertise while leaving the core business to languish.

Antonini fought back by using the Lee Ioccoca approach, appearing in his firm's TV commercials, walking through the aisles of a renovated Kmart store and assuring viewers that "if you don't have a new Kmart in your area yet, it will be coming soon."

The between-the-lines message was obvious—"I'm working on it."

Shareholders disagreed. By 1993, shareholder pressure had forced Kmart to sell Pace Warehouses to arch-rival Wal-Mart. One year later, the company had taken an $850 million hit and was planning to close 800 stores—500 more than previously planned. Dilution of its stake in its specialty chains was proposed and defeated by shareholders, who were past placation at this point.

By the beginning of 1995, thousands of Kmart employees had been laid off and management was literally decimated. Kmart had sold its majority stakes in Sports Authority and OfficeMax, and Antonini had been demoted from chairman to president (but still CEO)—a position he'd last held in 1986. On the first full day of spring in 1995, Antonini resigned from Kmart at the request of major shareholders.

I saw Joe Antonini about a week later in Bloomfield Hills, where my offices are located. I asked him about his resignation.

His assessment?

"The shareholders just refused to be reasonable," he said.

I suppose that's one way of looking at it.

Mi Capital Es Su Capital

Management decapitation is not the only action available to shareholders looking for action. Another is to approach management through the paycheck.

When he left Kmart, Joseph Antonini's reported salary was $893,000—respectable, but not enormous by American CEO standards, and certainly not out of line for a chief executive who'd been with the company for more than three decades. He hadn't been paid a bonus since 1992, and even that one was considerably less than his salary.

Many CEOs get more. Determining whether they'll continue to get more has been another popular approach for bringing managers in line with realities.

The time-proven philosophy of carrots and sticks has been resurrected with success by many companies.

Thus, in March 1995, about the same time that Kmart sent Joseph Antonini packing, *Business Week* was able to report that IBM had increased CEO Louis Gerstner's salary and bonus package by more than a third to $12.4 million, in recognition of a 30-percent lift in stock performance, while Salomon Brothers' Chairman Deryck Maughan saw his pay cut by 87 percent (to $1 million!) after the firm posted a near billion-dollar loss in 1994—the worst in its history.

Having your pay cut to a million bucks may not seem like much of a slap on the wrist, but everything is relative, and an 87 percent pay cut does tend to get one's attention.

Another contributing factor in Louis Gerstner's case is that IBM now requires its executives to hold significant investment in IBM stock. Thus, the managers' fortunes are locked in with, and bound to rise and fall with, those of the shareholders'.

A Cal-Berkeley study done in 1993 found that requiring executive investment does tend to lash the captain to the mainsail. Of 105 CEOs participating in the study, 58 lost more in stock value than they earned in salary and bonuses. Particularly for older executives, who are on the verge of cashing in their stock and retiring to Hilton Head, such a hip-pocket-ectomy is guaranteed to make shareholder interests and executive interests one and the same.

Chapter 10

Taking It Personally

When obstinate management and activist shareholders are just headlines in *The Wall Street Journal*, it's one thing. When you find yourself pulled into the maelstrom, it's quite another.

One time I found myself on the doorstep of one such situation. It began with a visit to an old haunt, the Detroit Club . . .

I can still remember the first time I heard of the Detroit Club. It was January 1967, and I, fresh out of college, had just gotten the first job of my financial career, a position as a research analyst with the investment firm of William C. Roney and Company.

The job was, as it is at every financial organization on the face of the earth, a grand misnomer. Research analysts don't analyze much of anything. The title is a glorified name for a clerk, and for people with degrees in finance, the job is a reality check, much like the comeuppance lawyers get when they arrive at their first firm, JD in hand, and are put to work filing legal briefs.

But the two positions have another thing in common: they are the apprenticeship one serves on the way to bigger and better things. Just as law clerks survive from day to day on dreams of winning that big case, investment research analysts eat, sleep, and breathe the investment dream—the hope of developing the Midas Touch. Like every recent college grad, I saw myself in those days as a veritable well of untapped potential. I was determined that I was going to get there—wherever "there" was—faster than any of my research analyst peers, and as I sharpened pencils, filed spreadsheets, and ran down quotes for my betters, I did so secure in the knowledge that it was all only temporary and there was light at the end of the tunnel.

For one brief, shining moment on that cold January morning, the light at the end of the tunnel was absolutely blinding.

I was carrying in the research department's mail when I heard someone call, "Hey kid! Come with me."

I looked up. I gulped. It was W.C.—William C. Roney. The main palookah. The company namesake.

My heart raced. This was it. The Big Break. W.C. had his coat on, so he was going out and he wanted me to go with him. To where? A big client? If W.C. was going *out*, it had to be someone of major importance—a Ford or a Fisher, someone of that ilk; the little clients all came *in*. I dumped the mail on an empty desk and raced to the closet, glad that I'd worn my good topcoat that morning.

"Where are we going?" I asked as we walked out onto snowy Woodward Avenue.

W.C. snorted.

"That snowstorm last night screwed everything up," he grumbled. "The power's out in every damn restaurant in downtown. So I called over to the Detroit Club; they're making up a hundred sandwiches for the brokers."

Sandwiches for the brokers. Fuel for the engine that ran Roney & Company. Damn. I was still a gofer.

But my disappointment was quickly replaced by curiosity. The Detroit Club? The *Detroit* Club?

It seemed to me that there had to be a word missing.

I'd grown up around Detroit, and my father, while by no means a wealthy man, had nonetheless enjoyed a fair success in the diamond tool business. Like most of Detroit's successful businessmen, he was a member of the Detroit *Athletic* Club. Mostly an eating and drinking club, the "DAC," as it's known around town, has enough athletic facilities to justify its name. There's a weight room, running tracks, a bowling alley, squash courts, and an elegant old natatorium where the club's resident swim team, the Water Beavers, traditionally dunk incoming presidents, suit coat, tie and all. The recently retired auto company executives who actually used the facilities in those days took their refreshments in a third-floor, casual-attire lounge incongruously known as the "Isle of Yap." Everyone else— the majority—had their drinks in the Tap Bar or the Grill Room, downstairs, on the ground floor. I knew all about the DAC. I couldn't count the times I'd lunched there with my father, or dined there with my family after Sunday afternoon swims. That had to be where we were going.

I looked up as W.C. and I scrunched through the slippery, foot-packed snow. We were headed down Cass.

"Uh, Mr. Roney?" I asked hesitantly.

"Yeah, kid?"

"Uhm—excuse me, but isn't the Detroit Athletic Club over on Madison?"

W.C. stopped. His face had the look of a man who'd gotten a bad oyster.

"The Detroit *Athletic* Club?" he said. "Yeah, kid, it's on Madison. But we ain't going there."

I must have still looked puzzled, because W.C. went on.

"Kid, the people who run this town are members of the Detroit Athletic Club."

I nodded. Sure. Everybody knew that.

"But," W.C. held up a leather-gloved index finger to make his point, "the people who *own* this town take their drinks at the *Detroit* Club. You clear on that?"

Clear? I wasn't; not at all. But I nodded anyhow.

"Good!" W.C. clapped me on the shoulder. "Now, let's go get those sandwiches."

Times Change

Decades later, I stood in the smoking room of the Detroit Club, scanning the front page of one of *The Wall Street Journals*, which sat in neat, well-pressed ranks with a variety of other newspapers on the big oak library table. Twenty-two years had passed since I'd come here to assist W.C. Roney in his noontime mission. In that time, the light at the end of the tunnel had arrived for me as a bright and beautiful dawn. I'd taken what I'd learned and applied it in my own business, and it had grown to the point where I no longer sought new clients. The people I represented had come to value my company as a firm that delivered consistently good return on investment, always better than the market as a whole, while zealously guarding their principle. It was a bright picture, indeed, with only one dark spot anywhere in the whole of it, and I had come to the Detroit Club on this April morning in 1989 to deal with that.

There was a rustle on the other side of the table as Bob Reichenbach, my thrift analyst, picked up a *Detroit News*, scanned the front page of the sports section, and put it back down again. He looked at his watch and looked up at me.

"You think our lunch date is going to make it?" he asked, an eyebrow raised.

I looked at my own watch. It made me think of when I was a kid, and I was going to the movies with friends or meeting some buddies at the zoo. My mother always gave me a dollar to carry in my pocket, so I had bus-fare home, just in case my friends didn't show or they were getting into shenanigans in which I didn't care to be involved. "Mad money," she called it; money so you could get mad and go home. Right now, getting mad and going home didn't sound like such a bad idea, and it struck me as ironic that I was here, at the Detroit Club, because I happened to be the custodian and representative of a whole bunch of "mad money"—only in a completely different sense of the term.

I glanced at the time once again.

"He's coming a long way," I told Bob. "Probably just running a little late."

Bob shrugged, nodded, and went back to his paper while I walked around the room, looking at the paintings. There were a lot of the types of things that you'd expect to see in a businessmen's club—seascapes, hunting scenes, landscapes rendered in the misty, foggy style of the Hudson River School. But it was the nameplates on the paintings that were most impressive. One contained the note that the painting had been purchased by the Club in 1889. Another was a donation, made in 1888. They were pre-auto industry, considerably so, which in Detroit amounts to about the same thing as prehistoric.

The Detroit Club had been around for a long time. But it had changed since the time when W.C. Roney had first brought me to the place. Back then, it had positively bustled. You had the sense, when you walked in the front door, that you were entering the nerve center of capitalist Detroit. I recalled the old days when I'd been with Roney for a few years and the firm had its annual meetings there, absolutely packing the second-floor banquet room with brokers. In the beginning of the evening, they'd be drunk with the opulence of their surroundings; by the end of the evening, they'd be drunker still on the club's scotch. We used to joke that you could save all the bad news for the end of those meetings—nobody would ever remember hearing it. Still, for all the joviality of those days, there was a very serious, solid side to the Club back then. Just being there meant that you had made it, and made it in a very big way, in financial Detroit.

Yet here we were, on a weekday, at a few minutes past noon, and you could fire a cannon through the place without harming a soul. The seat of power had moved elsewhere in Detroit. It had settled in what were formerly merely social clubs—Bloomfield Hills and Oakland Hills Country Clubs, out north of town, and on the east side at the Country Club of Detroit, and the Grosse Pointe Yacht Club. It spent its weekends out of town, up in Harbor Springs, near Traverse Bay. In these later days, memberships at the Detroit Club were held by the sons of former members—people who kept their chairs in the dining room out of a sense of loyalty or obligation, and by newcomers who didn't understand that the times had changed. As I looked around, I thought of New York's Algonquin Hotel, which had once hosted the famous Round Table, that daily convention of American literati. Today, the members of the Round Table are dead and gone, but the Algonquin is still visited regularly by English teachers and grad students, who come in search of literary ghosts and wind up looking at one another. Like the Algonquin, the Detroit Club had passed its glory days. The grand old Club had even developed a musty air, as if the old rooms with their green woolen carpets had been kept shut up and unused too long.

It was getting late. The man we were meeting for lunch was, I fully realized, not very fond of me. Perhaps he would even feel justified in snubbing me. I looked up at Bob.

"Maybe he's having trouble finding parking or something," I said. "Let's take a look out front."

We had just stepped into the entrance hall when the front door opened and our luncheon appointment arrived.

"Bob," I said. "I think you remember Ken Seaton."

Case Study: Detroit and Northern Financial Corporation

Kenneth D. Seaton was 59 years old in that spring of 1989. The CEO of both Detroit and Northern Financial Corporation (D&N) and its thrift, the D&N Savings Bank, Seaton looked the part of a business executive, and vaguely resembled, in my eyes, a latter 20th-century version of that archetype of Michigan businessmen, Henry Ford. He oversaw his firm's more than $2 billion in assets and directed its 51 offices from a shining, eight-story office building in the town of Hancock, amid the relative wilderness of "the U.P."—Michigan's Upper Peninsula.

Many who know the region liken the Upper Peninsula to a virtual country unto itself. The great bulk of the area lies north of the 45th parallel and so is, literally, closer to the North Pole than it is to the Equator. Isolated by the surrounding Great Lakes and the woods of northern Wisconsin, the region only truly became easily accessible from the rest of Michigan in 1957 with the opening of "Mighty Mac," the bridge across the Straits of Mackinac—at the time, the longest suspension bridge in the world. Prior to that time, most travel to the U.P. was by ferry boat or bush plane. In times of bad weather, one simply did not go there at all. If you talk to the people who live there, you'll often get the feeling that they liked it better that way.

The U.P.'s isolationist attitude began in the 19th century when copper was discovered in the gnarled old hills known as the Huron and Porcupine Mountains, and in the crooked

finger of the Keweenaw Peninsula. Like the later California Gold Rush, Michigan's Copper Rush turned paupers
into millionaires virtually overnight. In fact, when Horace
Greeley advised ambitious youth to "Go West, young man,"
he was speaking not of the Pacific Coast, but of Michigan's
Keweenaw Peninsula. In Greeley's time, it was the closest
thing there was to the pot at the end of the rainbow.

Flushed with their success, the citizens of Hancock,
Houghton, and dozens of other boom towns vied to grace
their communities with the trappings of civilization. Op-
era houses sprang up. Homes were built and imbued with
every facet of classic Victorian overstatement. U.P. society gleamed from every angle with the relative gaudiness
of the nouveau riche, and the pillars of the communities
tended to look down their noses at the wealthy of Chicago
and Detroit, those idlers who made their money in the slow
and tedious trades of selling grain, making carriages, running merchant ships, and slaughtering beef. The cream of
the U.P. had, after all, equaled the wealth of their southern
cousins in the space of mere months. That, in the minds
of the U.P. gentry, made clear which was the more capable
society.

In the manner of all booms, the copper rush went belly up
around the turn of the century. Feverish deep-shaft mining during the first World War played out all the easily
accessible ore in the Upper Peninsula. Shipping costs and
the logistics of distant smelters made what was left too
expensive to go after. Then the advent of strip mining in
other parts of the country made deep-shaft mining obsolete.

That was the final blow. Depression fell over the area like
a pall. People picked up and left, or followed subsistence
lifestyles, hunting and fishing for their food, and cutting
timber for pocket money. The children of the copper mo-
guls were left to live on their inheritances. Some were so
depressed by the change of events that they, too, lived as if
they were impoverished, even though they had hundreds
of thousands in the bank—usually D&N.

With the opening of the Mighty Mac, the area developed a new industry based on the ruggedness and beauty of the area. The children of the copper miners began to cater to tourists. But it was a grudging change of events. Wild northern winters kept the tourist season pitifully short; those who came outside the U.P.'s brief two-month summer were small groups—fishermen and snowmobilers. A parochial attitude was inevitable. Locals began to call themselves *UPers* (pronounced "you-pers"), and everyone else—even a summer resident—became a "lowper." Lowpers didn't belong. They were people from down south. Today in the Upper Peninsula, on evenings in the bars, when they don't think the tourists are around, you'll hear the citizens of the U.P. refer to the tourists as "trolls"— the people who live under the Bridge.

If the U.P. can be likened to another country, then Kenneth D. Seaton was certainly one of its princes. The lobby of D&N's headquarters building says this with pictures more adequately than it could ever be said in words: A floor-to-ceiling photo collage depicts the history and traditions of the region and there, amidst the images of mining equipment, pick-wielding Finns and pasty-eating Welshmen, Indian folk heroes, and the rugged Lake Superior shore, are pictures of Ken Seaton—with his family at a picnic; with his father at the building's ground-breaking; with his wife, Lois, on their wedding day. It is a blurring of family and corporation that would seem distinctly odd in most communities. In Hancock, where a Seaton had run the century-old thrift for 69 of its years, the link was seen as logical and natural. To many of the people who obtained loans and kept their deposits there, Ken Seaton *was* D&N, pure and simple.

He wore the mantle well. A hunter, skier, jogger, and all-around outdoorsman, Seaton kept fit with daily games of squash and racquetball, and he had—and some would say cultivated—a certain flamboyance about him. Midday strollers in Hancock were apt to see Ken out waterskiing during his lunch hour. This morning, Seaton, a former Navy seaplane pilot, had flown himself down to Detroit in an executive plane that D&N maintained for him. His shirts and suits were cut to accentuate the trim figure he kept, and he had, at most times, a bounce to his step, as if he could barely contain his own energy. This day, some of that bounce was gone, the only hint he gave that what we were about to have was anything other than a casual lunch between business acquaintances.

A young woman had come into the entrance hall behind Seaton. I stepped aside to let her pass. Instead, she just smiled back at me. She was very young, and I realized with a start that she was with Seaton. It puzzled me; had Ken Seaton brought one of his daughters along to what promised to be a rather rough business meeting?

Seaton solved the mystery by introducing her. The name almost immediately escaped me, but she was, it turned out, a public-relations person who had been retained by D&N.

"You don't mind if she joins us, do you, George?" he asked me.

I nodded to Bob Reichenbach, who saw the young lady into the library ahead of us. A public-relations person! I couldn't believe it. Did Seaton intend to conduct our conversation through a flack? I tapped him on the shoulder as he began to follow Bob and the young woman.

"Ken," I asked him, "what's with the P.R. lady?"

"Oh," he smiled back. "She's nothing—just someone who's going to be handling press contacts for us, things like that. I thought it'd be good if she listened in today. You know, sort of break her in to the job."

Now I was flabbergasted. Break her in to the job? She was going to get an earful, that much was sure. I stopped him again.

"Listen, Ken," I told him. "This is likely to get pretty frank today. I don't think you're going to want a third party listening in, you know?"

He remained silent. Maybe he *didn't* know.

"Tell you what," I offered. "If she wants to sit in for a general discussion, over the first part of the lunch, that's fine. But after that, she's got to go. We've got to be pretty candid here."

Seaton's brow furrowed, then he smiled.

"No problem, George," he said. "You want her gone, she's gone."

He walked over, whispered something in her ear, and she nodded and walked out. I remember wondering if she'd come down with him from Hancock, or if she was with a local agency. I hoped for the latter, because she stepped out on the streets of Detroit, and we never saw her again.

With that rather rocky start to things, the three of us went upstairs to lunch.

D&N's Trouble Begins

For the first 90 years of its existence, D&N Savings Bank had been a mutual thrift. Even if you aren't conversant in banks and thrifts, you know what a mutual thrift is if you've ever seen the movie *It's a Wonderful Life*. Remember the scene where the Bedford Falls Building and Loan officer misplaced a bag of deposits and there was a run on the thrift? And how Jimmy Stewart convinces the depositors to withdraw only what they need and to leave in what they can? At the end of that scene, he's left with two dollars, and he kisses the bills, because that's two dollars in the black, and so the thrift is still solvent.

That's a rosy, Hollywood explanation of how a mutual thrift works. The depositors are, in effect, the shareholders of the institution. They don't know that they are shareholders, and they don't get shareholder benefits: what they receive is interest, rather than dividends. But a mutual thrift is, like the Bedford Falls Building and Loan, basically a bank in which depositor money provides the capital for the institution, and the operation makes money by loaning from this capital and collecting a higher interest on these loans than the interest it pays out to savings depositors. And the surprising fact of the matter is that the mutual thrifts of this country were, for many years, very much like the Bedford Falls Building & Loan—humble little institutions run by paternalistic managers who viewed them as their own property. They didn't make a lot of noise, and eventually they built up mountains of assets.

When, eventually, these mutual thrifts went public, they were generally lucrative investments. The "shareholders" in a mutual thrift were, after all, the depositors, and the depositors didn't get anything from the sale but continued interest. In effect, when depositors were given the opportunity to buy shares in the newly converted-to-stock thrift institutions, they really bought their own equity back, and got with it all of the assets of the thrift—the use of monies deposited, the mortgages, the real estate owned, everything.

When a thrift converted to a stock company, nondepositor newcomers—like me—got the rare opportunity to buy shares at below book value. The new investors literally got something for nothing. The new investment funds coming into the corporation added to existing value and often doubled shareholders' equity, yet shares were sold to the public at half that new book value. Such a situation comprised a remarkable opportunity to buy value.

The downside was management. Imagine that you have a Jimmy-Stewart-type chairman of a thrift, whose family has run the place for nearly three-quarters of a century. Imagine that this chairman has come into the job by succession; he hasn't come within a hundred miles of Wharton on the way there, and he hasn't had to. It's his own show, and he runs it as he sees fit.

Then things change. To get extra capital, this benevolent, well-intentioned, paternal manager takes his thrift public and gets investor money. But all of a sudden, with this outside money comes outside scrutiny, and the thrift, that ran along quietly under the chairman's father, and his father before him, has people who are questioning how the place is being run. And the chairman gets upset. It's his thrift, isn't it?

The answer, of course, is that it's not. It stopped being the chairman's thrift when he accepted other people as investors.

There, in a nutshell, you have D&N. And there, in a nutshell, you have Ken Seaton.

Bad to Worse

The difference between D&N and the Bedford Falls Building and Loan is that the Bedford Falls B&L had competent management. Buildings and Loans, and Savings and Loans, were originally intended as community institutions. Well-run S&Ls still work this way; they know who they're getting their deposits from, and they know who they're loaning their money to. They're intended to be mortgage-lending institutions, investing money primarily in residential mortgages in their immediate communities.

After it had gone public, D&N had ceased to operate this way. Throughout its life, the thrift's board had been playing with other people's money; now they had money from other people who weren't even depositors. One wonders if they didn't see it as a denouement—a chance to spend the cash as they saw fit, secure in the knowledge that the investors were all trolls, down under the bridge somewhere, hundreds of miles away.

At any rate, D&N had gone from residential mortgages to commercial mortgages, and many of those had defaulted in a big way. Real estate owned, also known as "REOs"— real estate seized upon default—is supposed to be a very minor part of any bank's portfolio. With D&N, these REOs were numerous, and commercial real estate in Michigan was sagging, compounding the problem.

To make matters worse, the thrift had been putting money into investments such as collateralized mortgage obligations (CMOs). These derivatives, originally invented by Wall Street investment bankers, were instruments that looked like bonds, and sounded like bonds, but were not bonds at all. Most bonds represent portions of a loan made to a government or other credit worthy institution; CMO pools represented participation in *thousands* of loans made through thousands of individual mortgages.

In the best case, these instruments carried the hazard of not surviving to term: mortgage holders almost always have the option of refinancing and paying off a mortgage early, and in recessions, they do so often. But the problem with CMOs is that you own only the original mortgages, and not the replacement, so your capital comes back to you when interest rates are low and your reinvestment opportunities are poor.

In the worst case, mortgage holders can default. If the CMO is a package of shaky mortgages, and they all begin to go at once, the asset value of the security—the real estate backing the paper—drops as well.

D&N had also been getting itself into the purchase of whole loans and participation in loans made by other banks— with little regard to the solidity of the loan. Purchased loans usually arrived in the form of a six-inch stack of paper—the detail of the loan— topped by a check. The check was an earnest fee, tendered to the loan participant for assuming a portion of the obligation, and you could almost gauge the shakiness of the package by the size of the fee—the bigger the fee, the more likely you were to lose your shirt.

But D&N hadn't seen it that way. They saw the CMOs as high-yield investments backed by mortgages, and the purchased whole loans and participations as instant cash. And they were in the mortgage and money-lending business, right? A purchased loan fee was icing on the cake.

Some cake. Already, D&N was discovering how bitter it could be.

The Bomb Drops

The three of us—Reichenbach, Seaton, and I—went upstairs to the Detroit Club's third-floor dining room. Massively embellished with wooden ceiling beams and a lintel that seems to be three times the size of the door over which it stands, the room looks like something out of a Tudor castle. All the polished wood reflected sound far too well. Although there were diners at only about half the tables, we could clearly understand conversations halfway across the room.

Not wanting to start off with both barrels—particularly with other ears listening in—I took out a copy of D&N's annual report, and complimented Seaton on it.

"Why, thank you," he relaxed visibly, touching the report's gray-flannel-like cover. "We're quite proud of it."

I opened the report to the detail in the back.

"I particularly appreciate the good disclosure, like the disclosure on market value of investments owned," I said. "It says here that investments have gone from a little over $20 million underwater to about $50 million underwater. That's good for an investor to know."

Seaton said nothing. He knew, as I knew, that the disclosure had been mandated by increasingly tight restrictions on how thrifts report their earnings and losses. Still, D&N had done a good job of burying the detail; I'd only found it because Bob Reichenbach, as a CPA, has special expertise in reading such reports. I had no doubt that we were the only investors who both had the expertise and had taken the time to understand the true nature of D&N's own investment picture.

"Ken," I said. "I think you know we recently filed a 13-D."

Form 13-D is required by the SEC when an investor or investment group significantly increases its ownership in a public thrift. Our group had recently moved up to the point where we had slightly over 7.4 percent of D&N's stock.

Seaton nodded. He'd seen the notice of the filing.

"Our group now has 285,000 shares in D&N," I added.

He nodded.

"Then," I continued, "you'll understand our concern."

The rest of the lunch went quietly. We chatted about the industry in general and the outlook for the recession continuing. It was hard to get down to brass tacks; there were too many ears in the room. Finally, as coffee was being brought around and Seaton was signing his chit, I leaned toward him.

"Can the three of us speak privately?" I asked.

Seaton said nothing for a moment, and then nodded and got up. The three of us took our cups with us and walked into one of the club's private dining rooms. Seaton sat, I sat, and Bob shut the door.

"What's up?" Seaton asked.

"What's up is that my investors have had their pockets picked to the tune of $2 million dollars."

He looked pained.

"C'mon, George," he said. "That's paper. It goes up and down. It'll come back."

"I don't think so."

He sat up.

"Then why," he asked, "the 13-D? If we're such a lousy investment, why'd you increase your position?"

"Because we're now your single biggest stockholder, and that puts us in a position to do something about it."

Seaton forced a smile.

"But we're doing something already," he said. "We're altering our investment strategy."

I nodded at Bob.

"Show him," I said.

Bob brought out a document he and I had drafted, titled "Ed Opens a Gambling Parlor." The "Ed" here was Ed Burger, D&N's chief financial officer. The document showed, step by step, how, under Burger's strategies, losses in shaky "high-yield" investments had been followed by investments that indicated the promise of even higher yields—and a proportionately higher risk of going bust. Seaton stared at it for a moment.

"Don't you see?" he said. "It shows here we're fixing it; the higher interest will take care of it."

Reichenbach and I stared at one another. The man didn't get it at all.

"Ken," I said. "the return *on* the principal doesn't mean anything. It's return *of* the principal that counts. You're running a thrift, not a junk-bond fund. You can't afford to risk your shareholders' capital like this."

He still didn't look like he got it.

"So what do you suggest I do?" he asked.

"To start with, resign your position with the U.S. League."

He stared at us.

"That's crazy," he said.

The U.S. League of Savings Institutions is the industry group of the American thrifts. As such, it weighs in heavily in industrial and political circles, and Seaton that year had become vice chairman. Under the League's order of succession, he would become chairman in 1990, and the chairman was a big wig, with a capital "B," consulted by Congress and the president and quoted often by the press. Being chairman of the U.S. League would mark the pinnacle of Seaton's career.

"Ken," I told him, the little private dining room quiet around us, "your business is in trouble and you have a fiduciary responsibility to your shareholders to pay attention to that business. You simply can't do that if you're off hob-nobbing at the White House."

"You just don't understand," he told me. "That position will help D&N immeasurably."

"No," I said, "you don't understand. By the time next year rolls around, there might not be a D&N to be helped."

He smiled thinly.

"I think you're overstating the situation," he said.

"Another thing," I continued. "I think we should sell the company."

This one almost brought him to his feet.

He regained his composure quickly and said, "It's not the time to do that, George. Just give us some time. We'll pull through. We have for a hundred years, and we will again this time."

I wanted to ask him who the hell "we" were; Mark Twain once said that only monarchs and people with tapeworms were allowed to use the pronoun "we."

"Ken," I said quietly. "there are plenty of banks—banks like Comerica and Michigan National—that will pay handsomely to acquire D&N and get the deposit base. D&N's unrealized portfolio loss situation will actually be advantageous to them from a tax standpoint, and you have good depositor populations in several key counties."

He said nothing.

"Also," I continued, "I'm sure we can get you a seat on the board of the acquiring institution. You won't lose any face here; your investors will admire you. Your career will be secure."

"You're saying," he asked, "that it's not secure now?"

"I'm saying," I said, "that you are headed for public shame and humiliation. Why put yourself through that? Why put your family through that?"

He shook his head.

"It's simply not as bad as you think," he said, getting to his feet. "Just wait; we've weathered worse times. D&N will come through."

But you won't, I wanted to say. I held my tongue. The three of us took our leave, and Seaton led us out of the room.

On the wall opposite the dining room, there was a painting that had always caught my eye, one of the few in the Club that was not a landscape or a seascape. Painted by Frederick Church, it was simply called *Flapjacks*, and it showed a beautiful, sweet-faced young woman flipping pancakes as bandanna-wearing bears rushed in from all directions, carrying plates. I'd always admired the whimsy of it. Now I saw a darker side.

Bears were, after all, inherently dangerous animals.

So what would happen to the sweet-faced young woman when she ran out of pancakes?

Chapter 11

Heavy Artillery

Set aside for a moment the harsh financial realities of taking over a company by buying it out. Even if you forget for a moment that buyouts, especially leveraged buyouts (LBOs), all too often leave a firm heavily ridden with debt and ominous interest obligations, another point remains: no matter how sincere your wishes, buying an entire public company out is an open invitation for everyone to make you the Bad Guy.

I call it the "Snidely Whiplash Syndrome." In a buyout, the party doing the buyout is usually seen — or portrayed— as a megabucks bully (never mind that the money for the buyout is almost certainly borrowed), picking on the Little Nells of management. Local media present the picture in terms of "Us versus Them"; management paints the situation for the workforce as a case of raping the family.

While little publicized (for journalists, the "story" is gone from a takeover as soon as the new management is in place), the damage precipitated by such posturing may be as heavy—or heavier—than that caused by debt-loading the bought-out company. What the Whartons and Harvards of the world all too often fail to realize is that business is, at its roots, an extraordinarily human enterprise. Workforces who think Machiavelli has moved into the executive suite are probably spending more time on their resumés than they are on their jobs. The buying public, schooled on grape boycotts and *It's a Wonderful Life*, may turn their collective back on a firm that a buyout has rendered Politically Incorrect. And frankly, as they try to tug a debt-ridden elephant back from the edge of the financial precipice, the buyers may not think too much of one another after a couple of months, either.

. . .All of which adds up to a marvelous recommendation for Change from Within.

The instrument of that change is the proxy.

THE PROXY

The term, *proxy*, is actually a very old contraction of *procuracy*. That word in turn is descended from the Latin *procuratio*—the title of an agent of the Roman Empire retained by the emperor to manage the financial affairs of a province or to govern a territory. Thus, a proxy is an instrument empowering one person to act on behalf of another. It is often compared to the celebrated "power of attorney," but the comparison is inaccurate; a proxy merely designates an agent and instructs that agent as to the originator's wishes. Thus the office of a proxy (for the term applies to the agent of the action, as well as the instrument) is more of a representative than anything else. The entire proxy process is a miniature representation of the way a republican form of government works—or rather, the way it should work: the many express their wishes to the few, who act in behalf of their electors.

If you hold shares in a publicly traded American corporation, you have doubtlessly seen at least one form of proxy. This is the little pamphlet and ballot that arrive in the mail about a month or so before the annual shareholders' meeting. The pamphlet, particularly if it is a large corporation with the tonnage of a GM or an IBM, will probably contain propositions forwarded by shareholders that ask the share-holders to vote in favor of a resolution, usually one commanding the directors to do something that they don't want to do. The pamphlet will then contain a reply from the directors in which they very diplomatically imply that the originators of the proposition are disillusioned crackpots, and that to vote for what they suggest will prove the downfall of the company and the American Way of Life.

The meat of this type of proxy is, however, the election of directors. The same pamphlet that pooh-poohs the shareholder propositions will contain glowing descriptions of board candidates. And the little board-of-directors ballot will even go so far as to contain a box that says, more or less, "All of the above." In a concession to democracy, there will also usually be a second affirmative choice that instructs the directors to elect or retain "all candidates proposed by the Board with the exception of _____"— the blank being a little line with sufficient room for one name. It is said that Roger Smith, the former chairman of General Motors, was highly irritated by the frequency with which his name appeared on this little line, particularly in the final years of his chairmanship.

Many people assume that this ballot and its accompanying pamphlet arrive from the company itself. That is not exactly correct. The true source of this proxy is one step removed from the company as a whole; it is the *managers* of the company who initiate "management proxies," and managers conduct proxy campaigns in order to enable themselves to run things as they see fit.

Thus, boards get elected from directors selected by boards—or rather, by the chairpeople of boards. It's as if the president were to decide who was allowed to run for Congress; the balance of power takes a sudden plunge to the administrative side. Yet, as cockamamie as they may seem, such practices have been traditional in even the largest of American corporations. In business, government for the leaders has been alive and well for decades.

It takes only a small amount of imagination to see that the proxy is a two-edged sword. Managers can request proxies, but so can any other legitimate shareholder of a corporation. When that happens, when shareholder spokespeople and managers are competing for the endorsement of the many, a proxy contest ensues—sometimes with all the subtlety of a presidential election campaign.

Institutional Investment Tips Scales in Proxy Battles

Proxy contests were once derided in the financial world as the "poor man's buyout." The prevailing theory was that anyone who *really* wanted to change the management style of a company would just take out his checkbook and buy it, and those who lacked the means to do so probably weren't cut out to manage, anyhow. That was in the days when the vast majority of shares were held by individuals or family trusts.

A proxy contest in a company with a highly fragmented shareholder list is a laborious process, and one heavily slanted in favor of management.

Sometimes, there is the problem of discovering who one's fellow shareholders are. Shareholder lists have traditionally been open to scrutiny during shareholder meetings, but they have been open in only the most technical sense. I recall one time when I traveled cross-country to inspect such a list, only to be told when I approached the board that the time to inspect the list had come earlier in the meeting and that the window of time allowed for my inspection (had I been quick enough to spot the opportunity) would have lasted about 30 seconds. Under such a system, it's all but impossible to learn anything of substance concerning a company's ownership, even if one attends the meeting with one's own portable photocopier.

Another hurdle has been that conversation among shareholders has somehow managed for years to escape protection under the constitutional provision guaranteeing freedom of speech. Under long-standing SEC proxy rules, investors contacting more than 10 other shareholders first had to file for permission with the SEC. This was, of course, tantamount to waving a red flag before management, thus informing them that their positions are in jeopardy.

In years past, those attempting to circulate nonmanagement proxy material were likely to communicate with only the tiniest minority of their shareholder peers, and they were kept busy jumping through hoops while management communicated with the masses relatively unencumbered. It should surprise no one that management usually won.

The picture changed with the advent of institutional investing.

In 1990, Carolyn K. Brancato, chief economist at Columbia's institutional investor project, estimated that a little over 45 percent of the equity in U.S. companies was held by institutional investors—union pension funds, mutual funds, and the like. By 1992, *Business Week* magazine was reporting that institutional investors had gone over the top, accounting for 53 percent of ownership of all American stocks.

The difference, of course, is that while an individual shareholder may hold on the average a few hundred shares of a company's stock, the institutional investor typically has hundreds of thousands of shares in its portfolio. Among publicly traded companies today, there is hardly a case where the largest shareholder is not an institution of one form or another. This means that contacting the manager of one pension fund, or one mutual fund, may be more effective than contacting hundreds of individual shareholders. Moreover, a letter campaign to a broad shareholder list generally requires SEC clearance, while a phone call to an institutional manager does not. With this change in investor demographics, the proxy-contest playing field, while still not level, became less of a mountain in favor of management. For the first time, investor insurgents became more effective than the proverbial mosquito.

The difference could be seen in the aftermath. Leveraged buyouts, while the surest way to take control of management, generally leave companies as empty shells of their former selves, carrying huge debt burdens and only marginally competitive. Proxy contests often fail to unseat management but usually end up effecting change nonetheless.

Writing for *Investors Daily* in 1990, Vineeta Anand rated the 18 contests of that year's annual meeting season as amounting to eight management victories, three dissident wins, and seven settlement draws. But Anand went on to report that according to a study by Analysis Group, Inc., nonmanagement proxy contestants achieved their goals in 11 of 14 contests, regardless of whether they won the contests. One example cited was American General Corporation's board, which won their proxy battle yet decided only weeks later to put the company up for sale— exactly as investor insurgents had requested.

One University of Michigan study, which traced the aftermath of 60 proxy fights waged between 1978 and 1985, showed that fully 80 percent of the companies experienced changes in control within three years of their contest, regardless of the outcome.

Institutional investors are usually managed by individuals schooled in fiduciary responsibility and more willing to exercise the proxy option to protect shareholder interests. With institutional investing becoming ever more the norm in America, it would seem inevitable that the 80 percent figure will grow. The message is clear; sooner or later, proxy contests unseat inadequate managers.

When Management Needs Change

Inadequate management is, of course, the proxy contest's *raison d'etre*. In a *Business Week* commentary in April 1990, Judith Dobryznski and Eric Schine wrote ". . .It's Open Season on Yes-Man Boards." The writers succinctly summarized the situation that puts fuel in the proxy engine:

> What do shareholders want? The answer isn't that tough to figure. They want corporate boards to watch out for their (the shareholders') interests and management to do its best to increase value over the long term.

Dobryznski and Schine then went on to present a blueprint for directors who wished to stay on their boards. They advised them to:

- Push for a new strategy to increase shareholder value

- Set targets and deadlines for management

- Be prepared to change management, if goals aren't met

- Improve oversight of critical company activities

- Review their (the board's) own performance

Boards who don't follow this prescription will be more and more likely to be unseated by proxy, simply because, unlike its LBO cousin, the proxy contest does not run the risk of amputating value in order to effect change.

Moreover, proxy contests are considerably cheaper to mount. In April 1990, *Time* reported that the professional fees and expenses from buyouts and takeovers accounted for between 2 and 4 percent of the value of a transaction. The fee-and-expense "tax" on a proxy action, on the other hand, usually runs considerably below one percent.

Target: The Arrogant CEO

There is, of course, an alternative to any action—proxy, buyout, takeover, or otherwise: managers' use of the tradi-

tional director-appointment process to put vested interests on the board in the first place. But managers seem
terribly slow to learn the lesson.

I'm reminded of a seminar I attended in 1990, shortly before starting the proxy contest with Detroit and Northern.
The seminar was held by SNL Securities, a research firm
that specializes in thrift stocks (the firm's name is a delib-
erate play on "S&L"). Run by an incredibly sharp and garrulous fellow named Reid Nagle, SNL had noted a trend
toward proxy contests in the thrift industry and had invited several "market operators" (I've always bristled at
the term) to come discuss running such contests—not just
proxy battles per se, but *thrift* proxy battles.

For the sake of balance, Reid had invited a few thrift CEOs.
Most of these spent the two days of the seminar wander-
ing around with the jumpy, suspicious demeanor of a John
Bircher at a May-Day celebration. But a few of them spoke
up, and I remember one who stood, obviously irritated by
everything he'd heard, and debated with Nagle.

Nagle had just said that it was in a CEO's best interest to
pay attention when a major stockholder, especially one
who owned 9.9 percent of the company, had something to
say.

"Fine," this CEO replied. "So I give this guy an audience
and let him have his say. Then what? The next thing you
know, he'll be asking me to give him a seat on the board.
Just because he owns 9.9 percent. And the next thing you
know, it'll be open season on my board seats. Anybody
who wants to can buy 9 or 10 percent of the company, and
they'll want me to give them board seats."

This, unbelievably, was how he was putting it: they were
his board seats, and investors were asking him to *give* them
seats on the board he owned. I don't think he even heard
the titters running through the audience.

"Anyhow," the CEO asked Nagle, "say I do what this guy
wants. Say I give him a board seat because he's got almost

a tenth of the company. Then, say nine other guys come along, and they each have 9.9 percent, and I have to give them seats as well. Then where am I?"

"You," Nagle replied, "are exactly where you should be. You have a board of directors composed of people whose investment interests coincide exactly with the best interests of the company. There is no hidden agenda, no second agenda—what's good for the company is good for the owners, and vice versa. What you have, in short, is the perfect board of directors—perfect representation by the owners for whom *you* work."

Applause broke out in the seminar hall and the CEO sat down, scowling—this obviously wasn't how he'd intended things to come out.

I don't know if that CEO still has his company. I do know that, whether he likes it or not, he is eventually going to have directors who are major investors in his company. And he'll have it whether he gives it or they take it, whether he loses a proxy war or eventually gives in to scrutiny.

The only difference in how he gets there is whether *he'll* be there as well.

Chapter *12*

ESOP Fables

I mentioned earlier that I reject the popular notion that successful investors are gamblers. I do not see myself as a gambler. Nor do I see myself as the Grim Reaper.

This is an important point, because I want to make it very clear that this book is not a blanket invective against management. Nor am I advising investors to actively search for poorly managed companies and then turn a profit by either chopping heads at all levels or closing down the company and selling off the bones.

I am well aware that there are investors today who will disagree with me. Some investor groups specialize in seeking out those companies that have fallen into the hands of the managerially challenged; these investors then put in their own management teams or sell company assets for a profit. There are even a few investors who have developed a reputation for filing lawsuits to get management to run the companies as the investors see fit, to offer the company (or its component parts) for sale, or encourage the company to pay "greenmail" to make the investors go away. Irwin ("the Liquidator") Jacobs and—early on in his career—Carl Icahn were famous for this latter course.

Just as an honest man has nothing to fear from a lie-detector test, a healthy company with a good future has nothing to fear from what the press likes to call "takeover artists" or "raiders."

But the faltering or downsliding company had *better* have some investors who will call for management change if the rest of its shareholder base wishes to see something useful come from their investment.

Certainly, it is traumatic for a company or its management to be forced to sell off an old and cherished division, or to drop the new activities it had added in order to see "growth," or to even close its doors entirely and liquidate its assets.

But such courses are like chemotherapy for an individual suffering from cancer. They may seem debilitating and they may cause pain. But they are drastic measures taken to deal with a situation that is already certain to be fatal unless something is done immediately.

And—this is important—when investors rise up to confront management and wrest control away, they are not doing it to "hurt the company" or "ruin the business." The company is already injured, and the business already headed for ruin, or the investors would have no reason to take such drastic actions.

I have always seen traditional, true, long-term investors— among which I number myself—as farmers. We don't pick stocks because we want to pick a fight with managers. Rather, we invest in companies in which we *like* the composition and style of the management team.

Value investors are looking for Sleeping Beauties, those increasingly rare companies that have value far in excess of their market price, and that have the potential to see any number of future increases in both value and price.

My firm specializes in investment in a number of different industries, such as thrifts, banks and insurance companies, retail stores, information and database companies, and healthcare companies. I like to buy dollars for fifty cents, so we look in these areas for well-managed companies that, due to market preferences (such as the tendency of many investors to sour on thrifts after the Keatings scandal), are trading at about half of their actual value. We hold such companies until they reach about 70–80 percent of actual value—a point that may take some time to reach because, often, as a company's stock rises in price, its actual value is appreciating as well. In the meantime, like a farmer who has purchased fertile land, we are enjoying regular harvests in the form of dividends.

The majority of these companies never require intervention from either my firm or our fellow shareholders. My hope, quite frankly, is that such intervention will be unnecessary. After all, responsibility for the careful stewardship of the company lies with the board of directors; they are paid to look out for the best interests of the shareholders. When an investor has to take action to prevent or reverse a loss of value, that investor incurs cost (if nothing else, he is taking his eye off the ball in other areas in order to concentrate on this single company). That means the investor is paying over again for the service that the board was supposed to provide in the first place, and common sense says it is unwise to pay for the same thing twice.

The actions that we are discussing in this book, then— outside intervention with a company's board, suing the board, or conducting proxy campaigns to gain board seats or force the board to necessary action—are the Heimlich maneuvers of investment. You learn them and hope you won't have to use them.

How ESOPs can Benefit Management at Shareholders' Expense

Years ago, my firm made significant investment in M.H. Rhodes, Inc., a company based in Avon, Connecticut, that manufactured timers of all sorts, from parking meters to munitions fuse timers for the Department of Defense. The latter customer had been good for Rhodes, and my staff analysts and I could see value here well above the share price.

The company's chairman, Mark Rhodes, was one of those charismatic individuals, a virtual patriarch who enjoyed whole-hearted dedication from his employees.

When Rhodes retired from his namesake company, his parting action was to establish an ESOP—an employee stock ownership plan—for the workforce that had been so dedicated to him over the years.

A noble gesture?

Let me say, first of all, that—despite all the arguments that have been made in their favor—I have yet to see, in all my years of investing, an ESOP that worked. Most fail to improve a company's value beyond a point that it would have reached anyhow. Many ESOP-owned companies, like Eastern Airlines, just fail—period.

ESOPs fail because they are socialism in capitalism's clothing. Capitalists expect a company to provide a safe harbor for principal and a return on investment; socialists expect a company to provide income for workers at any cost necessary. The two philosophies are not good bedfellows.

Be that as it may, the mere establishment of an M.H. Rhodes ESOP was not a major stumbling block. *That* came in the way Rhodes put the deal together.

M.H. Rhodes, Inc., at this time, was trading at $10 a share. The company's value (my own calculations confirmed this) was more along the lines of $20 a share.

Mark Rhodes established his ESOP by selling his own stock to the employees—at *$28 a share.* He was making an out-and-out killing. But at whose expense?

Where did the employees get the money to fund this grossly overpriced ESOP? Mark Rhodes convinced M.H. Rhodes' board to have the firm borrow the money and then loan it to the ESOP.

Overnight, the company's financial structure went massively upside-down. M.H. Rhodes, Inc., which had enjoyed an intrinsic value twice its market price, was mortgaged well into the next century. My fellow shareholders and I saw our "stable investment" go from no debt to a debt level that was *six* times equity in the blink of an eye. This virtually destroyed the firm's ability to do business profitably from that time onward.

This was not a case that called for a proxy contest. The damage was already done, and besides, a proxy contest did not seem winnable; 55 percent of the stock now resided with the employees, who were happy—they had an ESOP! To correct the situation, I felt that I had no course of action open but to sue, so I obtained counsel in Connecticut and filed suit against M.H. Rhodes, its board, and the estate of its former chairman, who had died shortly after he screwed every single one of his shareholders.

For the uninitiated, let me warn you now that suing management is the shareholder's equivalent of diving head-first into the tiger's mouth. You might make your point, but you will be worse for wear at the end of it.

Fortunately, I was not alone in my lawsuit against M.H. Rhodes' board of directors and managers and their ESOP plan. I was privileged to have Max Heines as a co-plaintiff. Max founded Mutual Shares, the predecessor to the Mutual Series Fund, an extremely successful old-line value fund now managed by his protégé, Mike Price. Max is widely acknowledged to be one of the greats in value investing, and having him on my side was like finding out that Mickey Mantle has agreed to play on your company's softball team.

Even so, the lawsuit would be harrowing.

The first thing my Connecticut law firm told me was that in order to prepare for trial, it would have to assign several full partners to the case, and have them work night and day for three weeks, just to get ready for their first day in court. Full partners in Connecticut law firms—particularly those who specialize in corporate law—are not cheap. I quickly saw my legal bills mount into the hundreds of thousands of dollars.

M.H. Rhodes' board fought my suit using corporate funds. Since I was still a shareholder, I was, in effect, funding *their* effort, as well. To the other shareholders (the majority of whom were now employees and participants in the ESOP), I was portrayed as a malcontent filing a lawsuit that was costing them money. It was not a happy time.

If proxy actions are the Heimlich maneuver of shareholding, lawsuits are CPR. They are drastic, life-and-death actions that, when they do work, do so only at great cost.

M.H. Rhodes was my first major legal action against a company, and I was astounded by some of the questions my Hartford attorneys asked. Did I have skeletons in my closet—any criminal indictments, bad employment records, or extramarital affairs? My Michigan attorneys assured them I was, in their words "so clean he squeaks," and the Hartford firm said that was good—otherwise, relevant or not, it was sure to emerge in court.

Furthermore, since it was using its shareholders' funds to mount its defense, M.H. Rhodes' board appeared ready to fight down to the last dime. The pre-trial hearings dragged on and on.

At one point, the judge in New Haven, Connecticut, invited me—me alone—into his chambers and asked about my son, who was just about to start college on the East Coast.

"I'm asking," the judge said, "because even though you'll probably win this case, that boy of yours will have gotten his degree and will be well into graduate school before this case has completely run its course in the courts. Now, I'm willing to spend that time, if you want to. That's my job. But do you really want to spend the next four or five years of your life in courtrooms? And even after you win here, you know the company will appeal to a higher court. Do you want to pursue it that far? Do you think it's worth it?"

I was not the first litigant to discover that our legal system is not designed to mete out justice in court—it is designed to encourage out-of-court settlement. And settlements are arbitrated arrangements in which each side gives up more ground than it cares to.

I won—after six years in court—if you consider getting a few cents back on the dollar a victory.

I pass this story along as advice to anyone who plans on making a career of investing in companies and then "shaking up" the management. When board and managers fight—regardless of whether the battle is set in a proxy contest or the courtroom—they almost always do so with the funds of the company at their disposal, and at little personal expense. They almost always have more bullets than the investors. Even if they do not, they are not buying bullets with their own money—the investor usually is.

I pass along these courtroom war stories and this "ESOP fable" because I think it contains a moral worth learning—think about the consequences of what you're doing.

Too often, investment with the intention of forcing a change in management seems to me about as logical as going out of one's way to catch a disease, just so you can fight it. The cost doesn't justify the action. Even when you win, you lose. The lawyers (on both sides) always win, of course.

This is not to say that my firm and I are never again going to campaign for the breakup of a failing company, or apply pressure to get a board to live up to its fiduciary responsibilities, or campaign for a board seat and a change in management, or even sue a board and its managers if the situation calls for it.

All of these actions are justifiable in certain situations. In some cases, it would be a moral outrage to stand by and do nothing while a company's governing body does potentially irreparable harm. From a company-ownership standpoint, it certainly is more responsible to act than to do what most unhappy investors do—they sell their stock.

But one key here is to lessen the need for such actions by using common sense in your investing in the first place. And the other is to develop the ability to distinguish between short-term setbacks and those actions that really and truly threaten the livelihood of a firm for the foreseeable future.

Chapter 13

The Fast Lane

Some people see shareholder activism—shareholders speaking up to boards and holding them accountable for their actions—as democracy in action. Others see the movement toward greater shareholder involvement as a classic example of the inmates running the asylum. Regardless of which way you lean, the definite trend is that the shareholder voice has become both stronger and more compelling in recent years, and institutional investors have been at the heart of it.

This wasn't always the case. In years past, pension funds accounted for the vast majority of institutional investors. Pension funds were generally closely affiliated with a single company or corporation, and corporations tended to take care of one another. In this climate, it was a decidedly unwise career move for a fund manager to speak out against the management of a poorly performing company. Those who spoke up were open to chiding from the managers of the firm whose pension they managed. Threats of moving the pension to another manager—or, at very least, the implication of such threats—were common in such events. Under such conditions, the most a manager could do with a losing company was "vote with his feet": sell the stock.

Things Start Moving

Two things happened to change this climate.

The first was the greater enfranchisement of *union*, as opposed to company, pension funds. Unions are not disinclined to criticize corporate managers; some would claim
that the only reason for a union's existence is to do exactly
that. Unions, moreover, are schooled on the principle of
common good. The combination of these elements—a tradition of management criticism and a virtually intuitive
ability to measure corporate performance by how the company benefited its stockholders—made union pension
funds virtual hotbeds of shareholder activism. Add to this
the fact that social issues have schooled union funds in
the intricacies of shareholder politics (witness the staggering number of Northern Irish and South African refer-
enda that have cropped up at shareholder meetings over
the last two decades) and you had, so to speak, motive,
means, and opportunity. Combined, they added up to
proxy actions aimed at unseating ineffective managers.

The other thing that changed the institutional climate was
the growth and proliferation of mutual funds. Virtually
unheard of by the individual investors of an earlier generation, mutual funds have come to be seen by the public
as a very comfortable halfway point between the savings
account and the individual stock portfolio. As they became popular, such funds offered an option to taking one's
financial life in one's own hands—one could put it, instead, in the hands of someone who supposedly knew what
they were doing. As word got around, and the general
public learned that the right mutual fund could provide
both stability and a better return than that available at the
corner First National, mutual funds became part of the
common vocabulary.

In years past, people had participated in the stock market,
purchasing individual issues. With the growth and popularity of mutual funds, people no longer "played the mar-

ket." Instead, they played the *managers*. Magazines sprang up to track those managers with the ability to beat the market. Investors, in turn, learned to pull out and find another fund if the one they'd chosen was not performing as expected. In fact, Dreyfus, Fidelity, and others encouraged people to do just that, fielding entire platoons of funds, and offering its customers the option of switching from one Dreyfus fund to another with less hassle than one would have in switching banks.

This sent a bold and obvious message to mutual fund managers: get your fund performing or get another line of work. Those who found their golden geese turning to turkeys were highly motivated to correct the situation.

THE INSTITUTIONALS AWAKEN

Harry DeAngelo, professor of business at the University of Southern California, is one monitor who has noticed the shift in institutional involvement. Widely cited in years past as an expert who saw institutions staying out of the proxy-contest picture, DeAngelo feels that the climate has now changed.

"My perception is that things have changed significantly," he told me in a recent conversation on institutional involvement, "and they started to change right around 1983. In the GAF proxy contest, a dissident showed that he could go up against management, where there was significant institutional stake, and actually win.

"I'm not really sure why institutional investors have been coming around," he continued, "other than the fact that there has been increasing acceptance of hostile takeover amendments, and also increasing pressure on institutional types for performance; both of those factors would make them more open to considering a vote against management. I still think that there are pressures on them; they still get the heavy pressures not to go against management, but I guess I just think that it's less so, or that the two pro-change factors are sufficient to get them to go with a dissident."

DeAngelo and his wife, Linda (also a USC business professor), have studied a number of proxy contests and are generally seen as the accepted authorities on outcome research. Their findings refute the snowball's-chance-in-hell conventional wisdom surrounding proxy contests. The bottom line? The DeAngelos have found that in any given proxy contest, there's a better than 2-in-3 chance that a dissident or dissident group will affect some change in the board of directors.

This doesn't necessarily mean that the dissident faction will gain board seats. But it does mean that even in cases where management "wins" the contest, there is an overwhelming tendency for directors to resign seats within the following three years.

"You could probably say that there is a better chance for dissident groups to affect changes in companies as time goes on, if you phrase the statement very carefully—that is, if you control for the attributes of poor performance on management's part," DeAngelo told me. "I don't have the data for that, but I'm making an informed guess on the basis of what I've seen. Actually, if you look at the incidents of 'success' over time, you'll probably find that success rates haven't gone up; they've gone down. However, what I think has happened is that dissidents have become a lot bolder over time. They've seen some success, so they've been willing to challenge companies like Sears in proxy contests. Firms that one would previously have thought inviolable are now at least vulnerable to challenge."

The bottom line, DeAngelo says, is that the proxy challenge is now standard-issue in the institutional investor's arsenal. And the reason it's there is because proxy challenges have proven to be effective instruments of change.

"I guess it's possible that dissidents are succeeding in gaining board seats because shareholders are now becoming more accustomed to seeing proxy solicitations from groups other than management—that such a solicitation no longer seems odd to shareholders," he told me when we last spoke. "But that wouldn't be my first guess. I think the difference is that shareholders have seen dissidents have some *effect*—not just that they've seen more of them. Certainly, the institutional investors—the people who manage those accounts—are pretty sophisticated people, and it's not that they didn't previously know what a proxy contest was; I think they were doing calculations of these accounts, these money management accounts, and the people that run these plans didn't want to be branded as renegades."

FULL SPEED AHEAD: UNITED SHAREHOLDERS' ASSOCIATION

Some people, on the other hand, don't mind being branded renegades at all. In 1986, T. Boone Pickens founded the United Shareholders' Association (USA), and the principal reason for USA's founding was nothing other than finding more effective means of shaking some bottom-line sense back into corporate America.

T. Boone Pickens, the Voice in the Wilderness

I'd first met Pickens in the early 1980s when he came to speak to a group of investors and portfolio managers at the Detroit Athletic Club. Boone, who had already mounted raids at Phillips Petroleum, Gulf Oil, and several other companies, was raising his visibility among investors generally and attempting to gain support for his pro-shareholder cause.

At the time, Boone was riding a wave of popularity among a rather narrow group of us who were vocal and zealous advocates of corporate governance and shareholder rights. We'd admired him in print; in person he set us on fire. When Boone spoke about the need for corporate owners to regain control of their property, I stood on my chair and led the cheers. The Reverend Pickens was preaching fire and brimstone to the managerial sinners, salvation to the shareholder faithful.

In the months and years that followed, though, I realized that very few of those who had attended Boone's talk really shared my zeal for shareholder rights. It was one thing to applaud when Boone lambasted million-dollar CEOs for their miserably poor performance and quite another to take on corporate managers on their own turf. Fear of failure, hesitance to resist the powers that be, the presence of a bank director on the board of a target company—for whatever reason, many bank trust managers found it politically impractical to side with Boone in his proxy fights.

Fortunately, I never suffered from such inhibitions. It helped greatly that I ran an independent investment management firm, and so I didn't have to worry about a boss who might be part of the interlocking directorships of the Fortune 500. This left me free to speak for what I believed in, and I knew that if people like Pickens could be given enough support from shareholder ranks, the CEOs and boards of public companies might finally start to get the message.

In the early 1980s, as Ronald Reagan and Margaret Thatcher were taking their conservative rebellion into the mainstream of political thought, shareholder democracy, too, was being elevated. But it was an embryonic movement, with few participants. At that time, I came very close to running a proxy contest against Nathan Rosenfeld, CEO of Jacobson Stores. My analysts and I had determined that the price of Jacobson's stock—about $10 at the time—was less than one-fifth of its potential value, simply because the company's management was performing poorly. My clients and I had accumulated about 20 percent of the outstanding stock when I heard through a mutual friend that Rosenfeld had been diagnosed with terminal cancer.

A fair fight is one thing. But nothing, not even the prospect of a 400 percent return, could convince me to wage a proxy fight against an elderly man dying of cancer. I put on the brakes; Rosenfeld died shortly thereafter. His son, Mark, implementing many of the steps I'd advocated, went on to build the company to the point where the stock, adjusted for splits, crested at the equivalent of $200 a share.

Still, even though my proxy fight against Jacobson turned out to be the proxy fight that never was, my efforts had attracted attention and glowing approval from Pickens' corner. It was obvious to both of us that we were fighting for the same cause.

Later, when I'd not only waged a successful campaign at D&N, but out-polled management by four-to-one among the independent shareholders, the United Shareholders' Association was again in my corner. Pickens and his people were firm in their support during the campaign, and wild with their applause when I won. They remain friends and allies to this day.

"I think it's safe to describe the general shareholder's position as ludicrous when Boone first started the organization," Cari Christensen, USA's executive director, told me. "The deck was heavily stacked on the side of management; the people who actually owned companies had lost their voice."

That, Christensen says, inspired USA to set up an agenda geared toward regaining some measure of shareholder voice.

United Shareholders' Association Motivates Changes in SEC Regulations

"It was one of the things Boone looked at when he founded USA," she said, "so it was always there, as a goal. And it was embodied in a proposal that we eventually sent to the SEC, suggesting a number of revisions to the rules governing how shareholders can interact with one another and effect change in their companies."

The changes USA proposed included an easing of the restriction requiring proxy filings whenever more than 10 shareholders gathered to discuss an issue. USA also proposed that the SEC make it more difficult for companies to "camouflage" poor performance, by requiring companies to compare their performance to that of peer companies whenever a proxy statement is issued. Finally, USA asked that the "we/they" stigma of dissident candidacy be removed; at the time of USA's founding, a dissident could run as an individual, or could propose replacement of an entire board, but could not run as part of a "mixed slate" of managers and dissidents combined. What USA suggested was a contingency that allowed dissidents to keep valuable board members and include them as a part of a revised management team on dissident proxy statements.

USA's proposal was eventually codified as a series of proposed changes submitted for public comment by the SEC in June 1990.

"We commented," Christensen said. "We not only sent our own letters from USA in support of the changes, we encouraged our stock-holding members to do so, as well."

The USA commentary was so positive and so resounding that it triggered reactions from the corporate community.

"The Business Roundtable (a pro-management association) got involved late in the process," Christensen recalled in a conversation we had just a few days after the reforms went through. "They even went so far as to arrange meetings with Bush's secretary of the treasury, Nicholas Brady, to put forward the argument that the proposed changes could adversely affect the value of the dollar on the international market. And then, after we'd made our comments and the Business Roundtable had made theirs, the SEC withdrew the proposals."

It seemed to have been a shareholder defeat.

"We figured that was it, that we'd lost," Christensen said, shrugging. "The SEC issued a statement saying that they had received so many comments that they had decided to withdraw the proposals while they studied the comments, but we figured that was just the usual government white-wash. We thought it was dead."

The SEC, it turned out, was engaging in a rare spurt of bureaucratic veracity. They had, indeed, received a great deal of comment on the proposed rules changes. In fact, they had received some 1,200 letters of comment: in SEC terms, a virtual avalanche of public opinion, believed to be the largest ever received by the SEC on a single issue. That they actually were reading and reacting to commentary became apparent a year later, in February 1992, when they issued a revised set of proposals. These included most of the changes suggested by USA plus a number of stipulations requiring disclosure of executive compensation.

"We were overjoyed," Christensen recalled for me. "The revised proposals were, in our estimation, even strengthened beyond those that had originally been sent out for review. It was one of the first hints we'd been given as to how Richard Breeden (then newly appointed SEC chairman) might be leaning, and it was very, very pleasant, indeed."

After a year in hiatus, the SEC rules changes began to move along quickly. There was some rumor that the sudden interest in shareholder voice was triggered by the fact that 1992 was an election year, but Christensen said, "I have a hard time believing that. You know, I'm a Republican, and Ralph (Ralph Ritworth, USA president) is a Republican, and Boone, of course, is known for all the work he does supporting the Republican party. But I honestly have to say that we got as much support from the Democratic members of Congress on this proposal as we did anywhere. The Democratic Congress was behind us, and so was Dan Quayle's office. At the same time, there were some speculative letters coming out of the Treasury that contradicted Quayle's advice. So you'd really have to say that this issue was crossing party lines. I don't believe it was politically motivated."

USA went aggressively to work, supporting the revised SEC proposal and helping to publicize the cause. Along the way, some interesting confrontations arose.

"We were very interested in allowing mixed boards— boards composed of a mixture of outside directors and managers—to be proposed on dissident proxy statements," she told me, and I agreed with that sentiment. In one of the studies done by Harry and Linda DeAngelo, it was found that mixed boards, with their combination of management expertise and outside-director diligence, tended to produce the best results after a proxy contest. But apparently the DeAngelos' studies weren't very popular in the corporate world.

"The Business Roundtable and their supporters came back and said that they opposed such a provision because it could disrupt 'the collegiateness of the board,'" Christensen told me. "And we said, 'You're absolutely right—that's exactly why we want it! We *want* to disrupt the collegiateness of the board.' It almost got hilarious, at times."

In June 1992, Breeden's office announced that new proposals could be expected in October, and he was as good as his word. The revised rules were issued on October 15, 1992.

The changes actually made were those proposed earlier in the year, with one exception: a proposal requiring extensive disclosure of executive compensation was modified so it was considerably less detailed. But that, Christensen insisted, did little to lessen the worth of the revisions.

"Actually, detailed disclosure of executive compensation was never part of USA's original proposal, anyhow," she revealed. "We felt such a measure could be counterproductive, since it could encourage shareholders to try to micromanage and set executive salaries through some sort of shareholder referendum. And that's not what we were after; we were trying to come up with a more effective way of putting together responsible boards.

"I mean, executive compensation disclosure is good in one sense," she elaborated, "in that it's very visible, and it lends credence to the suspicion that things are out of whack. In that sense, it's really a convenience issue. But it's a symptom, not a problem. After all, if Paul Lego (Westinghouse chairman and CEO) is getting a salary out of proportion to his contribution, is it Paul's fault that he's making so much money? Of course not—it's the fault of his board, and particularly his compensation committee."

That focus—making board members accountable for their errors—is, Christensen says, one of the factors that was made abundantly clear less than two weeks after the SEC proxy regulation revisions came out, when the General Motors chairmanship and board were shaken up by outside directors.

"That double-whammy—first the proxy changes, and then the change at GM—sent a clear message to directors," she said. "It told them that it wasn't just chairmen and presidents who were going to be held accountable for their actions, it was board members as well. It put them in a spotlight, and it kept them there."

This aspect of the new investor climate—the realization that change is not only possible, but probable—is, I feel, the greatest benefit of the SEC proxy reforms. Prior to the reforms, shareholders had to go through the hassle of proxy filings just to have a conversation with any significant number of their peers. It was like mobilizing an army: once you got it rounded up and ready, you almost felt like you had to use it. The reforms gave shareholders the freedom to talk—among themselves and with management—without having to go to "red alert." That's why, even though some people are predicting an epidemic of proxy fights, I think the great bulk of future management change will come from *conversations* between shareholders and directors, rather than contests between them. When I mentioned this to Christensen, she agreed with me, and offered this example:

"We have a program at USA that we call the 'Target 50 Program,'" she said. "It was Boone's idea to pick out the 50 companies that we felt were the most blatantly mismanaged and to put pressure on them to do a better job. The first year we did it, we were largely ignored. The following year, we were getting some response.

"In 1991, we actually sat down and met with 25 out of the 50 companies on the list," she said. "And I don't mean we had functionaries coming in—in many cases we had CEOs coming in to see us. Paul Lego, for instance, came in to meet. And in many cases, it went beyond meetings. We actually sat down and reached agreements with 15 companies."

It seems obvious to me that with proxy reform, the trend cannot help but get stronger.

Christensen and I talked about the reforms and their effect in the autumn of 1992—far in advance of the usual proxy season—but she told me then that in that year's 'Target 50' program, six of the 50 targeted companies had already been in touch with USA. I saw this as a sign that directors were getting a message—talk it out now or fight it out later. I asked Christensen for USA's opinion. Did they think that the climate had changed in America's boardrooms?

"We think," she replied with a smile, "that these guys are waking up and smelling the coffee."

Chapter 14

Red Flags

This book, and the idea behind it, is actually a contradiction of sorts. While I strongly espouse shareholder activism when necessary, I nonetheless find the necessity to be extremely distasteful.

Shareholder activism is a redundant practice—when a shareholder has to reach for the reins on a runaway corporation, he or she is doing something that management should have done in the first place. Redundant practices burn money. Proxy fights, especially, burn money. Even in the best of all possible outcomes—the dissident shareholder carries the day, wins a board seat, and is able to exercise persuasion that helps or saves the company—that victory will have been won only after management has attempted for months to stave off the incursion (using company money) and the shareholder has spent a small fortune (which the company will likely have to reimburse) to get the seat. Meanwhile, the company's competitors, who (presumably) do not have to deal with a proxy contest in their midst, can pursue advancement in the marketplace, happy in the knowledge that the contested company's market eye cannot be completely on the ball.

Don't get me wrong. Faced with the alternatives—extraordinary losses or even total failure—shareholder activism and proxy campaigns are often necessary evils. But wouldn't it be wonderful if management could have done the right thing in the first place? Wouldn't it be nice if all that money were being invested toward a totally positive end, rather than being spent on attorneys and proxy solicitors?

Don't fly off the handle unless you know where you're going to land. That Midwestern aphorism is especially appropriate in the case of shareholders considering activism or intervention in corporate governance. After all, even the most benign forms of activism—a sit-down with management or a meeting with the board—are going to force a company's leaders to turn, at least temporarily, away from the business in order to concentrate on the internal dynamics of their organization. Before you force such a shift in perspective, you want to be sure it's necessary.

Just as a doctor looks for signs (outward evidence of trouble) and symptoms (vocalized complaints) when searching for evidence of disease, the wise shareholder looks for signs and symptoms and weighs them all before concluding that a company is sick. The remainder of this chapter discusses some of the things that my staff of analysts and I look for when we suspect something's amiss.

STOCK PRICES DROPPING

Elementary perhaps, but in the long run, market price trends are often a reliable indicator of where a company is going.

When you track market prices, it's always important to do so in comparison to value. In temporary circumstances, a company's stock will sometimes trade at prices in excess— sometimes considerably in excess—of actual value. Rumors may have it that the firm is on the brink of releasing a product that will revolutionize the industry, or the company may be suspected of being a takeover target for which a rival is willing to pay a hefty premium.

When, for whatever reason, a stock price is too high relative to value, an eventual downward stock-price adjustment is inevitable.

One famous example of such an adjustment took place a few years back with Timberland Boots, a footwear and clothing company that, for a variety of reasons, became trendy. Following the Lemming Principle, investors began buying Timberland shares, fueling the increase in price. When the stock finally fell like a casserole to its proper level, industry papers thundered about the "setback" to Timberland and the "shakeup" that followed. In reality, there was no setback, and any shakeup was unnecessary. Timberland stock went to where it should have been in the first place, where it more closely reflected the intrinsic value of the business.

Over time, a company's stock price will closely approximate its intrinsic value and track the underlying progress of the business. In the short run, however, stock prices are generally determined by two human emotions: *greed* and *fear.*

Greed is the urge to make a quick or painless buck: "This stock is going up in price, and I think it will continue to go up—I'm going to buy in and ride it to the top."

When greed is dominant, you have bull markets. At the top of the bull markets, quite logically, greed is widespread and optimism is rampant.

Fear operates on the declining side: "I'm going to lose my shirt; I've got to get out now."

Dominant atmospheres of fear produce bear markets. At the bottom of a bear market, quite logically, fear is most widespread and can deteriorate into out-and-out despair.

In the long run, stock prices are determined by the fundamentals: a company's earnings, dividends, cash flow, sales, book value, return of equity, and—most importantly—a firm's ability to generate free cash flow, which is a reflection of the economics of a business and its management's talent.

Investment for anything other than the long term is foolhardy. When you're speculating on short term market movements and your stock takes a nosedive, you shouldn't be any more upset than you would be if your favorite horse failed to place at the track; in both cases, probability was working against you.

By the same token, if sound analysis leads you to believe that a company has a certain value, but the stock is selling well below it, you have, if you are wise enough to take it, an opportunity to benefit from the spread that temporarily emerged between the low price and the higher value. Successful investors invest according to what's rational, not according to what's fashionable.

Indeed, often, a stock in decline can be a terrific opportunity for wise shareholders to take a position, *particularly when the price decline is associated with some temporary corporate problem*. But *temporary* is the key word here.

The most famous example is the New Coke fiasco. Back in the 1980s, Coca-Cola management decided to try to strengthen their market position by changing the flavor of their flagship soft drink. Unfortunately, the public decided that "New Coke," as the product was called, had about as much charm as swilling mouthwash.

New Coke was a marketplace disaster, and Coca-Cola stock, while it did not crash and burn, certainly headed for the basement in a hurry.

The cool head in the midst of this was superinvestor Warren Buffett, who reasoned that Coca-Cola had, over the decades, been an extraordinarily fine company with a bonafide economic franchise in its name, distribution system, and long-standing customer base.

Buffett reasoned that, if *he* knew New Coke was a mistake, Coca-Cola's management certainly had to know it, and had to do something about it.

So, bit by bit, Buffett put approximately a billion dollars into Coca-Cola, buying stock at depressed prices. When the company reintroduced its time-proven formula as Coke Classic, the stock price readjusted accordingly. A half-decade or so after the New Coke episode, Buffet's billion-dollar investment was worth upwards of $4 billion.

LOW RETURN ON EQUITY

This again, is a number that has to be analyzed on a long-term basis. A quarterly setback is not the end of the world. But a low annual return is cause for concern. And consistently low annual returns are the economic equivalent of an alarm bell.

To a certain point, return on equity can be viewed against industry yardsticks. Certain industries (the automotive industry is one) are so capital-intensive that their average returns on equity are going to be lower than those of most industries. And when the industry offers long-term stability, many investors feel a return on equity slightly below average is entirely acceptable.

I, personally, have a target that I look for in return on equity, and that target is 20 percent, without a lot of debt leverage. That's what I want, and so—even though I live in its backyard—I do not invest in the automotive industry. The Big Three just cannot consistently produce the necessary ROI figures. It's against the nature of the beast.

CHRONIC RESTRUCTURINGS

As I write this, I am in the midst of watching a local Michigan company that is undergoing its third reorganization in five years. Amazingly enough, this firm's stock price has gone up at each reorganization announcement (even though it falls shortly thereafter). Hope springs eternal among institutional investors, and the market is quick to interpret reorganization as a sign that management has admitted its mistakes and is about to fix them.

But what if the problem is not fixable?

The company to which I alluded is in the business of engineering and light manufacturing. In recent years, it has entered into several large contracts with the auto companies (*them* again!), subcontracting engineering responsibilities, and in many cases, hiring whole blocks of former auto-company engineers—the same people who did the job now being contracted out—in the process.

I would forward the suggestion that this is not a business proposition. This is a wager. The company getting the contract is betting that it can manage a certain job better— can even manage the same workforce better—than the larger corporation for which it is doing the work.

The real winner here is the auto company. It wouldn't have subcontracted the work if it thought it could do it effectively in-house. Instead, it has found a firm willing to take on a losing proposition: the odds are stacked against that being successful, and no amount of reorganization is going to change those odds.

Constant reorganization is a sign of frustration and panic. Almost always, it is an indication that a company has lost its focus. The problem is not how it is running its business, but what business it is trying to run. The solution for this local company is to stop trying to make lemonade out of lemons, and to return, if at all possible, to the type of business that made it grow in the first place. If it does not, its stockholders are in for a rough ride.

CONSISTENT YEAR-END MANEUVERING

Firms will sometimes put the bloom on a bad year by crashing projects to completion before year's end (so revenues can count in that year and not the next) or by carrying expenses forward, so they accrue toward the following year and give the current year's profit a net lift.

This accounting magic (I call it "ledger-demain") is perfectly acceptable if a particularly bad year is followed by one that shows every sign of being very, very good. The two periods have a net leveling affect, and shuffling income and expenses evens things out to reflect that.

But when year-end accounting magic becomes a standard business practice, that's a sign that management is trying to put Band-Aids™ over bad business practices, and it's also a sign that something has to be done.

EXODUS OF KEY PERSONNEL

This is "scuttlebutt research" (as the great investor Phil Fisher used to call it) in its purest form. No one knows where a company is headed better than its key people. If they are leaving ship, either they are being lured away by competitors (and the company is not responding adequately to a market threat), or the ship is obviously in the process of sinking.

Departing employees are more than an indicator. They are also a source of information. Conversation with them is (provided they've not been gagged by a severance agreement) a useful way of gathering data for further analysis.

PARADES OF CONSULTANTS

"An expert," someone once said, "is anyone with a briefcase more than twenty-five miles from home."

When experts show up in succession at a company, it's a sign that management has lost its way. They don't know what to do, and they're trying to find someone who does. This is either a signal that the company needs new management or a signal that the business has changed and management must likewise change or pay the consequences.

Nontemporary Problems

Companies that made carriage wheels were, at one time, very profitable. You don't see many of those companies anymore.

Markets change, climates change, and products and services obsolesce. There are excellent arguments in favor of a company sticking to and focusing on the product, service, and philosophy that made it great, but when the world changes in a dramatic way, the company must change or it will wither and die. At such a fork in the road, it is a rare and wonderful management team that has the adaptability and flexibility to make the necessary changes.

The common factor among all of these "red flags" is analysis. To be properly understood, any of these situations requires investigation, reflection, and consideration—really, just common sense and a basic understanding of business and financial analysis.

Sometimes, problems take care of themselves (New Coke), and shareholder activism does nothing more than take everyone's eye off the ball. But in other cases—to continue the metaphor—shareholder intervention is the only thing that can possibly save the game.

Chapter *15*

The Better Part of Valor

IF you can keep your head,
while all about you
others are losing theirs,
then, obviously, you don't understand the situation. . .

These words, inscribed on a plaque traditionally given to graduating midshipmen at Annapolis, underline a point that is critical to anyone considering a proxy campaign.

It's imperative, before you spend time and money forcing a company to come to a vote at the annual meeting, that you know what you're up against. A proxy campaign is an election, and like any election, will be won by the side that has the greatest share of active supporters—shareholders, in this case. In the business of proxy campaigns, understanding the situation entails analyzing the shareholder base and determining, to as great an extent as possible, the amount of support each side can count on. . .*before* forcing things to a vote.

A dissident shareholder could, after all, spend hundreds of thousands of dollars of his or her own money on a proxy campaign by the time the company's shareholder meeting rolls around. You'd hate to get to that point, go through

143

the vote, and then realize that you never had a chance to begin with.

A simplistic example: Let's say you've invested in an underperforming company, and you'd like to conduct a proxy campaign to get representation on the board of directors with the eventual hope of changing company management. But when you analyze the shareholder list, you quickly realize that the CEO of the company owns 41 percent of the stock, and his mother owns an additional 10 percent. Assuming the CEO's mother loves him, this is an unbeatable combination, and your best course is probably to sell your shares, take your losses, and move on.

Shareholder analysis isn't always that simple, of course.

CALCULATE YOUR CHANCES

There are two main types of shareholders in virtually any corporation's list: individual and institutional. The individual shareholder is the one everyone thinks of—the person who pays for a share, and gets a certificate with his or her name on it that he or she either keeps in a safe-deposit vault at the local bank or leaves on deposit at his or her brokerage house. Institutional shareholders are pension funds, mutual funds, bank trust departments, insurance companies, and other professional money managers.

Both those types of shareholders are fairly easy to locate—they're on the list that the company must provide to any significant shareholder with a good reason for requesting it. But these shareholders have become less common in recent years.

Today, many shareholders never actually see a stock certificate. They buy through a broker and have the stock registered in the broker's name. This type of shareholder, known as a *beneficial shareholder*, still has all the rights and privileges of stock ownership, but the stock is simply listed as belonging to a client of, say, Merrill Lynch. The company doesn't automatically know who the stock belongs to—only Merrill Lynch does.

Recent changes in SEC regulations have provided a *nonobjection clause*, under which Merrill Lynch can release the names of beneficial shareholders to the company if they have signed a release saying they don't mind. The release is one of a number of pieces of paper that a person typically signs when becoming a client of a brokerage, and the vast majority of stock owners—80 to 90 percent—sign the release and become *nonobjecting beneficial owners.*

Nonobjecting beneficial owners have become a shuttlecock of sorts in the business of proxy contests. Brokerages at one time did not have to release these names to a company at all. Recently, SEC regulations have changed, and the brokerage can be required to release the names if the company so requests (there are actually firms that specialize in the business of gathering such lists). Often, companies—particularly companies that fear a proxy fight—will make a point of *not* requesting such a list. The reason for this is that the law does not require a company to release (to a dissident shareholder) information the company itself does not possess. In such a case, the dissident party (if they want the votes) is left to their own devices and will have to spend their own time and money trying to ferret out these "mystery owners."

For years, institutional shareholders wanted nothing to do with dissidents conducting proxy contests. The logic went something like this: "Company managers are businessmen, and as a fund manager, so am I, and dissident stockholders are bomb-throwers who waste everyone's time and money, so I'm going to vote with management."

In the last decade or two, that climate has changed. Modern fund managers realize that responsible portfolio management goes beyond buying and selling, and it often requires hands-on intervention in the direction of the companies they own. In fact, many of the largest proxy fights of recent years have been initiated by institutional investors. With the growing significance of institutional shareholding (they already own some 53 percent of all American stock), institutional shareholders have become major—possibly *the* major—factors in most proxy campaigns.

SOLICITING PROXIES IS A TOUGH JOB, BUT. . .

Figuring out Who's on First—and, more importantly, who's on whose side—can be a complicated process that will in almost all cases require the assistance of an experienced proxy solicitor (see chapter 17). This is why it's important to have the help of such a solicitor long before you ever try to recruit your first vote: a solicitor can often look at a list and say, "I know these guys; they always vote with management," or "These are people who will listen to a good argument," or "These guys have hated this company's management for years—they're a slam-dunk to go with us."

Sometimes, strange things can move a shareholder to your side of the table, and this can happen all the way up to the time when a vote is taken. I had this illustrated for me when I conducted my campaign against D&N's management.

Chapter *16*

Down to the Wire: A Proxy Fight

"*The Wall Street Journal*?" the man in the drugstore asked. His expression was one to which I'd become quite accustomed in Hancock—a combination of curiosity at having an out-of-towner in his establishment and consternation at being asked for something out of the ordinary. I was beginning to think of it as the "Hancock Look."

"That's right," I said. "*The Wall Street Journal.*"

He gave me the Look again.

"Well, what do you want *that* for?"

That gave me a moment of pause. I'd at least scanned the *Journal* every morning for the better part of three decades. It was hard to categorize just *what* I read it for. It had become something like breakfast; I just *wanted* it.

"Well," I told the man behind the counter. "I like to read it for the financial news."

"Oh." The Look went up a notch or so in intensity and became an out-and-out scowl.

"*The Wall Street Journal,*" he muttered. "I don't think we've ever seen one of those in here."

Suddenly, he brightened.

"Try over at the bank—at D&N," he said, smiling in satisfaction. "Betcha they'll have one over there that you can look at."

"Thanks," I nodded.

I didn't stop in at D&N. I didn't think I'd be too welcome there that morning. Besides, the way things had been running over at D&N, it wouldn't have surprised me to learn that the folks *there* had never seen a copy of *The Wall Street Journal*, either.

WHO'S ON FIRST

In general, newspapers seemed to be a medium that were *looked at*, rather than *read*, in Hancock and its environs. The *New York Times* was as rare as *The Wall Street Journal*—a request for the Sunday *Times* was certain to earn one the Look and the explanation, "This is *Michigan.*" And even such Michigan standards as the *Detroit News* or *Free Press* were only available as yesterday's news. Hancock newsstands were a good 10-hour drive by truck from downtown Detroit—and that was in good weather. So the previous day's paper was usually as fresh as news got. I learned that the hard way in a party store, through a conversation that sounded a lot like the old Abbott-and-Costello "Who's on First" routine:

Me: I'd like a *Free Press*, please.
Storeowner: There you are.
Me: But this is yesterday's paper.
Storeowner: That's right.
Me: Don't you have the current edition?

Storeowner: This is the current edition.
Me: It's *yesterday's*.
Storeowner: That's right.
Me: But I'd like *today's* paper.
Storeowner: Come back tomorrow.
Me: I can't get today's paper until tomorrow?
Storeowner: That's right.
Me: At which time, it will be yesterday's paper . . .
Storeowner: Uh-huh.
Me: Doesn't that strike you as odd?
Storeowner: (Says nothing—gives me the Look).

I suppose that aspect of Hancock—a place so distant from anywhere that it only got yesterday's news—explained a lot about the people, the town, and the sad state of D&N. It takes less time to drive to Iowa—three states away from Detroit—than it does to drive from Detroit to Hancock. And sociologically, it might be even more distant than that.

Hancock residents weren't very apt to talk with outsiders about anything except fishing, deer hunting, snowmobiling, or the best places to see fall colors. But if you could get them to discuss their own views on life, you were likely to get opinions that most 20th-century businesspeople would find strange; even alarming.

When it got down to the nitty-gritty, people around town would say that the purpose of business—any business— was to employ people.

NORTHWOODS SOCIALISM

"But what about profits?" I'd ask them. Weren't profits important? And they'd nod vigorously, saying, of course, profits were important. A business had to have profits. Everybody knew that. But when the subject came around to a business going under, they would universally decry it as a disaster for the working man, a black-hearted evil wrought by the firm's corporate masters. To put people out of work, simply because a firm wasn't making money? In Hancock, this was thought of as an attack on the common working Joe. Even businesspeople often had difficulty in seeing that the alternative—bleeding the owners dry to keep an unprofitable business running—was just as bad, and in fact, made considerably less sense. In Hancock, you put in your time and you picked up your paycheck; no one seemed to think much, or care, about where the money came from before that.

Another virtually universal opinion around Hancock was that "the government"—a term encapsulating both the state and the federal legislative bodies—wasn't doing enough for people. Mention any problem, from the lack of heavy industry in the U.P. to a weakness of the dollar versus foreign currencies, and the response you'd most likely hear would be something along the lines of "the government ought to do something about that."

They were so common in the diners, bars, and pool halls that they'd be conspicuous by their absence—these philosophers in Mackinaw jackets, guys with beer bellies, beards, and ball caps, who felt that corporations owed people jobs and that economic problems were best handled through legislation. And yet, if you were to tell one of these Northwoods economists that what he was saying ran contrary to the principles of capitalism, and that he was identifying himself, through his opinions, as a dyed-in-the-wool socialist, he would very probably be inclined to ask you out into the parking lot so the two of you could settle the matter with your fists. It was hard to say which Marx was more of a role model in Hancock—Karl, Harpo, or Zeppo.

Some people have gone so far as to say that it's an ethnic trait; that this northernmost corner of Michigan, being settled predominantly by Finns, has followed a Finnish standard of economics. I personally think it's more a product of geography; like Finland, the U.P. has a small tax base, difficult logistics, and an often severe climate. Together, the three are a harsh incubator for capital tendencies; it's simply easier to look outside for the money.

PROXIES AND PUDDLE-JUMPERS

But the people of the Upper Peninsula looked outside for little else. The same protectivist tendencies made them skeptical of any change wrought from outside, particularly any change coming from "Detroit" (the name used in the U.P. for virtually the entire southeastern corner of the state).

I got a taste of that the afternoon before the proxy contest, during the flight up from Detroit's Metro airport.

It was a Northwest Airlines commuter airlink flight, a flight actually operated by Mesaba Airlines (the name always reminds me of what Tonto called the Lone Ranger).

I was well aware that my peers—the downstate people already on D&N's board—would doubtlessly be flying up in their own planes, in planes leased from private-pilot cronies, or in private charters. But I had a couple of reasons for flying commercial.

The first was a matter of principle. Leasing airplanes, and turning the leases in on directors' expense accounts, seemed to me a slap in the face to a business that was losing money, particularly a business that was losing money because of misdirection.

The second was because I'd learned the hard way, years before, to only fly with pilots who made a living behind the controls of an airplane. My father, my brother, a family friend, and I had gotten into a little Piper Cherokee-Six in Detroit with a real estate broker who was going to show us some property up near Traverse City, in the northern tip of Michigan's Lower Peninsula. There are two kinds of private pilots: those who have been rated, somewhat like commercial pilots, to fly using instruments and radio homing frequencies, and those who are only "visually rated;" i.e., they can fly to whatever they can see out of the window. Our real estate broker/pilot was the latter, and he flew into a snowstorm where, of course, he couldn't even see the propeller. But rather than turning around and heading back to Detroit, he tried to tough it out and take us through on instruments he wasn't trained to use. In very little time, we were lost, and flying around in circles, burning fuel. The real estate broker tried to land the plane on instruments, with disastrous results; the broker was killed outright, I suffered a broken back (in five places) and a crushed foot, and everyone else came out with similarly severe permanent injuries.

People are always trying to get me to go with them somewhere in their private planes, assuring me it's perfectly safe. But when I tell them about my close call, they always turn around and tell me about *theirs*, and they all seem to have at least two. So I have an ironclad rule: if it doesn't come with a professional pilot and a beverage service, I don't get on board.

Mesaba Airline's 7:35 p.m. flight from Detroit's Metro airport qualifies on both counts, but just barely. The plane is a classic puddle-jumper: ceiling so low that you have to board looking like Quasimodo and an interior consisting of one row of cramped seats on one side, an aisleway so narrow that you have to walk by shuffling sideways (turning the resemblance to Quasimodo up a notch or two), and a double row of equally cramped seats on the other side. And the flight was a *long* puddle-jump: three-and-a-half hours to Marquette (another Upper Peninsula town), and a layover there before continuing to Hancock.

There were seven of us going up to wage the proxy contest, yet despite our confirmed reservations, only one seat showed up as open when we got to the airport that evening. Ken Altman, our solicitor from Hill & Knowlton, finally shoved a huge briefcase full of proxies into my arms and said, "Here. We'll drive up, if we have to. But just in case we don't make it, be sure these get presented properly."

So I got on board as the door was closing, and my first reaction was to mutter, "What the hell . . ."

The plane was half empty. But when I protested to the aircrew, they just insisted that I take a seat, so I did (the briefcase under my feet, my knees somewhere up by my chest). We sat on the runway for three-quarters of an hour as my mind raced. Had Seaton and company bought out the plane in an attempt to keep us out of Hancock? Frankly, it didn't seem beyond the realm of possibility. I never did find out what had happened, because, eventually, it seemed to dawn on the crew that there was still room on the plane, and we went back to the gate and picked up the rest of our people.

Anyhow, when we finally got under way, it turned out that my seatmate was a woman with a bank in Marquette. When she found out that I knew something about her industry, we chatted. About halfway up the state, the conversation turned to D&N, as she put a hand on my arm and whispered conspiratorially, "Well, you've heard about the big doings up in Hancock tomorrow, haven't you?"

I played dumb.

"What doings are those?" I asked.

"Oh!" She looked around and whispered, "Some fat-cat Jew from Detroit, a guy named Schwartz, is trying to take over the bank. He's coming up with lawyers, solicitors, the whole nine yards, and there's going to be this big proxy war."

"Wow," I said. "And who is he again? Some Jewish guy?"

"Named Schwartz," she nodded. She rubbed her fingers together. "You know how those people are; they want to take over the world. And it's a shame. D&N is such a pleasant, old-fashioned institution. They really do a great job; really take care of their people."

"What about their stockholders?" I asked. "Do they take care of them?"

She shrugged.

"Beats me," she said.

We talked a little more, the pilot announced our approach into Marquette, and she asked where I was going in town. I replied that I was continuing on to Hancock, and she asked me what was happening in Hancock.

"An annual meeting, " I said.

She turned her head.

"What kind of annual meeting?" she asked.

"Shareholders' meeting."

"But the only shareholders' meeting going on there," she said, "is D&N's."

"That's right," I told her.

We were coming in for our landing.

"It's been nice talking with you," I told her. "Let me give you one of my cards."

I think she knew what was coming, because she took it cautiously. When she saw my name, the color dropped from her face.

"Listen," she said as we got up from our seats. She looked around. "I've got to tell you something. Some of my very best friends happen to be Jewish."

"Of course they do," I smiled.

I thought about telling her that I'm a Roman Catholic, but I didn't.

It didn't seem germane.

ALL THREE LINES

We got in late to the Copper Crown Motel: Hancock's best (and only) hostelry. We'd booked 10 rooms, all together, and—after the incident with the "overbooked" airplane— I was relieved when we got our keys without any problem. Altman and some of the others made calls out to businesses on the West Coast, but everyone was dead tired. The proxy contest wouldn't start until two the next afternoon. We left most of the last-minute business for morning.

There were other hotels in Houghton, Hancock's sister municipality across the river, but we'd chosen to stay at the Copper Crown because it was only two blocks from D&N's headquarters. I discovered that may have been a mistake when I came back from my fruitless search for a *Wall Street Journal*; when I walked into the adjoining rooms we'd booked as a command center, both Altman and my dad were tapping the cradles on telephones.

"What's wrong?" I asked.

"We can't get outside lines," my father told me.

That was grim news. Hill & Knowlton had been working with our firm for better than a month, collecting the proxies we'd need for the afternoon meeting. But a proxy is, when you come right down to it, a favor, and many investors don't give them the highest priority. When you ask for a proxy, if you have a good argument, you'll probably get it. The problem is getting it in time. And we had several large investors who had not yet delivered their proxies to us. A telephone was our only way of rounding up those critical, last-minute votes.

I went down to the lobby.

"We can't get any outside telephone lines," I told the lady behind the desk.

She gave me the Look.

"Well you know," she told me, "you people are already using all three lines."

That took a moment to sink in.

"*Three* lines?" I asked. "But this motel has to have at least fifty rooms! You mean there are only three outside lines?"

She nodded.

"Used to be just the one," she said. "But folks complained. So we got three. Always was enough. Until this morning."

That explained it. Ken Altman and Cindy Dickinson, my operations manager, each had a fax machine running out of his/her room, receiving proxies. That left just one line open for phone calls.

"What'll we do?" Ken asked me.

I checked my pocket for change.

"I'll find a pay phone," I told him.

Man in a Phone Booth

And that was how we gathered the final proxies. Ken and his people called the smaller investors from inside the hotel, and Rick Nelson and I found pay phones to contact the larger ones, reversing the charges whenever it was someone we knew fairly well. The rest we charged to my home and office phones. Meanwhile, Bob Reichenbach and Cindy were driving furiously back and forth between the hotel and the gymnasium where the proxy contest was to be held, dropping off briefcase after briefcase of proxies.

It was bizarre. I remember standing in the phone booth outside the Copper Crown Motel and calling Bruce Ballard, a broker at Shearson Lehman down in Detroit. Bruce and one of his broker colleagues, Alan Hubbell, had been very supportive of my intention to put some shareholder voice on the board, but I'd yet to receive their proxies. So I was just in the middle of my pitch, on how I wanted to be a director of D&N and do a good job of representing the interests of him and his shareholders, when a pickup truck backfired and stalled on the street across from me. Two or three cars came to a halt, and somebody began to lay on the horn.

"George," Bruce interrupted me. "Where the hell *are* you?"

And when I told him I was standing out in the April cold, calling from a phone booth in Hancock, Michigan, he nearly busted a gut. After a solid minute of laughter, he was all but out of breath, but he said, "Listen, buddy. This is terrific. I don't know many people who'd go all the way up there and make calls from the street corner, just to look out for their investors. I'm going to get on the phone, George, and in the next hour, I'm going to speak to every one of my customers and secure their proxies. And then I'm going to get my legal department and my proxy department to drop whatever they're doing and give your proxies top priority. You'll have them by one this afternoon."

Bruce Ballard was a man of his word. Shearson's proxy department held more than 600,000 shares of D&N stock—far and away the largest single block of the thrift's shares.

Ironically, Seaton and his board had thought that since Shearson was D&N's investment banker, those proxies were as good as theirs. As it turned out, something like 90 percent of the Shearson proxies came in on our side of the fence, and they came in, just as Bruce had promised, at one that afternoon. It was enough to turn our edge into a landslide.

GUNFIGHT AT THE O.K. CORRAL

High noon came two hours late that day, and the O.K. Corral was a high-school gym.

We had finished almost all of our phone calls by eleven-thirty or so, but the fax machines were working overtime, churning out proxies as they poured in from all over the country. As we gathered the final batch from the floor, where they had spilled over, we suddenly realized that we had nothing to carry them in. Every box or briefcase we'd brought was already over at the shareholders' meeting. It was twenty minutes to two.

"Here," Cindy Dickinson said. She'd run next door to her room and emptied out her suitcase.

"You're a trooper," I smiled. My dad had a car waiting out front, and I sprinted to the curb, the decidedly ladylike suitcase in my hands.

"The room buzzed." You know how they always say that in books and newspaper articles? It usually struck me as affected, but I realized the appropriateness of the phrase as we walked into the Hancock high-school gym. The place sounded like a beehive; all the faces turned our way as we entered. You could make out individual voices occasionally, and they all were saying the same thing: *There he is.*

My father was walking a short distance ahead of me. A pleasant-looking, older gentleman, he seemed the typical professional retiree, in town to attend the annual meeting and take in some sight-seeing in the Upper Peninsula. No one had yet discerned that we were together.

They greeted him warmly at the registration desk, and looked on, smiling, as he signed in.

"Walter G. Schwartz," he put in the space marked *shareholder's name*. A murmur arose around the registration desk. And then Dad wrote, in the space marked *shares owned*, "350,000."

The word spread like wildfire through the hall. Schwartz's old man was bankrolling him, buying him a seat on the Board!

Actually, of course, my father's holdings were relatively modest. He's always been one of my investors, but never to the degree that you would say he was bankrolling me. And his holdings in D&N were all through my group—the 350,000 shares he registered were proxies that had been entered under his name.

Still, it didn't take more than a few seconds for the news to travel up to the front of the gymnasium, where Seaton and his board were presiding over the meeting. I saw Seaton speaking to the directors next to him, all of them whispering furiously and glancing back in my direction.

Jeez, you could almost read their lips as they said it, *this guy is serious; he might actually pull it off!*

Then I stepped up to the registration area and plopped Cindy Dickinson's suitcase down on the desk. I opened it, and a faint cloud of Chanel No. 5 came wafting out. But no one seemed to notice that. What they were all staring at were the bundles of proxies—hundreds of them. By the looks on their faces, you'd have thought they were staring at a suitcase full of thousand-dollar bills.

David Joswick, our attorney from Miller Canfield, had been badgering D&N's counsel to let Rick Nelson and me address the shareholders. When the proxies were registered, they relented.

It was a very strange meeting. First a fellow in work clothes stood up and gave a short, disjointed little speech about how credit unions were getting the short end of the stick, and that was a shame in his book, because credit unions were really the salt of the earth, and they stuck up for the little guy. And you could tell that he really believed in what he was saying; he was pretty worked up over it, and he actually looked half-exhausted when he sat down. He even got a smattering of applause.

Nobody had the heart to tell him that D&N was a thrift, not a credit union.

Then the president of Soumi College came forward and spoke about the wonders the Seatons had worked for the community and the shame that it would be if the control of a community institution like D&N was wrested away by strangers who cared nothing for Hancock, and nothing for the bank. After a few minutes, he'd progressed from saccharine to out-and-out cloying. It was obvious that Seaton was a major benefactor of the college. One wondered if the foundations for "Seaton Hall" weren't being laid at that very moment. But the college president's words were striking a chord with the patently partisan crowd of 250 or so in the little gymnasium. When he asked them to "not be intimidated by these people from downstate who were trying to take away their company and tell them what to do," heads nodded in agreement.

When my turn came to speak, I almost wished I hadn't asked for the opportunity. The group there looked so haggard, so defeated. They had the empty, hollow faces one associates with Eastern Europe, the beleaguered expressions of people who only faintly comprehended what was going on around them.

Still, I tried to explain to them that what they were participating in that day was a democratic action, an opportunity for the people who owned the company to speak out
and have a say in how it was run. I tried to emphasize that
I was running for a directorship simply in order to serve
those interests would most benefit *all* of the shareholders,
and that the obligations of a director were to look first to
the shareholders' interests, and last to his own personal
benefit. I tried to stress the importance of fiduciary responsibility, but I can't say I got through. The looks on the
faces in the crowd seemed to say, *here we go again—this
guy's going to take over <u>our</u> company, and there's nothing
we can do about it.*

When Rick spoke, he echoed my sentiments. But the
Hancock shareholders weren't getting the message. They
couldn't get the message—they were numb.

AFTERSHOCK

In storybook terms, it would be nice to say that they
counted the votes at the meeting, Rick and I were welcomed onto the Board of Directors, and we set about re-
constructing the company.

It didn't work out that way.

There were some 3,700 shareholders involved in the contest. We'd agreed to let D&N's auditors oversee the count,
and it turned out to be a far larger job than they'd ever
overseen before. They ended up taking the paperwork back
with them to Chicago and working on it for several days.
By that point, of course, the meeting was long over. I was
back in my offices in suburban Detroit, and my staff was
shaking their collective heads at the size of the phone bill
we'd racked up over the months of March and April.

Finally, the results came out. To no one's surprise, Rick Nelson and I had been elected to the board by a sizable majority of the shareholders.

To everyone's surprise, Seaton and the board promptly challenged the results and demanded a recount.

I swear, when I heard the news I was ready to choke the life out of somebody. The proxy contest had been audited by Seaton's *own people*. How could he challenge the results? What was he hoping, that they'd misplaced a steamer-trunk full of proxies? It was absolutely infuriating to hear that, in some school-boy scheme, they were going to spend D&N further into the red, paying for a recount in hopes of keeping the board an exclusive club for themselves.

Of course, even after the recount, Rick Nelson and I were on the Board. I called Rick to congratulate him, and he said, "I appreciate that, George. But I've got to tell you, this is about the only congratulations either one of us is likely to get. We've got us some ticked-off people up there in Hancock."

"Well, Rick," I told him. "You know what? Maybe it's about time . . ."

Chapter 17

Marshalling Your Forces

Proxy campaigns are stimulated by differences of opinion: the CEO or general manager has one idea of how to run the company; the dissident shareholder has another.

In a perfect world, these differences would be taken to the shareholders in a straightforward manner. Management would state its case, the dissident his, and the shareholder body would be asked to decide who was right. It would be like the Lincoln-Douglas debates—straightforward, simple, candid, and totally above board.

Unfortunately, the political system dispensed with such simple solutions years ago, and so has the world of corporate politics. A proxy campaign is, quite literally, a political process—an election—and proxy campaigns are waged with all the serpentine actions and legerdemain of a political campaign.

In such a climate, the dissident who tries to go it alone is doomed to the same failure as a political candidate who tries to run for office based on nothing more than personal opinion—however right it may be—and charisma. As anyone who has ever been involved in politics knows, it is a machine that is fueled by people—lots of people—and successful proxy campaigns will involve the orchestrated efforts of a variety of talented individuals.

Think of yourself as the general manager of the campaign. The issue that you are carrying to the shareholders—be it election of yourself or another responsible individual to the board, or a forced shift in company policy—is your candidate. To see that candidate successfully into office, you'll need a variety of help.

Proxy Solicitor

Proxy solicitors are the key allies to any successful campaign. Solicitors are retained both by the company and the dissident party, and the opposing solicitors look at a company's shareholder constituency, determine which individuals or institutions are swayable to their party's point of view, and attempt to gather sufficient votes to carry or defeat an action (depending on which side the solicitor is working for).

When considering a proxy campaign, the proxy solicitor is one of the first allies you should seek. Experienced solicitors can save you weeks of wheel-spinning and hundreds of thousands of dollars in misspent funds.

This is because an experienced solicitor knows not only the process by which a campaign must be conducted, but the climate in which it will be conducted, as well.

What is the constituency? Who's leaning which way? The CEO's mother, if she owns stock in the company, will probably vote with her kid. Assuming you've kept in touch at Christmas, your mother will vote with you. But the rest of the shareholders might be something of an enigma. An experienced solicitor will be acquainted with the leanings of at least some of the individual investors, and most, if not all, of the institutional investors. Knowing which ones are approachable—which ones will listen to a dissident point of view—enables you to concentrate your efforts in those quarters where you have the highest probability of success.

One reason for obtaining a solicitor up front is that the solicitor is the individual who can best help you determine whether you are championing a winnable cause. Two items of information provided by solicitors—the probable inclinations of the shareholder body and the amount of time and money that will be necessary to gather a majority from this body—will help you make the hard decisions of whether you wish to proceed with an action and whether you have sufficient resources to do so.

How good a solicitor do you need? "The best" may seem like a logical answer, but that's not necessarily the case. It all depends on your acquaintance with, and rapport with, your fellow shareholders. For a smaller company with a minimal number of shareholders, most of whom you already know, you only need a solicitor who is sufficiently up-to-date on SEC rules to guide you through the mechanics of the proxy process. With a shareholder body that is largely an enigma, more solicitor horsepower becomes necessary.

If you need a top-notch proxy solicitor, some of the best advice as to who to use will probably come, believe it or not, from your friends who are company managers. Better solicitors work, for the most part, on the side of management, simply because companies generally have deeper pockets than dissident shareholders. Top proxy solicitors, as of this writing, demand as much as $300 an hour for their services, and they are worth it if they can reduce your overall expenditures in a campaign.

ATTORNEYS

I use the plural here because unless you're fortunate enough to find a firm that is sufficiently multitalented to handle all aspects of a proxy campaign, you stand a good chance of needing to retain two forms of counsel throughout the course of the action.

The first one you'll need is a firm versed and experienced in current SEC regulations. We compare proxy campaigns to political elections—in all truth, the regulations governing communication with and the solicitation of shareholders are more involved than the rules governing the electoral process. SEC regulations have seen more changes in recent years than election rules, as well.

Communication with shareholders is literally censored by the SEC. Actually, it goes beyond censorship: unless your intended communication meets certain criteria, the SEC simply won't allow it to go out. All such communication must be submitted to the SEC, and they review it according to guidelines that, although they have been amended in recent years, are still slanted heavily in favor of management.

A law firm specializing in SEC affairs will both know what's acceptable and be prepared to argue on your behalf. As in many aspects of law, SEC regulations are often open to interpretation. A good and persuasive attorney can gain you more leeway in your communications with shareholders, and this can be a critical difference when it comes down to the final vote.

The second type of attorney you'll need is a talented litigator. There are only two types of proxy campaigns—those that involve lawsuits and those that involve the threat of lawsuits. Good litigators can help to make your campaign one of the latter, which is a much less costly way to go.

Throughout the course of a campaign, you may find yourself both initiating and defending yourself from legal action. Simply because regulations require a company to produce certain information does not mean you are going to get it; you may have to sue to get that which is rightfully yours. By the same token, simply because you are right does not mean you are impervious to suit; the threat of lawsuit is one of management's favorite defensive mechanisms, and you can expect to have your mettle tested.

Again, in both cases—SEC specialists and litigators—the best firms are most often retained by companies, and company managers are good people to go to for recommendations. I have seen campaign-related legal fees that run anywhere from $125 per hour to $600 per hour.

These can mount up. There's the old story about the attorney who dies and goes to heaven and is met by Saint Peter with a brass band and a crowd of dignitaries. The lawyer asks what all the fuss is about, and Saint Peter tells him that they are celebrating the fact that he has lived longer than any other human, having reached an age of more than 2,000 years. When the lawyer objects and says he was only 70 when he died, Saint Peter looks in a book and says, "Sorry. Our mistake. We were going by your billable hours."

If you are in a position to conduct a proxy campaign, you have long since learned the lesson of that story, and you know enough to audit your legal bills and question dubious hours. Even so, proxy campaigns can generate enormous legal costs. A proposed letter to shareholders may go through multiple submissions to the SEC—and multiple editions and related meetings—before it is allowed to go out. This is the one constant I have seen in virtually every proxy contest. In each one, the participants have consistently underestimated their eventual legal costs. Forewarned is forearmed.

Proxy campaigns cannot be conducted without proxy solicitors and attorneys. These are the minimum resources necessary for the action, and if you are entertaining such an action, you should be prepared to spend some money in both areas.

In addition, most campaigns will, depending on the talents you either have personally or have available to you in-house, require additional assistance in three areas.

INVESTMENT BANKERS

Investment bankers are credible sources of information on company value and performance. They can also act as brokers, buying and selling companies in much the same manner as real estate agents buy and sell property.

In taking your case to the SEC and your fellow shareholders, you will be making certain allegations: "XYZ Company is underperforming. . ." or "The company's return on investment in area X is not what it should be. . ." Such allegations must be backed up by data—first, to pass SEC muster (regulations will not allow the communication of unsubstantiated claims); and second, to convince shareholders that yours is the cause with which they should side.

A good investment banking firm will have at its disposal the analysts necessary to value a company and make credible comparisons of it and other firms in its field. If the purpose of your campaign is to eventually break up and sell off the assets of a company that is beyond redemption in its given field, investment bankers can help you achieve fair returns on those sales.

Investment bankers are not cheap. The threshold price— the minimum amount of money that an investment banker is going to need to get involved with a proxy campaign— has been $50,000 to $100,000 in recent years. More involved campaigns with larger companies will have larger threshold prices, and $500,000 is a figure often budgeted for such services.

PUBLIC RELATIONS

Flacks, spin doctors—the nicknames by which PR people are known is indicative of how they are often perceived. Public relations is the area of a proxy campaign in which an investor is least likely to be versed, for the simple reason that PR practices run contrary to those that the financial world uses on a day-to-day basis.

Finance and economics are objective sciences. They deal with facts. Is a company profitable? The answer is there in black and white. You can answer it with a number, and if you cannot, then you don't truly have an answer at all.

Public relations, on the other hand, deals almost entirely with opinion—not, for instance, "is a company profitable," but "is a company profitable *enough*." Such questions can be argued with numbers, but cannot be answered with them.

The last century has seen numerous attempts to introduce objectivity into the field of public relations. Surveys measure public perception and trends. Focus groups assay the probable effectiveness of any given action. Measurements are taken before and after a public relations campaign to gauge its effectiveness.

In the end, all of these are nothing more than the quantification of opinion, and PR remains an essentially black science. As such, those of us who live in the world of numbers tend to view it with skepticism and even discount it.

Nonetheless, opinion—the basis of public relations—is, in the end, the thing that fuels the economic engine. Recessions are not primarily caused by a lack of money; they are caused by a widespread lack of confidence. Escalating prices for real estate or any given commodity are caused by the economic factors of supply and demand, which are both influenced by consumer confidence.

A proxy campaign is a formal contest based on a difference of opinion, and public relations is the field in which opinion is shaped and swayed.

Do you need a PR agency to wage a proxy campaign? It's easy to say "no." After all, we all tend to think of ourselves as persuasive.

But, to be perfectly frank, few investor groups have the necessary skills to perform adequate PR work. PR people are simply better at this stuff.

You also have to look at your competition. Does the company have a PR department or agency? You bet they do. Are they going to be working on the side of management? You bet your eye teeth.

Bear in mind, as well, that shareholders are, by and large, conservative people, and they tend naturally to think of dissidents of any stripe as kooks. Management is going to encourage such an opinion, forcing you to take the battle uphill.

In smaller campaigns, where you know most of the shareholders very well and your reputation precedes you, you actually may be able to dispense with public relations. But this is the exception, not the rule. Often, PR is essential to a successful campaign.

Even though PR may be the telling factor in a contest, public relations is often the area of least expense, simply because PR talent is not all that expensive, relatively speaking.

What will a public relations agency charge you to conduct a campaign? The snide answer is, "All that you have budgeted," and there's some truth to the statement. Agencies tend to scale actions according to the resources you have available, and low-cost actions, such as targeted assistance in your letters to shareholders, can often work as well as newspaper ads or gimmicks.

If you retain a PR agency, you can look at $10,000–$25,000 (plus expenses) as the cost of admission. Where you go from there depends on the amount of negative PR that the company is going to direct against you. Defending yourself from a smear campaign can quickly mount up the bill.

ACCOUNTANTS

In a proxy campaign, the basic role of an accounting firm or department is to help you understand numbers and financial statements, to interpret the more in-depth reports (the 10Ks and 10Qs), and analyze financial data.

Many investors—particularly those who invest for a living—will not require such elementary assistance. You long since learned to do such things yourself (or to have it done by your in-house resources), or you wouldn't be in this field.

But accounting plays another role in a proxy campaign: that of keeping track of your own campaign costs.

At some point in a proxy contest, it usually becomes expedient for you to register as a committee (your SEC-specialist attorney can handle this) and proceed that way, rather than running the campaign through your own personal checkbook.

Independent accounting then becomes extremely useful for a couple of reasons.

One is that you almost certainly will want to try to recoup your expenses for your efforts. In virtually all successful campaigns, the dissident will be able to bill the company and receive compensation for the money he or she has spent on the company's behalf.

And even unsuccessful dissidents will often be able to recoup at least part of their expenses, on the basis that the proxy threat eventually resulted in the institution of better management practices within the company, and so imparted value. This is a high-road type of argument, and you may have to threaten or even mount a suit to get your money, but it is usually at least partially successful.

As for those funds that are not recouped through such actions, you will almost certainly be eligible for tax relief, since the cost of threatening or conducting a proxy campaign is a legitimate cost of business. Independent accounting from a reputable firm can speed and streamline your tax efforts.

By the way—when we discussed attorneys earlier, did I mention tax law? A word to the wise. . .

AN ARMY TRAVELS ON ITS STOMACH

What does this all cost? Obviously, by this point, you realize it ain't cheap.

Proxy campaigns are not for the faint of heart. The smart-aleck answer to the cost question is, "More than you think it's going to cost," and that, in almost every case, is true. Even those experienced in the field generally find that their final costs usually exceed what they'd budgeted at the onset: it's the nature of the beast. On top of all the expertise necessary, there are other costs to consider; the typical proxy contest for a medium-size company will eat up about $10,000 in postage alone.

You must also budget in your own time. A successful proxy campaign is going to require enormous amounts of your own attention and effort. You may as well look at it as a full-time occupation for the duration of the contest. During this time, you will not be able to concentrate to any great extent on other business matters.

Bottom line—most proxy contests have a six-figure price tag and, for larger companies, seven figures is not unusual.

Again—not for the faint of heart.

Why, then, would anyone in their right mind consider such a thing?

A primary reason is generally that the alternative—doing nothing—would be even more costly. This, together with the possibility of recouping expenses at the back end, can make a campaign a reasonable business decision, despite the enormous costs involved, both in money and personal effort.

Chapter *18*

Saber Rattling

Without revealing my political stripes, I must admit that I was highly amused by the diplomatic maneuverings conducted just prior to the change of government in Haiti in 1994.

As you'll recall, that was the year the Clinton administration sent a delegation to negotiate with the military strongmen who had been ruling the country ever since a coup a couple of years earlier.

Several tactics were tried.

Emissaries from the Oval Office promised safe passage to the dictators if they'd only have the good grace to Get Out of Dodge. Retirement havens were offered (in Panama, which, as it turned out, had apparently not been consulted about this option). Jimmy Carter waxed eloquent about human rights and political decency.

All of which budged the bad guys not one iota.

Then Colin Powell took the Haitian generals aside and let them in on a little military secret. Paratroopers were on their way from the United States. Warships carrying assault helicopters had been deployed. AWACS control aircraft and surgically capable stealth fighter/bombers were in the air. Full-scale invasion was a matter of hours away, and Powell told the generals, in excruciating detail, what Uncle Sam had planned for them and their banana-republic excuse for an army.

The exact words of that conversation are uncertain, but it seems the phrase "Stone Age" may have been dropped more than once.

All of a sudden, a miracle happened. The unbudgeable budged. Concessions were made. Retirement in Panama suddenly looked pretty damn good. And Haiti changed governments—to steal a phrase from T.S. Eliot, "not with a bang, but a whimper."

My point?

Nothing will change a human being's mind faster than the news that he or she is about to get his or her literal or figurative butt kicked.

This, my friend, is information that you can use.

Keeping Costs to a Minimum

The dissident actions in which I have participated, and all of the contests in which my colleagues have participated, have had one thing in common: the campaigns wound up costing much more than one would have imagined at the onset.

True, you can often get reimbursed for at least part of what you spent to effect change in a company—sometimes, you can get back all of it (more on this later). But you'll never get back the time you spent on telephones, at meetings, and away from your loved ones and family.

Still, in all this, there is a solace of sorts. As much as you dislike the inconvenience and expense of an impending proxy fight, the company's board of directors and managers are going to dislike it even more.

So, when all other avenues have failed, unveiling the news—that the paratroopers are (so to speak) on their way to Port au Prince—just may be enough to cause a change of faith on the company's board.

MAKE IT EASIER ON YOURSELF: START NICE

Notice that I have said, ". . .when all other avenues have failed. . ."

This is important. Stubbornness and pride are at the root of practically every altercation in the course of human history. From the standpoint of one's own self-image, it's far preferable to feed the other fellow shot and steel than it is to swallow your own pride. And, once convinced that they are on The Side of Right, most leaders—political or corporate—will go adamantly into battle rather than budge.

That's why it's better from a psychological viewpoint (and a damn sight cheaper, as well), to phrase your first requests for change in a corporation as just that—requests. A broom-the-bastards condemnation is going to do nothing but throw up the bulwarks.

Start by identifying the problem. Let's say Acme Cola, the beverage company in which you have long held interest, has decided to build an amusement park. This is a pet project of the president and CEO, who has long dreamed of a Cola World to which American families would make annual pilgrimages, enhancing the image value of the core product while adding another profit center for the corporation. But neither the president nor his board have any expertise in creating amusement parks and, as a result, numerous extraordinary expenses have been incurred. The original intended site of the park has been moved twice due to environmental concerns, and now the revised location threatens to be too far from major interstates to attract visitors in the numbers originally projected. The "World of Fizz" theme has bombed with focus panels, and the revised themeline, centering around a cute rodent character, has little to do with the company's beverage product and so will not result in any lift of image. Meanwhile, this change of plans has delayed the park opening for two years, generating negative publicity for the company. Moreover, potential union troubles threaten to make day-to-day park operations twice as expensive as originally projected. Meanwhile, Acme's major competitor, Beta Beverages, has taken advantage of this ongoing distraction and assumed leadership in the business' core marketplace.

Put yourself in the place of Acme Cola's president. His cherished dream has become a money pit. His product has fallen to second place in the market. The media is laughing at him. And, to him, the problems are the result of a long series of incremental setbacks. He didn't know that the first two proposed sites were going to endanger wetlands. He could never have predicted that the original theme would bomb with the public (and, in his heart-of-hearts, he thinks that perhaps the focus research was flawed, and "World of Fizz" could still prevail). And he never in his wildest dreams imagined that it would take so long to get an amusement park going, and he never suspected that it might pull him away from the core business of the company. From the president's viewpoint, he's the victim of circumstances beyond his control.

Which is pure bull, of course. Cola World was a stupid idea from the get-go, and as its author, the blame lies entirely on the president's doorstep. But if you, as a stockholder, tell him so in no uncertain terms, you have attacked him personally, and he will automatically group you with the myriad other hindrances which have plagued him from the beginning of the project.

The alternative is to present yourself as an ally with a solution.

If you own or represent a significant number of shares, you may be able to get a private meeting with this executive. If you don't own enough shares (or he's simply not taking callers these days) you can still write the fellow a letter.

Either way, the message should offer him an honorable way out. Perhaps you suggest that a task force be formed to find an amusement park company that would purchase a trademark license from Acme Cola. The resulting endeavor will pay royalties to the company in good years, with no downside to it in the bad. In the meantime, freed of responsibility for the park, the president and his managers can turn their attentions back to their core business and help restore the company to full profitability.

SEND STRONGER SIGNALS

Will he listen? Probably not. But by taking the high road (and documenting this contact and your proposed solution), you've made it more difficult for the company to paint you as a Black Hat in days to come.

If the managing executive doesn't budge, your next communication is to his board of directors. Again, if you are a major shareholder, you may be allowed time to speak at a monthly board meeting. Even if you are not granted an audience, you can still write a letter to each member of the board (whose names will be listed in the company's annual report). Tell them what you've proposed, and ask (in somewhat less concessionary terms, this time) that either your idea or a similar action be taken to alleviate financial pressures and allow the company to concentrate on performing to its full capabilities.

The chances are that your sentiments will echo thoughts that the board members have had for quite some time. They may even use your entreaties as a catalyst for effecting change; although, if they've sat idly by while the president has fouled things up for this long, that's rather unlikely. But the point is, by again presenting yourself as an ally with a we're-all-on-the-same-side solution, your hat (while possibly a bit grayer) will still not be black. More importantly, all of the people on the management team and the board now know who you are.

EN GARDE!

Once you've asked nicely, and nothing has happened, it's time to start rattling the saber.

Start by requesting a 10K for the company's last several fiscal years.

Form 10K is an SEC requirement for publicly held companies. It differs from the annual report in that rather than giving a "snapshot" of a company's financial state at the end of the year, the 10K goes into considerably more detail, breaking out salaries, employee benefits, building costs and occupancy, advertising costs, data-processing costs, and so forth. The annual report is a rosy picture of reality—or at least the picture of reality the board wishes to send to the shareholders. The 10K presents more of an impartial, accountant's point of view, and it is the document a dissident shareholder would use to begin building a case against the way the company is managed.

There are two ways of getting the company's most recent 10Ks. One is to get them from the SEC (they'll charge you a nominal processing fee, usually $15 per report). The other is to request them from the company itself.

You want to do the latter.

Details for getting a 10K from the company are usually contained in the annual report. The company, unlike the SEC, will usually send a 10K to a shareholder for nothing, but your reason for going this route is not to avoid forking over $15 to the SEC.

The reason you want to request the 10K from the company is to *let them know* that you're asking for it. Most publicly held companies of any size have an investor relations department that handles such requests, and this department usually summarizes the requesters in a list given regularly to the board. In some cases, a "watch list" of potential troublemakers may be kept in the investor relations department, and a request from anyone on this list will trigger instant phone calls to the board.

Once you have the 10Ks, begin requesting 10Qs for the same years, as well as the completed quarters of the current year. A 10Q is a more detailed version of the company's quarterly report—a new 10Q must be filed with the SEC no more than 45 days after the close of each quarter.

Assuming the firm has had good years preceding the bad, be certain your requests for 10Ks and 10Qs include operating periods in advance of the company's episodes of poor performance. The message this sends to the directors is this: "I am building a case to show that this company is performing below potential, and I intend to demonstrate that the business practices to which I've objected are the reason for the poor performance."

By this point, little will have happened. You've told the managers and the board of directors that you think the company should be run differently; they either don't agree or have not been sufficiently motivated to act on your suggestion. You've also made it known that you are assembling your evidence (in the form of the 10Ks and 10Qs), but, so far, no one else knows of your actions.

Which is why you now re-contact the company's investor relations department and request a copy of the corporate charter, articles of incorporation, and bylaws.

Charters and bylaws, again, can be obtained without the management's notice by going to the SEC. The reason you want to request them from the company is that you again want them to notice that you are obtaining this information, *which contains the regulations governing such items as the calling of special meetings by shareholders and the majority required to approve a change of control for the company.*

Finally, re-contact the investor relations department and tell them you want a list of shareholders—both the shareholders of record and nonobjecting beneficial holders (people or institutions who have their certificates held at a brokerage house rather than having them personally issued, and who have signed releases allowing the brokerage to include their names on shareholder lists).

You may not get this. For one thing, you need to be a significant shareholder (in the S&L industry, the minimum requirement to make these requests is a minimum $100,000 investment in the company, held for a period no less than six months). And even if you're entitled to make the request, you'll need to state a reason for it (the correct, qualifying poker-face reply is, "for the purpose of communicating with other shareholders").

At this point, you'll have become a pain in the rear end which can no longer be ignored. The board and management team will be on the verge of doing one of two things: either asking you what you want, as a prelude to changing the way it's running the company; or girding itself for battle.

To up the ante, you can also begin making inquiries with proxy solicitors: asking how much they charge per hour, how much time they feel it will take them to contact the shareholders, and whether they will be able to assume you as a client. Similar inquiries can be made at public relations agencies.

The reason for going shopping like this is that most proxy solicitors work for companies rather than dissidents. The same goes for PR agencies and law firms. And even though there are conventions of confidentiality that govern such contacts, word does tend to get out on the street when some-one is shopping for help on an upcoming proxy campaign.

The message being sent is, "I'm willing to spend some money to get things changed in this company."

Perhaps the opposite is true. Perhaps you don't want to spend a lot of money.

Indeed, at this point, you have not. If you've done your communications with the company, its managers, and the board by letter and telephone, and your initial consulta-tions with proxy solicitors, PR firms, and law firms have been free, your only out-of-pocket expenses have gone to pay the company for reproducing the shareholder list (and I've never known this to exceed the company's own costs). Even if you've made personal trips to visit the manage-ment and speak with the board, it's still unlikely that you're out-of-pocket more than $5,000.

But the opposition doesn't know that you've gone as far as you care to. You've forced them to wonder what you're up to. A referendum at the next annual meeting? A pro-posal to sell the company? Are you trying to get elected to the board (and oust one of *them*)? Are you going to make so much noise that word gets out into the trade press?

What are you holding—a royal flush or a pair of deuces? Will the paratroopers jump when they get to Port au Prince? Or to put it in the words of Dirty Harry, "How many shots did I fire? Was it five or six?. . . Do you feel lucky today?"

Make them feel squeamish enough and the company's management and directors may blink. They may give in and do what you want, without requiring you to go into a proxy contest and *force* them to do it. That's a win/win: you haven't spent a ton of money to effect this change (you've certainly spent less than what the company has been losing for you, or you wouldn't have gone to this trouble in the first place), the company is on its way to greater profitability, and neither of you is going to spend the better part of the next year trying to win votes and discredit the other guy.

WHAT IF THEY CALL YOUR BLUFF?

On the other hand, the company (particularly if it has considerable resources at its disposal) may decide to call *your* bluff. It may stay mute and allow you to proceed to the next step, if you wish. Now is when you have to decide if you want to spend the money and buck management, shut up and put up with a sub-performing investment, or sell your shares and take your losses.

At least, if you decide to take the former course, many of your ducks—the 10Ks and 10Qs, the shareholder request, and the initial consultations with the necessary people to assist you—will already be in their row.

Chapter 19

Bizarro World: Foreign Companies

The story circulating in American business circles a few years ago went something like this:

Three businessmen—an American, an Englishman, and a Japanese—were traveling in the Middle East when they were kidnapped in Beirut and held for ransom. The kidnappers' deadline came and went, but the businessmen's governments had held the line, and no ransoms were forthcoming. Finally, the kidnappers had had enough and they decided to execute their hostages. But first, they told the businessmen, they would grant each of them a final request.

The Englishman considered his final request for almost half a day. Finally, he decided.

"I would like," he told his captors, "to have a proper English tea, with scones and clotted cream."

The Japanese businessman ruminated upon his options for two hours and then he, too, came to a decision.

"I would like," he said, "to deliver a short lecture on the superiority of the Japanese method of management."

When it came the American's turn to choose, he did not have to consider his final request at all.

Nodding at the Japanese businessman, the American told his captors, "I want you to kill me before Fujiwara, here, starts talking. . ."

In that little story lies a very large kernel of truth. We Americans take an almost pig-headed pride in our desire to avoid listening to the Japanese.

It's a pride born in ignorance. Our superficial observations of the Japanese have given us a cartoon-like perspective on them. They seem to us almost comically serious and consumed by protocol—especially on the golf course. The typical Japanese corporation operates with what seems to Western eyes an ant-like devotion to the organization, with virtually no concern for self. American businessmen, many of whom pay only lip-service to the precepts of sexual equality, are nonetheless themselves appalled at the low status afforded most women in the typical Japanese corporation.

Japanese businesses look to western observers something like Bizarro World in the old Superman comic books— they dress like us, and to some extent act like us, but in the details, we find them little short of weird.

All of which makes their numerous business and economic successes particularly irksome to the typical Westerner.

THE WRONG SIDE OF THE TABLE

My curiosity was piqued a few years ago when I had a series of meetings with a Japanese company. One of the Americans with whom I was working at the time had done business for several years in Japan, and he was guiding us through the intricacies of negotiating with individuals who not only spoke a different language, but came from what, to us, was a foreign culture.

We were hosting a Japanese contingent at an American office, and our conference room had been readied for an all-day working session. We'd taken the usual steps to offer hospitality to our guests. Refreshments were waiting on a sideboard, pads and paper had been set at each place on the table, and a VCR and overhead projector were waiting in case our guests had any audio/visual exhibits they cared to share during the course of our meeting. We also arrived at the conference room early, and our group naturally went to the far side of the table, to give our guests a shorter and less awkward walk when they entered the room.

"No, no," my Japanese-savvy associate said when he came into the room. "Quick, move before they get here! You're sitting on the wrong side of the table!"

In Japan, he explained, the hosts sat on the side of the table closest to the door. This way, if an attack came by way of the door, the hosts were in a better position to defend their guests.

We switched sides, and got a little chuckle over the idea of a bunch of guys in gray flannel suits being called upon to mount a defense against whatever amorphous threat might come barreling through the conference-room door. But the more I thought about this concept, the more intrigued I became. I looked into the matter.

In western society, we have several quirks that extend back to the days of King Arthur (or beyond). Our mode of address to a man we respect is to call him "Sir," a title that finds its roots in the days of chivalry. The title we give our superiors, including our ultimate theological superiors, is "Lord"—another throwback to feudal times. Even our military salute finds its roots in the days of knighthood. A knight in armor would raise his face-shield to show respect and nonaggression to an ally, and today's salute is a pantomime of that action.

All of these items become a touch quaint when they're explained, but pass virtually without comment in our daily life. They've been with us for so long that we never seem to question them. They are nothing more than remnants of our feudal past.

Japan's feudal past came much nearer to modern times, and evolved to a point never approached by the hierarchies of western culture.

Feudalism was the status quo in Japan as late as the 18th century. The country ran under the aegis of a wide number of warlords who kept their positions with the help of extensive private armies and who operated as benefactors to the common people living in their domains. Indeed, even when Perry landed in Japan in the 19th century, the trappings of feudalism were common. There were courts where aristocrats received visitors; the gentry carried swords as symbols of authority.

If truth be known, feudalism never died in Japan; it simply evolved.

For centuries, there were three classes of people in Japanese society.

The people of the land—farmers and fishermen—occupied the base of the Japanese feudal system. They kept the engine running, formed the largest part of the population, and lived in subservience to the upper classes.

Next came merchants and craftsmen, who were a necessary go-between in service to the ruling classes. Members of the merchant class were accorded certain privileges. They were, for instance, allowed to wear swords in public. But (and the Freudians among you may do with this information what you will) the swords they wore were not allowed to be as long as those worn by the ruling class.

The ruling class was known as the *bushi*. These were the military class, fiercely loyal to their warlords, and almost totally selfless in their devotion to cause. Their beliefs were codified in a set of principles known as *bushido* (literally, "the way of the warrior"), and a member of the bushi class would rather perish than violate a single precept of bushido. The most famous story in all Japan is that of the 57 samurai whose master was killed. They sought out and killed their former master's enemies and then, out of shame at the fact that they had allowed their lord to perish, all 57 committed suicide. Their graves are still decorated to this day.

In Japan, Business Is War

The point is, while we westerners have only vestigial remnants of our feudal past, the principles of bushido are very much alive in Japan today. And in the evolution of Japanese society, the captains of industry are not, as we might assume, the descendants of old Japan's merchant class. Japanese corporations are run by people who live by the code of the samurai.

A Japanese would not tell you this—not because he would be secretive about it, but simply because it is so much a part of the fabric of his daily life that it would not occur to him to comment on it. Like our respectful titles and our military salute, the roots of the system may no longer seem conspicuous.

But they are still very much there. People in Japanese corporations operate with a selflessness that would seem almost deviant in the American workplace. A Japanese underling is happy—overjoyed—when his boss receives the credit for something the minion did; he knows he will be rewarded later on in his career path, just as his predecessors were rewarded by their warlords for faithful service.

The primer for aspiring corporate types in Japan is the *Go Rin No Sho* ("The Book of Five Rings"). The author, Musashi Miyamoto, was not a businessman at all, but a master swordsman whose style of fighting, *Ni-Ken Ryu* ("the two-sword school"), elevated him to the status accorded Wyatt Earp in our legends of the Old West. The *Go Rin No Sho* is a book of instruction on military strategy and tactics; it is used today in Japanese business schools as practical allegory for dealing with competitors in all walks of life.

The Japanese, in essence, view business as war. The motive is not profit; the motive is victory.

Even a smattering of knowledge of *bushido* puts you in a much better position to understand Japanese business and businesspeople. The virtual reverence that many Japanese show toward golf, for instance, owes itself to another *bushi* principle, that there must be a soft or artistic side to balance out the aggressive nature of a warrior.

To this end, the samurai of old always practiced an avocation to keep them well-rounded and to avoid monomaniacal concentration in one endeavor (Miyamoto himself was a woodcarver of considerable repute in addition to his skills as a swordsman). To the Japanese, golf is a sort of art form. A long drive or a tricky putt is a thing of beauty in and of itself, and so it nicely provides the yin/yang balance called for by *bushido*. And tradition calls for them to approach their avocation with the same seriousness that they show to their principle activity. A Japanese golfer *has* to take his game seriously—otherwise he is implying that he doesn't take business seriously, either.

If you are starting to form the notion that they play by a different set of rules in Japan, you are getting my point. And nowhere is that point more true than in shareholder politics.

In the United States, most investors realize that the SEC requires certain filings when any single entity reaches a certain equity position in a company. For instance, there's one filing required when a party owns 5 percent of any single corporation, and a second filing required when ownership hits 10 percent. By the time an individual person or institution hits that point, it's expected that they will be exercising considerable influence over the company's future and may even cause a change of control. A 5 percent stake will earn you a board seat on most corporations in America today. A 10 percent stake will virtually guarantee it.

Consider, then, the case of T. Boone Pickens—no slouch whatsoever in the American investing scene, and virtually the Carrie Nation of investors' rights. I mentioned earlier that Pickens' group, USA, has been extraordinarily effective in shaping the manner in which American corporations are run. In addition, Boone Pickens at one time had a reputation as the most effective raider in America, sweeping through Gulf Oil and Phillips Petroleum with the confidence of Sherman descending upon Atlanta. When Pickens talked, American industry not only listened—it obeyed.

Such would not be the case in Japan.

ILLUSTRATION: PLAYING BY DIFFERENT RULES

Koito Manufacturing Company, Ltd., is to Toyota Motor Corporation what GE and Lucas are to western automakers. If it lights up and it's on a Toyota car or truck, Koito probably makes it, and back in 1990 that put lights in T. Boone Pickens' eyes.

One story has it that, in analyzing Koito's performance over a number of years, Pickens saw it as an underperforming company, paying low dividends and posting profits that were considerably under those enjoyed by counterparts elsewhere in the industry. Seeing value and potential well beyond that reflected by the prices at which Koito was trading, Pickens, with the help of a Japanese speculator, began buying Koito stock with an eye toward increasing profitability and realizing a windfall.

The other story has it that Pickens realized that Koito's main customer, Toyota—which itself had a 15 percent equity stake in Koito—would see outside incursion as a threat and be required to defend itself from a raid upon what amounted to a captive supplier.

Whether the motive here was shareholder activism or plain old American greenmail, the point is, it didn't work.

Toyota, again, had a 15 percent holding in Koito. Pickens was at *20* percent when he demanded a seat on Koito Manufacturing Corp.'s board.

No soap.

Pickens increased his holdings while Toyota remained motionless in their 15 percent equity position. Finally, Pickens hit a 26.4 percent stake in the Japanese supplier— a clear 11.4 percent seniority to Toyota's position, but still he could not convince the other shareholders to give him what would come as a matter of course in any American corporation. He was forced to stand idly by as the tail— Toyota—wagged the dog.

Where did he go wrong?

What T. Boone Pickens had run straight into was *keiretsu*— another by-product of Japan's very recent feudal history and its *bushi*-oriented business philosophies.

American corporate politics run in a sort of king-of-the-hill fashion. The party with the strongest equity position generally gets to run the show, and the motivation is the best possible profit from any given situation.

The closest thing we have in the west to *keiretsu* are mutual-defense pacts like the North Atlantic Treaty Organization. In NATO, while there might be some players who are larger than others, the organization runs more on its own will than on the whim of any single member. Its aim is to keep all of its members healthy through unified re-pulsion of threats.

Keiretsu traces its roots back to those days in Japan when provincial warlords were both competing with one another for power and constantly defending themselves from in-vaders who mounted regular incursions from Korea and China. The costs of keeping feudal armies on constant alert was enormous, so these warlords formed regional al-liances among themselves, negating the need to defend themselves from infighting and making it easier to mount national defenses on a sort of National Guard basis, with each warlord contributing a modest portion of troops and munitions to one unified regional military force.

This why-can't-we-all-just-get-along/let's-take-care-of-each-other attitude translated over into the corporate world in the form of *keiretsu*. Remember, under *bushido*, the goal is not profit (that is the goal of an underclass). Bushido revels in victory, and Japanese businesses aspire to this goal because if victory is achieved, profit is inevitable. *Keiretsu* is mutual investment for the sake of allegiance, and this is the wall against which T. Boone Pickens ran.

Pickens' request—that the Koito shareholders elect him to a board seat from which he could hold sway (and presum-ably increase prices) against fellow-shareholder/principal-customer Toyota—was roughly equivalent to Japan ap-proaching the United States and asking us to team up with them in a trade war against Canada. Regardless of whether we would profit from such an action, we would never con-sider it because Canada is a long-standing neighbor and ally and, as such, we owe it considerable loyalty.

Just as we would never consider turning against Canada, the Japanese—who consider honor and loyalty paramount to virtually everything else—would never consider sell-ing out a partner in a *keiretsu* alliance. Pickens' wave of money broke upon an iron shore, and Koito went on vend-ing automotive lighting to Toyota and taking only a mod-est profit.

For Pickens, if you'll excuse the pun, it was "lights out."

There's one very old western maxim that applies here, and this is it: Know who you're getting in bed with.

I know that I am seen by some of my peers as being virtually parochial in the way I pick my investments. I rarely invest in companies outside my native Midwest. Many of the firms in which my clients and I hold stakes are in my home state of Michigan, and I invest only in those industries in which my staff and I have expertise and an advanced level of understanding. I live near Detroit and I don't have a penny in Silicon Valley because: a) it's on the West Coast, and b) I haven't the foggiest notion as to exactly what it is they *do* out there, so I have no means with which to gauge the actual worth of their companies.

If that's parochial, I plead guilty. But "parochial" has proven to be both steady and safe for me, and the rewards have been both consistent and considerable.

That being the case, I haven't bought into any *keiretsu* alliances lately. Nor do I intend to.

As seductive as the world of international investment and finance may seem, I do not, as a rule, advise my clients to invest overseas.

Perils of International Investment

This is not a matter of pure national pride (although, I must admit, there's a bit of that in there as well). It's a matter of common sense. My staff and I have accumulated decades of knowledge on American investment precepts and regulations, and it seems to me foolhardy to follow temptation into areas where that knowledge will not, and cannot, serve us.

It's not just Japan. International investment is fraught with perils unknown to those whose holdings lie entirely with U.S. companies.

I've already given you my opinions on the doomed-to-fail nature of ESOPs. Consider, then, the state of corporations that operate in highly socialized countries. Socialized industries are really nothing more than federalized ESOPs. They do not exist to make a profit; they exist to provide a livelihood for the constituency. I won't say whether that's good or bad, but I will say that I cannot see a way to make a good investment in it.

Add to this the fact that a corporation is only as strong and as permanent as its native government. In the Third World, in particular, even the most excellent investment opportunities live under the shadow of the fact that they could be nationalized under a change in government.

If overseas investment were the only way, or even the best way, of seeing a good return both of and on one's principal, I would probably feel otherwise. But the fact is that I do not see investment outside the United States as a necessary evil. Profitable investment is both possible and predictable without ever having to stray outside those companies trading on our own listings and exchanges.

Of course, if your field of expertise is in some area that winds up emigrating offshore—one example that comes to mind is the field of statistical process control, which was invented in the United States but only came to fruition in Japan—then you may have no choice but to assume some risk and engage in overseas investment. If that is the case, I would strongly urge you to have the courage to admit your own ignorance and seek the counsel of an investment professional (not merely a broker, but an analyst/counselor) who is schooled in, and preferably lives in, the country in which your investment will be made.

Shareholder activism works in the United States because the corporate climate here is both rooted in democratic capitalist principles and geared toward a bottom-line profit motive. Value and worth are the means by which we measure businesses, and businesses exist to make money for their shareholders.

Those points, while they might seem laughably clear to all of us, do not apply across the board overseas, and the American investor would do well to be clear on this before he sends his investment dollar touring.

Foreign Companies in the U.S.

What about foreign concerns that trade in this country? Are they playing according to American rules, or is there an accent with which one must contend?

T. Boone Pickens has gone out of his way to claim that, at least in the case of Japan, the illness is being exported. In 1991, Pickens formed the Mid-America Project (MAP), a coalition of economists and American business and labor leaders, to investigate and campaign against the incursion of *keiretsu* principles in the United States. Among other things, MAP released a report entitled "Keiretsu, USA: A Report on Japanese Cartels in Mid-America." The report alleged that nearly 1,200 Japanese-affiliated auto companies and automotive vendors, operating in the American Midwestern auto belt, were engaging in anticompetitive collusion. The report stopped short of accusing the Japanese of out-and-out violation of SEC regulations but did say that the spirit of their actions here amounted to virtually the same thing as a plain, old-fashioned trust.

If MAP is right, then even the American subsidiaries of these Japanese corporations are running, not to make a profit for their shareholders, but to effectively and noncompetitively serve the concerns that they fuel, and to shore up formal *keiretsu* alliances that exist back home in Japan.

If MAP is right, Americans investing in such companies are actually offering themselves as unwitting hosts to a parasitic situation in which return to shareholders is relegated to secondary importance.

This, in turn, leads us to ask the same questions about American subsidiaries of corporations that have their roots in socialized countries, or American companies dependent upon parent companies in shaky Third-World nations.

At the peril of sounding xenophobic, I would suggest that such attributes must be taken up in the course of risk assessment that any prudent investor must exercise before purchasing shares in a company. In my own case, I must admit that I lean very heavily toward American companies that are also American-parented.

"Buy American" might sound, to some listeners, milksoppy and patriotic, but you know what? I don't mind in the slightest being called a patriot. And when it comes to stewarding your investment, it's also a lot less of a shot in the dark.

Conclusion

Using the Power

Today there is still a world in which the right to vote must be purchased—the corporate world. The shareholders of a company are the anointed few who alone have the right to determine whether that company will succeed or whether it will become a footnote. And the multiplied franchises of their shareholders are what eventually determine if industries will be strong or weak, if economies will be prosperous or recessive, and if life for people in general will be a thing of joy or a litany of despair.

Power is meaningless unless power is used. The shareholders of today's corporations wield a combined power that would humble the greatest armies ever known to man. Yet, to exercise this power, shareholders must recognize who they are—the true owners of the companies that make our industries and our world run.

Passivity in ownership is not a sin. But it is most certainly a shame. To read a report, to listen to a concerned fellow shareholder, to mark a proxy—these are things that take moments. But they can have both momentous and long-lasting results—positive results.

I have one last wish for you; one challenge.

The wish is for you to truly realize that the company in which you own stock is not some amorphous concern that belongs to some nameless, faceless entity. That company is a palpable organism, capable of success or failure, and that company belongs to its shareholders. That company belongs, at least in part, to you.

Earlier we asked the question, "Whose company is it, anyhow?"

Now you know the answer.

In your heart, you knew it all along.

It's *your* company.

And now the challenge:

What are you going to do with your company?

Suggested Reading

Brandes, Charles. *Value Investing Today.* Homewood, Illinois: Business One Irwin, 1989.

Buffett, Warren. *Compilations of Letters to Shareholders of Berkshire Hathaway.* Copyright Warren Buffett.

Fisher, Kenneth. *100 Minds that Made the Market.* Woodside, Calif.: Business Classics, 1993.

Fisher, Phillip. *Common Stocks and Uncommon Profits.* Woodside, Calif.: PSR Publications, 1984.

_____ . *Conservative Investors Sleep Well.* Woodside, Calif.: Business Classics, 1975.

_____ . *Developing an Investment Philosophy.* Woodside, Calif.: Business Classics, 1980.

Goodman, George [Adam Smith, pseud.). *The Money Game.* New York: Random House, 1967.

Graham, Benjamin. *The Intelligent Investor.* New York: Harper & Row Publishers, 1973.

_____ . *Security Analysis.* New York: McGraw-Hill Book Company, 1988.

Hagstrom, Robert, Jr. *The Warren Buffett Way.* New York: John Wiley & Sons, Inc., 1994.

Kilpatrick, Andrew. *Of Permanent Value.* Birmingham, Ala.: AKPE, 1994.

Klarman, Seth. *Margin of Safety.* New York: Harper Business, 1991.

Lewis, Michael. *Liar's Poker*. New York: W.W. Norton & Company, 1989.

Lowe, Janet. *Benjamin Graham on Value Investing*. Chicago: Dearborn Financial Publishing, 1994.

Lynch, Peter. *Beating the Street*. New York: Simon & Schuster, 1993.

————. *One Up on Wall Street*. New York: Simon & Schuster, 1989.

Mackay, Charles. *Extraordinary Popular Delusions and the Madness of Crowds*. New York: Harmony Books, 1980.

Monks, Robert. *Corporate Governance*. Glasgow: Harper Collins Publishers, 1994.

————. *Power and Accountability*. Glasgow: Harper Collins Publishers, 1991.

Neil, Humphrey. *The Art of Contrary Thinking*. Caldwell, Idaho: The Caxton Printers, Ltd., 1976.

O'Glove, Thornton. *Quality of Earnings*. London: The Free Press, 1987.

Perritt, Gerald. *Small Stocks Big Profits*. Chicago: Dearborn Financial Publishing, 1993.

Schilit, Howard M. *Financial Shenanigans*. New York: McGraw-Hill, Inc., 1993.

Schwed, Fred, Jr. *Where Are the Customers' Yachts?* Burlington, Utah: Fraser Publishing Co., 1985.

Smith, Adam. *Wealth of Nations*. Buffalo: Prometheus Books, 1991.

Soros, George. *The Alchemy of Finance*. New York: John Wiley & Sons, Inc., 1987.

Stewart, James. *The Den of Thieves*. New York: Simon & Schuster, 1991.

Train, John. *The Money Masters*. New York: Harper & Row Publishers, 1980.

————. *The New Money Masters*. New York: Harper & Row Publishers, 1989.

Index

nonobjecting beneficial, 145
obligation of, 6, 22
passivity, 199
power, 199
shareholders' committee
contacting, 33
forming, 40
Smith, Roger. *See* General
Motors (GM): decline of
SNL Securities, 112
Nagle, Reid, 112
socialism, 118, 149
Southern California real estate,
65-66
speculator, defined, 21
Stempel, Robert C. *See* General
Motors (GM): decline of
paternalism of, 72
resignation of, 70
stock market, predicting, 12
stocks
pink-sheet, 14
price trends, 136, 138
selection of, 20

T

Thermo Electron Corporation,
39-40
Timberland Boots, 137
Toyota Motor Corporation,
191–193
tulip mania, 66–67
Twain, Mark, 50, 62

U

U.S. League of Savings Institutions, 102
unions, 124
United Auto Workers (UAW),
70, 73
United Shareholders' Association (USA). *See* Pickens, T.
Boone

V

valuation, methods of, 15
value
as basis for investment, 15
defined, 15
liquidation (LV), 15
net present (NPV), 15
private-market (PMV), 15
value investing, 14–20
guidelines for, 17–20
method of, 20
value investment, 15, 114

W

Wal-Mart, 81
Wall Street, 11
Wall Street Journal, 6, 14